Being Mary?

Being Mary?

Irish Catholic Immigrant Women and Home and Community Building in Harold Hill Essex 1947-1970

A thesis awarded degree of PhD
Social Studies Centre
Anglia Ruskin University
Cambridge

Aenne Werner-Leggett

eleven
international publishing

Published, sold and distributed by Eleven International Publishing
P.O. Box 85576
2508 CG The Hague
The Netherlands
Tel.: +31 70 33 070 33
Fax: +31 70 33 070 30
e-mail: sales@budh.nl
www.elevenpub.com

Sold and distributed in USA and Canada
International Specialized Book Services
920 NE 58th Avenue, Suite 300
Portland, OR 97213-3786, USA
Tel: 1-800-944-6190 (toll-free)
Fax: +1 503 280-8832
orders@isbs.com
www.isbs.com

Eleven International Publishing is an imprint of Boom uitgevers Den Haag.

ISBN 978-94-90947-76-7

© 2012 Aenne Werner / Eleven International Publishing

This publication is protected by international copyright law.
All rights reserved. No part of this publication may be reproduced, stored in a retrieval s, or transmitted in any form or by any means, electronic, mechanical, photocopying, recording or otherwise, without the prior permission of the publisher.

Printed in The Netherlands

ACKNOWLEDGEMENTS

Firstly I would like to acknowledge the debt owed to the women who were willing to contribute their time to this thesis. There would have been no thesis without their brilliant stories. I would also like to thank the community of Ursuline Sisters of Brentwood especially the archivist who was always at hand and made me feel so welcome. Also a kind thank you to the two Catholic parishes of Harold Hill and the St. Ursula's primary school, in particular the former Headmistress Mrs. O'Connor and Fr. Martin for their initial support. Plus the secretary of St Edwards Church and the archivist of Brentwood House who was always there to give me the much-needed files also deserve thanks. The advice and knowledge from the staff of the Romford Central library was of great comfort to me.

This thesis would never have been completed if it wasn't for the help and support of Dr. John Pollard and Prof. Bronwen Walter who really pulled me through when it looked too difficult and a far too hopeless task to achieve. They have been full of enthusiasm and advice and I would have never got this far without their supervision. Their support and encouragement was way beyond their line of duty. All their input, e-mails and visits (even all the way here) I will never forget, it made it the experience worthwhile. Thank you I learned so much.

Outside the academic world and the fascinating world of dusty archives I am in much debt to my friends, family and colleagues and even patients for their support and kind words of encouragement and the arranged days off, no matter how busy the community was that week. Finally a special thanks to Steve for checking sloppy work, Rosie for all the cups of tea and Georgina for letting a stressed mum into her teenage world. Thanks for putting up with me and trusting it to be over soon.

Being Mary? Irish Catholic immigrant women: home and community building in Harold Hill, Essex

This study explores the lives of Irish immigrant women in the newly-built Harold Hill Estate in Essex in the post-war period, with reference to the influence of the cult of the Virgin Mary upon those lives. It analyses the roles which they played in their families and in the community. In so doing, it examines how the cult of the Virgin was used to prepare these women for motherhood, and in a wider context, for their supportive and caring roles in their families and community.

The thesis explores an under-researched area by use of the oral testimonies of Irish women, a diary of one of them and local archival and newspaper material. By allowing Irish women to discuss their lives, we are able to understand them and through their own lives, their contribution to the community can be examined. The archival and newspaper material provides insights into the building of the estate; the views of the local community; highlights the presence of the Church and the activities of the Diocese, thus augmenting the material provided by the oral testimony. It also makes it possible to explore the importance of Catholic education and Catholic teaching on the family unit and the position of women.

This thesis shows how the lives of women on the estate were affected by migration and differed from the lives of mothers and grandmothers in Ireland, as many undertook paid work outside of the family, and raised their children without the support of extended families. It also shows that changes in lifestyle were also the result of contact with the English community, through places of work and intermarriage ('mixed marriages').

Important conclusions that may be drawn from this study include the finding that despite all the changes arising from migration, these women held to their cultural beliefs and practices particularly connected to family and parish life, and deployed these in their activities within their communities. They continued to use the image of Mary to instruct their daughters and teach them obedience so that Irish Catholic culture continued to be reproduced in the subsequent generation. However the women drew on a far richer and more varied version of Mary's role than the rigid stereotypical ones prescribed by the Church. In their 'acting out' of Mary they actually performed roles which were more akin to the role performed by 'the Mary's' in the Gospels. By examining the influence of Irish Catholic women both inside and outside the home, the research suggests that localities represented as 'English' working class neighbourhoods and 'English' Catholic communities may contain a crucial Irish dimension that is usually overlooked.

CONTENTS

- Acknowledgments   v
- Abstract   vii
- Contents   ix

- **CHAPTER 1: INTRODUCTION**   1

- Aims of the Study   1
- The Origins of the thesis   1
- Contribution of the Study   3
- Key Themes   4
- Structure   5

- **CHAPTER 2: CONTEXTS and LITERATURE REVIEW**   9

- Irish Immigrant Women in England: reasons for leaving Ireland   9
- Position of women in Ireland   14
- The relationship between the Catholic Irish State and Irish migrant women   17
- Identity, Irish Catholic women and faith   21
- Irish women and their relationship with the Virgin Mary   27
- The influence of Irish Catholic migrants on the development of the Catholic Church in England   33
- Catholicism in England in the early 20th century   38
- The Importance of Schooling   40
- Local context of Harold Hill: the history of its building and growth and its relationship to Irish settlements in London   45

- **CHAPTER 3: METHODOLOGY**   69

- The Theories behind the method of oral history   69
- Oral history and psychoanalysis   74
- Position of the historian in the interview   76

- Culture and the use of language — 77
- In conclusion of the use of theory — 80
- Irish immigrant women and methodology — 81
- Research design — 83
- The research respondents — 86
- The process of interviewing — 88
- The selection of the sample — 90
- The diary as a source — 91
- The interview analysis: the tools of the story teller — 92
- Space to tell a tale — 94
- Dirty linen and alcohol: the outcome — 97
- Translating hostilities — 98
- Archival and related source materials — 99
- Conclusion — 103

- **CHAPTER 4: FROM EAST LONDON TO HAROLD HILL** — **107**

- The Irish community in East London — 107
- A doctor's practice in East London — 115
- Socialising, the Church involvement and the Irish highly educated community members — 119
- Religious life in East London — 122
- The impact that the Second World War had on the Irish community of East London — 123
- New Housing Programs — 129
- The Greater London Plan — 133
- New Communities — 138
- Choosing a Site — 139
- Diocese of Brentwood and schooling — 144
- A new life — 147
- Conclusion — 150

- **CHAPTER 5: IRISH WOMEN IN THEIR HOMES** — **157**

- Family life — 157

- Siblings and gender roles — 171
- Sex and Catholicism — 175
- Religious traditions and the Virgin Mary — 184
- Conclusion — 188

- **CHAPTER 6: CATHOLIC IRISH WOMEN IN HAROLD HILL** — **193**

  - Harold Hill residents — 194
  - Reasons for leaving Ireland — 195
  - Paid work in England — 204
  - Irish communities — 210
  - Urban Irish clustering — 214
  - Catholic education in the Diocese of Brentwood and Harold Hill — 215
  - Harold Hill mass centres and serving priests — 219
  - Helping the parish and parish social life — 222
  - Involvement in processions on the estate and fundraising — 230
  - The Need for Catholic schools — 234
  - Responsibilities of parents — 236
  - The Catholic Education Council — 236
  - The Need for Catechists — 238
  - The history of the Ursuline Sisters and education — 242
  - The Ursulines of Brentwood — 243
  - A Catholic School for the Harold Hill Estate — 244
  - The Beginnings of St Ursula's School — 247
  - The Building of St Dominic's — 248
  - The Junior School is opened — 250
  - Conclusion — 254

- **CHAPTER 7: CONCLUSION** — **263**

- **BIBLIOGRAPHY** — **271**

CHAPTER 1: INTRODUCTION

Aims of the Study

The study explores the importance of the ideology of the Virgin Mary to the cultural beliefs and practices of Irish immigrant women living in the newly built Harold Hill Estate in Romford, Essex, in the post-War period of the late 1940s to 1970s. It examines ways in which Irish women's Catholic upbringing continued to affect their lives after migration and contributed to the development of the urban communities in which they lived, through their roles as mothers and the extension of these caring activities into voluntary and paid work outside the home. It therefore makes visible the wider significance of women's daily lives in the creation of new suburbs as a consequence of massive 'slum clearance' in the immediate post-War period and highlights cultural differences within 'English' working-class neighbourhoods.

The research is multidisciplinary, drawing on cultural history, geography and sociology. It seeks to link literature on Catholic religiosity, women's studies, migration and community studies in order to investigate the relationship between women's personal and public lives. It analyses ways in which an immigrant community has retained its distinctiveness because of its religious difference from the 'host' population in which it has settled, but this difference is usually invisible and unrecognised. There are parallels here with the Muslim community in Britain, although that is highly visible and often treated as exceptional. This study brings an important new perspective onto understandings of the persistence and nature of cultural difference.

The Origins of the Thesis

The thesis is set in the first person because my involvement in the Harold Hill community is central to the development of the thesis. In February 1988, I had moved to the Harold Hill Estate in Romford and noticed that there were many Irish women active in the two Catholic parishes on the estate. What was more surprising was that their involvement was completely overlooked. As a foreigner from a Dutch Catholic background it felt different to me and I started to wonder if that was because the Catholic community had an Irish atmosphere to it rather than an English one. One of the differences from my Dutch parish was the place the Virgin Mary had in the lives of particularly the Irish female worshippers. It was this experience that led me to explore the importance of the Virgin Mary to these women.

Alongside this interest in the importance and significance of the Virgin Mary, as a nurse I was also interested in the closure of "Warley", a psychiatric hospital in Brentwood, as a significant number of nurses working there from the 1950s onwards were Irish women. This was also the case in the local hospital and children's home where I used to work. There were also active Irish women religious who taught and helped parents in the parishes raise their children. It became clear that many Irish women were very active in the local community who by choice of profession and their numbers made a huge impact on the community as a whole.

What makes Catholics distinctly different to the Protestants was not that they were unable to quote from the Bible, but that they believed so firmly in Mary. The Protestants I met used to think that we, Post Second Vatican Council Catholics, regularly worshipped our saints but this worshipping never featured in our home, school or even the parish church. But the love and veneration of the Virgin was not only a correct observation, it mattered.[1] For little girls Mary stood out above all else and she was in a way the human face of the Church; she was the female side to this masculine organisation where only men could hold important offices in the community, men religious at that. For laywomen, Mary was the only friendly female face that the Catholic Church had allowed. As she was important to women, she was also important to their children; children often had a little medallion of our Lady of Lourdes pinned to their vest so that no harm could come to them. She was especially important because in their younger years the only thing that most girls knew was that one day they would become a mother.

The history of Irish women in England has often been viewed from the outside and they were mostly seen as a social problem; Irish immigrant women especially do not often feature in historical research. Therefore the achievements of Irish immigrant women are pushed outside the realm of general history although their numbers had a large impact on particular areas in England. They were the reason behind an ever-growing Catholic Church and contributed to community spirit within that church. Further, as they raised their children and worked in local schools, hospitals and children's homes, they influenced the social life of their area.

Many single Irish immigrant women moved to the South East of England and in particular to London to find work. Their numbers increased as the demand for domestic workers increased: in London there were 1,630 Irish born women for every 1,000 Irish born men in 1921.[2]

The reasons Irish women emigrated often differed from those of men. Their place in Irish society was far more vulnerable than that of their male counterparts. Their position at the family farm in Ireland was less favourable than that of their male siblings as they were never to inherit. The role model of the Virgin Mary dictated what was expected of women in Ireland and restricted their movements in society.[3] Women were perceived as having a subordinate role and what their position in Irish society meant to them can only be explored if they are allowed their own space in research.[4]

After the Second World War the Harold Hill Estate in Romford was built as a result of the slum clearance of East London. This created an increase in Catholic worshippers in a mainly Anglican area as many of the new residents were either of Irish descent, or were Irish born. The authoritarian and male nature of the Catholic Church allowed very little room for documented evidence of achievements of women in the Catholic Church in general, and the attitude to the Irish nation of the English Catholic Church suppressed the successful presence that the Irish community in Britain held.[5]

Contribution of the Study

This research contributes to cultural history, in particular to that of immigrant women. How society places women will influence how women are able to place themselves. Childhood memories, the connection with Ireland and the importance of the Virgin Mary connects with the future these women wrought for themselves.

The research also contributes to oral history as it explores unwritten history, which challenges the mythmaking of governments and institutions like the Catholic Church. Interviews are important because not a lot of information finds its way into history about women in general; working class women and immigrant women especially are often denied a voice.[6]

The research contributes to local knowledge and understanding because local archives of a small community can allow an insight at the level of micro history whereas larger national archives often lose sight of individuals involved in historical processes and their influence on the local community. Its contribution also lies in the examination of local planning and the work of Abercrombie, who was responsible for the relocation of 'slum dwellers' to estates outside London after the Second World War.

Finally the thesis has a wider significance; it is a recognition of the positive impact of immigration on community building. It will contribute to the understanding of cultural differences in white English speaking communities, which are sustained within their own cultural environment without being identified as significantly different from the secular English population.

Key Themes

These themes form the basis of the presentation of the thesis. The most important of these was the place that the Virgin Mary held within the lives of the Irish immigrant women. The Irish community in particular had a very close bond with the cult of Mary. The second theme is the upbringing in Ireland because of the values and traditions that these women took with them. In this thesis the focus is more on the Irish traditions they brought with them and of the influence that these Irish traditions and values held within the lives of these women in Harold Hill. This is essential to understanding the experience of migration of Irish women to England. In fact it was for several women a two-stage migration, initially to East London followed by relocation to the Harold Hill Estate and therefore the thesis will spend time also looking at the Irish community in East London.

The women's understanding of Mary and the continued embracing of values from back home connects with the third theme; the way they dealt with being mothers without their own mothers or families to aid and support them. It researches women's home-based role in the community of Harold Hill. This flows into the fourth theme: what work these women chose, paid or unpaid, in this community and how they were active community builders on this new estate. This final theme also explores their role within the education of Catholic children on the estate. In a sense the themes are closely linked to the life cycles of the women whose stories are examined and these themes are taken up in the literature.

Structure

In this section of the introduction, the chapters which follow are outlined to indicate the structure of the thesis. In the first section of chapter 2, three sets of literature are reviewed; general literature on emigration of Irish women to England and the position of women in Ireland with a reference to the Catholic Church and Irish migrant women are explored. It critically views material that highlights the complex reasons for migration on a personal, family and community level. The ways in which the literature has influenced this research are outlined, and in addition the importance for more research in this area is stated. Then two sets of literature are critically reviewed; literature on identity and Irish Catholic women and their relationship with the Virgin Mary, highlighting the gaps in the literature and the influence of these materials to this thesis. This is followed by two sets of literature that examine the influence Irish Catholic Immigrants had on the Catholic Church in England and Catholicism in the early 20th century with a special reference to the commitment by the Catholic Church to education for the Catholic working classes where the available material is critically examined. Finally, the last section of the chapter discusses the research material of local studies in the local context of the Harold Hill Estate in Romford, Essex. The gaps and importance to research this area are discussed here.

Chapter 3 offers a critical discussion of my experience collecting oral history data through an engagement with current debates within feminist methodologies and general oral methodologies. It also discusses critically my experiences in locating achieve data on various locations and the difficulties encountered in locating and obtaining access to archives of Catholic bodies. It examines the importance of collecting data of oral and archive material and the uses of both in one study and pays particular attention to the relationship of the narrator in the research and the place of the interview and the dynamic between the interviewer and interviewee. The main purpose of this chapter is to explore the processes in which this thesis was developed.

Chapter 4 critically discusses the importance of the movement of the immigrants from East London to the Harold Hill Estate and looks at the lives that people lived in East London and examines movements and migration pattern of the women examined. It also provides the reader information of the locality of Harold Hill and the development of that estate as a backdrop in which to read and understand the women's stories explored in the thesis.

Chapter 5 is primarily based on women's narratives exploring the lives lived behind closed doors, in which the reader enters the private domain of interviewees. It explores the traditions that continued behind closed doors and explores the impact that the Virgin Mary had on those lives. It compares the lives they lived on the new estate with the family life from which they came and how this compared in their view. It examines the position of the young women and their development to become mothers themselves, raising their own children. The chapter critically reviews the ideals of the Catholic Church on family life and its expectations of women herein. It examines the use of the Holy Family as a model by the Church, in exhortations to instruct and to live by its example.

Concentration on women in the wider community and their interaction with that community is explored in chapter 6. This examines the influence of these women in the wider community and the impact that they had on the building of a Catholic working class community on the new estate exploring the presence of a Catholic working Class Irish identity within a working class English area. It focuses on rebuilding lives and a community with fundraising and community effort at is basis. The chapter also explores the difference the women highlighted between their lives on the estate and the lives they had left behind examining for instance the relationship with the parish priest on the estate and that back in Ireland. It seeks to explore the importance of school and church building and the desire by the Catholic Diocese to educate the children of the new arrivals in Catholic Schools and the involvement of the Ursuline Sisters in the school building. It seeks to explore but also to emphasise the importance of the Irish women and their impact on the area and their involvement in community building. But it also seeks to explore the impact Catholic teaching had on choices of paid or unpaid work of women and their role in the community and examines how this influenced their choices. The concluding chapter brings together the main ideas and main argument developed through the chapters and the conclusion that the thesis arrives at.

Footnotes

[1] Post Vatican Council 1962-1965
[2] Walter, B. (2001) *Outsiders Inside, Whiteness, Place And Irish Women*, London p. 127
[3] Beale, J. (1986) *Women in Ireland: voices of change*, London p. 51-52
[4] Dowd, A. (1994) *Women in rural Ireland in the Nineteenth and early Twentieth Centuries*, Cambridge
[5] Hickman, M. (1995) *Religion Class and Identity: The state, the Catholic Church and the Education of the Irish in Britain*, Aldershot, England
[6] Kofman, E. Phizacklea, A. Raghuram, P. Sales, R. (2000) *Gender and International Migration in Europe*, London

CHAPTER 2: CONTEXTS AND LITERATURE REVIEW

Because of the interdisciplinary nature of this thesis, many different sources have been explored and considered. In order to research Irish immigrant women in England, we have to examine their reasons for leaving Ireland and key aspects in their lives including the places they settled and employment. This chapter will examine how other research addressed the relationship Irish women had with the Catholic Church and what faith women brought with them from Ireland, especially their relationship with Mary and the differences they encountered in England. In addition, research that examines the Catholic Church in England and explores how much of its success can be contributed to the influence of Irish immigrants will be discussed. Finally, the research available on the local context of Harold Hill and the history of its development and growth and its relationship to Irish settlements in East London will be examined, as it contributes a new spatial dimension to the study of the Irish in Britain.

Irish Immigrant Women in England: reasons for leaving Ireland

Migration is a process in which individuals and often also entire communities are caught up. This has often been a process whereby large industrial powers contribute the economic pull factors and poverty in agrarian countries the push factors. Embedded within this process are many more complex reasons for migration on a personal, family and community level including an often under-researched religious dimension. Irish immigrant women can give important information about the reasons for leaving and inform us and provide us with an insight into the lives of migrant women. Women's experiences in Ireland should be taken into account in examination of their lives in Harold Hill and are important to the thesis as this contributes to the picture of the background of the women on the Harold Hill Estate.

Research on migrants used to be gender neutral as Kofman, Phizacklea, Raghuram and Sales highlighted when they explored migration to and within Europe:

> *"Most studies appeared to be gender neutral while utilising models of migration based on the experiences of men. Women, where their presence is acknowledged, are often treated as dependants, migrating under family reunion, and their contribution to the economies and societies of destination countries ignored."*[1]

Gender specific research has made important discoveries about the reasons for women to leave their homeland. The early researchers were mostly sociologists like Guyot, Padrun, Dauphinet, Jospa, Fischli, de Mestral, Giudici and Scheidecker who pioneered research on women migrants who migrated to Western Europe from Italy, Portugal, Morocco, and Algeria.[2] Their research was particularly valuable to this thesis because it highlighted the strong position religious faith held within the migrant cultures and the weaker position of women within their community and family. More recent work on the influence of religion especially in migrant Muslim communities has been conducted by Hoffer in which he explores the way in which Muslims explain mental illness and where the basis of their beliefs are formed by the understanding of the Koran.[3] What Hoffer shows is the complexities of migration when the religious background of the migrants differs from the host society. Very complex dilemmas involving health, for instance, are not understood, as they remain a hidden part of the migrant lives. This is strengthened by the negative racial attitudes towards the migrants based on their religious background. Because a woman's position in religious contexts is often connected with her position in the home and the family, her position is often either hidden from view or she is rendered silent and the assumption is usually made that she is more likely to be a victim in her own culture. Jonkers examined the relationship of professional health workers and Moroccan mothers and discovered the views of these women were often perceived as static and passive by the health workers, a view that proved incorrect with reference to women in the sample.[4] At the same time women's visibility as Muslims, for example, when using the Islam dress code is seen as an insult to western society unlike the Hijab of the men. In contemporary western European media the portrayal of non-western migrants plays on the fear of the unknown so that migrants with a religious background are conceived as different and therefore a threat. This is also represented by media and some politicians as a unique and new situation. But in Irish migration similar attitudes existed in England, in the nineteenth century when English populations were confronted with Irish Catholic migrant workers who, because of their Catholic faith, were seen as a threat to English society as Hickman pointed out in her research in *Religion, Class and Identity*:

> *"Religions in Britain influenced public policy formation, often decisively, in the 19th century; and have continued to exert a degree of influence in the present century. This much is usually recognised. However, the articulation of religious issues with ethnic issues tends, incorrectly, to be viewed as a recent phenomenon. For example, in recent years demands for Muslim schools to be given voluntary aided status have prompted much discussion. A central assumption in the debate is that the issue of segregation of a minority is being raised for the first time in British education."*[5]

Irish migration can therefore serve as a case study for the importance of religion in the relationship between migrants and the host society. Gray wrote a paper on migration policies in *Migrant Integration Policy* after a conference, which was held in Bundoran, Co Donegal during the Irish Presidency of the EU, January - June 2004, by the Department of Social and Family Affairs. It had the support of the European Commission on the topic of 'Reconciling Mobility and Social Inclusion'.[6] A key element of the conference was learning from Ireland's history of emigration. It also focused on the policies that were put in place to support immigrants. Gray refers in her paper to research by Lyberaki, who writes that in the case of Albanian migrants in Greece, the majority are Muslims and therefore are of different religious background than the Greek majority. Comparisons can be made with the Irish immigrants in English society. But also in the case of the Albanians social policies had little effect as the global economy is changing so rapidly, policymakers are often too late in their response. However Lyberaki argues that migrants themselves prove to adapt informally but successfully to the rapidly changing labour market.[7] If any lessons need to be drawn from the Irish migrants it would be that migrants in general as Lyberaki points out are often adapting and surviving successfully on their own accord. As one important reason for their success Lyberaki argues:

> *"Transnational migrant networks, operating across national borders and connecting people who live in different localities, produce various kinds of cross-border, trans-local flows which are now facilitated by the near-instantaneous character of communication: from the physical movement of migrants between countries of origin and destination to the movement of remittances, information, commodities and values."*[8]

This connects with the argument Hickman makes when she writes that Irish migrant workers were very quick to organise themselves without the help from governmental bodies or the Catholic Church:

> *"It is true that the Irish were dislocated after migration, as Lees (1979) also points out; but, once here, the Irish quickly established their own means of social organisation, particularly for finding work and lodgings."*[9]

Although the religious background of the migrant is often viewed with suspicion, the religious bodies themselves are usually not involved with the successful adapting of immigrants and often not even present at the early stages of migration, but their social structures prove to be the source of their success. This thesis will examine how Irish women established social networks and organised themselves into new communities. Lyberaki believes that for a part where migration into European countries today differs from migration in the past is the large number of women who are active as independent actors in this process.[10] Therefore the history of migration of a large number of single Irish women to Britain becomes important to study. In the case of Irish women the majority arrived in Britain as labour migrants.

Irish migration to Britain and the relationship between the two countries is complex because of Ireland's colonial past, bringing the Irish within the fold of the British nation on the one hand but marking them as 'other' on the other. This immediately connects with male migrant imageries, as Walter and Hickman describe how the masculine imagery of Irish men hides the presence of Irish women in Britain.[11] In British society the stereotypical view of Irish women is that of being housewives and as mothers of large families.[12] As Walter explains, women were likely to socialise within the safety of their own Irish community and particularly in their own Catholic parish, which made them less visible to Protestants, and therefore the indigenous population.[13] This is very relevant to the research on Harold Hill and more research needs to be done that looks at these issues. Hickman describes how the Church was important to many Irish migrants as a place to socialise, but they also had been able to organise themselves without help from the Church and Irish pubs and dance halls were often found within Irish communities, particularly in London as this research will show.[14] In Harold Hill however, which was entirely residential in character, social life centred very much on the church to socialise or organise social events. The influence of the Church can also be traced back in the work of the women religious who played a major role in the education of Irish children.

Socialising was something that women also did at their workplaces. Most women migrated to London because of the work available. But wherever they moved to and what lives they lived, was always closely connected with the need for such female workers.[15] For instance Irish women contributed to the production of textiles in the English factories; were nannies in the homes and as nurses played an important part in the health sector as Walter explores.[16] The Irish female migrants were more often single than female migrants from other countries and were often better educated than Irish male migrants, as the historian Fitzpatrick highlighted.[17] But similarities can also be found to other migrant women, such as the importance of faith and the powerful position the Church held in their society which is comparable to some Muslim societies from Moroccan or Kurdish origin.[18] MacAdam argues that some Irish women emigrated to escape their inferior position within their own society where they did not conform to the expected stereotypical women's role placed on them by the Catholic identity of Irish society, as examples she refers to:

> *"Unwanted pregnancies and same sex relationships were problematic within Irish society."*[19]

The ban on divorce and the strong position of the family made life difficult for women who did not fit the criteria, for instance single mothers, as Jackson explains:

> *"A woman who gave birth to an illegitimate child was shunned and ostracised by the community and a quick emigration to England was a resolution to her problem from the post-famine decades to contemporary times."*[20]

Position of women in Ireland

For some women leaving their homeland was the only option open to them. Irish society left very little work open to women and poverty was a direct result for many women. Poverty and health problems were closely connected as the infant mortality figures of Dublin in the 1926 Census show: In North Dublin City the average death rate per 1,000 children between one and five years was 25.6 and in the more prosperous suburb of Dublin, Drumcondra the death rate was 7.7 per 1,000 children.[21] The connection between health issues and migration is reflected in the stories of the Irish women of the Harold Hill Estate, as they referred to fears about infant mortality and the fear of death by outbreaks of diseases based on experience as will be discussed in the thesis. But health does not always improve after migration. When studying health issues of migrant communities, social constructions are often overlooked; this can help explain how choices of the individual often connect with formed social relationships. For instance reasons for leaving can connect the individual with her society. In their study on Northern Irish women and abortions in England, McEvoy and Boyle argued that psychology and psychiatry tended to approach abortion as a health issue for the individual ignoring the relationship between the social context in which women experience abortion and their responses to it. In their paper they revealed strong links between the women's experience and the very negative public constructions of abortion in Northern Ireland.[22] Some of these women only ever visited England to undergo an abortion or decided to stay for a short period but others stayed permanently in England.

Other interesting papers published on the health of Irish migrants include that of Ryan on depression in Irish migrants living in London. Ryan claims that the migration of Irish men and women was often unplanned as they carried a range of physical and mental health problems.[23] Tilki discussed alcohol abuse in Irish migrant men and the connection to finding work through the social contacts in the pub: a topic also discussed by the women on the Harold Hill Estate.[24] She argues on the importance of research:

> *"In order to address problem drinking among sections of the Irish community in Britain requires that the context and the experience of being Irish in Britain be understood by policymakers and practitioners so that health promotion and therapeutic interventions are effective in addressing this issue of concern."*[25]

In a paper on Irish migrants with dementia and British Heath Care, Tilki argues that:

> *"In addition to economic factors, a significant proportion of Irish men and women migrated to escape abuse in institutions or the family which had a bad effect on their mental health but also their isolation in British Health Care means lack of adequate help."*[26]

The reasons for leaving are well explored in Tilki's research but also the impact that migration often had on the migrant is highlighted and shows the importance for in-depth research on migrants' lives. However the importance religion played in the lives of the migrant, especially the women needs further research, faith was vitally important to Irish migrant women as they continued to struggle with health issues, which is often ignored. Women would pray to the Virgin Mary with their rosaries to protect their families from diseases with which they were all too familiar, as they were taught the see the Virgin as a powerful healer and protector of infant lives. They connected prayer and the powers of Mary with the faith and wellbeing of their families.

Research collecting data on the health status of Irish migrants was explored by Owen, the study researched settlement patterns and socio-economic circumstances.[27] The study was wide in scope and shows Irish migrants were still less well off than their white English counterparts. This connects with the areas in which Irish migrants settled and the poverty they encountered there. This also became apparent in this thesis where the poverty in East London will be explored in chapter 4. Ryan and Tilki both highlighted in their research the mental and emotional stress the migration process brings: for instance in women when they raise their families completely cut off from their own mothers. The connection between health issues and migration needs to be explored still further.[28]

Reasons for leaving often connect with lives lived in farming communities for many of Europe's migrants. To Irish women farming was often an important aspect of the migration. After its independence Ireland had remained a rural society with small-scale independent farms that supported a dominantly agricultural economy until the end of the 1950s. This agricultural economy had been shaped after the Famines of the 1840s and the Land Wars of 1880 with a land-inheritance system that left only one son to inherit.[29] Home rule would slow down emigration but it can be argued that the family farm with its strong links with the Catholic establishment and its reputation for self-sufficiency was keeping the large scale emigration, mainly from rural areas, in place. The Irish government, however, continued to criticise those who were leaving, referring to it as a selfish and above all voluntary act.[30]

For women it was difficult to find some future in Ireland for themselves as the options to marry were limited. For some, the religious life must have felt as one of the few options open to them. What made it even more complex was that Irish society placed women in three main categories; that of virgin, that of mother and that of prostitute.[31] Women were meant to marry and become mothers and since the Irish Free State was established the marriage bar was put in place, prohibiting married women from paid employment in various occupations. Thus paid work outside the family farm was very difficult to find but the changes in farming had already reduced employment amongst women before the independence of Ireland. The creameries for instance, which were introduced to the Irish countryside in the 1880s, were intended to improve butter making on the farms but they created much hardship amongst farmers and took work away from women, particularly in Munster, increasing unemployment amongst women.[32] Bourke refers to the period 1890-1914, before Irish independence, as an important period in which a shift took place from women's labour in the fields into the home. She shows how, in this period, their position within the employment market deteriorated: married women came to be increasingly dependent on their husbands' earnings, while economic opportunities for unmarried and widowed women collapsed. This trend then continued during the early 20th century.[33]

The relationship between the Catholic Irish State and Irish migrant women

In order to understand migrant women's lives, it becomes important to consider not only why they migrated but also to understand their past, the culture they grew up in and the traditions they passed on to their children. The Irish Republic established in 1922 was predominantly dependent on subsistence agricultural activity and with its patriarchal outlook it held limited opportunities for employment, particularly for women. Much more research has now been conducted to get a clear picture of what lives women led in Irish society. Luddy for instance collected more than 100 sources and documents relating to the public and private aspects of women's lives in Ireland during 1800-1918.[34] Daly highlights how the 1926 census returns for single women aged 14 and over, indicate that less than half of all Irish women in this age group were in employment.[35] This did not include women who supported their husband in the family business.[36]

As Brown points out the Irish Catholic Church played a major part in the shaping of the Irish society:

> *"Accordingly from the years of the devotional revolution onward Irish Catholicism increasingly became the badge of national identity at a time when the Church also felt able to propound doctrines that enshrined the rights of private property."*[37]

The overwhelming majority were Catholic and since the Famine Catholicism had become more and more the badge of Irish identity. After the Famine, during the 1850s, the Roman Catholic Church re-introduced visual aids and intensified the use of these devotional aids such as the rosary, shrines, beads, religious medals and holy pictures. Pilgrimages, processions and retreats were popular and religious feelings were more openly displayed as part of Catholic emancipation.

It was this Church that the Irish Free State inherited, and that continued to give its full support to the Irish Free State Government. The government and the Church believed in the important role that the Church had to play in the new state. Protestants that had continued to live in Ireland after independence often migrated as a result or became isolated from their Catholic neighbours.[38] Throughout the 1930s until the late 1950s, both government and Church believed that it was possible to apply Catholic principles to every aspect of secular social life and in doing so creating a thoroughly Christian society.

The work of Cairns and Richards examines Irish culture through the eyes of Irish writers which demonstrates the complexities of that Catholic society.[39] They refer to authors and playwrights after the independence of Ireland. In a reference to plays and nationalism they argue that:

> *"What was expected of nationalist drama is nowhere better revealed in the productions of Maud Gonne's patriotic women's organisation Inghinidhe na hEireann ('Daughters of Erin'), which included amateur dramatics in its activities. The group had sponsored the first production of Yeats's Cathleen Ni Houlihan in which Maud Gonne had played the title role, and it is that play's advocacy of sacrificing individual desire for national advancement which characterised the movement's other propagandist productions."*[40]

This also shows the importance of women playing their part in this new Irish society mainly by suppressing their own needs and desires and supporting the needs of others.[41]

Brown's research looked at many different aspects of Irish cultural history that illuminated to some extent the position of the Church in Irish society. He highlights how the rural middle classes of Irish society influenced the Church in the early 20th century as they sent their sons to the national seminary of Maynooth, something that was reflected in the atmosphere of the place:

> *"Maynooth, County Kildare was the national seminary where sons of shopkeepers and farmers were sent to. Journalistic sources*

suggest that the social tone of Maynooth in the period of the early 20th century was somewhat boisterous and uncultivated, dominated as it was by young men from the land, and that the education provided was rather less than culturally enlarging in its anti-intellectualism and sexual prudery, confirming the values in which so many young men had been reared.'[42]

This also highlights the middle class background of the clergy and the interest of the Church lay with large property owners.

Murphy argues when trying to place the importance of the Church in the history of Irish society that the matter is so complex that it remains difficult to examine.[43] It is important to explore how this then transfers into the lives of migrant women in England. In this thesis views of individual women on Catholic issues will be researched. Lee's study critically explores how the power of the Church in Ireland influenced the position of women since the Famine.[44] In the decades after the Famine women were increasingly thought of primarily as mothers. The idealisation of mothers particularly towards their sons becomes clear in Valiutis' study. She refers to a speech delivered by Eamon De Valera at the death of Margaret Pearse, the mother of Patrick and William Pearse the famed revolution leaders of 1916, in which De Valera compared her to the silent Mary. In his speech the success of the two leaders of the revolution is related to the devotion of the mother who can endure the pain watching history unfold. The women themselves remain silent.[45]

Important research has been conducted in which the stability and the role of mother and family life have been examined more closely. McCullough argues with regards to the familial ideologies that unlike the myths such as those encountered in the speech by De Valera, family relationships were often very complex especially on family farms where rivalry amongst siblings was commonplace.[46] These rivalries led in many cases to friction and involuntary migration and stability was not always present. The American anthropologists Arensberg and Kimball who researched communities in Co Clare and in particular gathered detailed information on farm work contributed to the myth of this stable Irish family-based society in research in 1931.[47] They believed it to be a very stable community despite the fact that at the time small family farms were struggling to survive and poverty was mostly the outcome of this constant struggle.[48] The rural ideals of family life and the family farm were so important to Irish society that this filtered through in urban society which became clear in the work of Humphreys when he researched the *New Dubliners*.[49] His research concluded that Dubliners had in many ways kept their rural identity: this meant very strong fixed roles for men and women also within the cities.

Irish urban society even kept many rural expressions in which the position of women becomes clear. O'Dowd's cultural research looks at the proverbs in which animals and people were compared, and women were often placed in a negative light, highlighting the lower position women held in rural Irish society. She writes:

> *"The beliefs and dictates enshrined in proverbs not only attempted to define women, but also curtail their activities in issuing exclusions and prohibitions from women's participation in certain events."*[50]

Women were seen as unlucky in various places of work and therefore to be avoided in those professions. O'Dowd places these proverbs alongside the tasks of women in farming and how their position outside the family home decreased.

Nash examines the position of the Irish woman in rural paintings and photographs and in 1910 the colour of a woman's dress was seen as important enough to be part of a national debate (red was preferred as it was vibrant) but after the establishment of the Irish Free State the women seem to disappear altogether out of the pictures.[51] This research can give a glimpse of the lives Irish women lived and the Irish society that they left behind. This could help explore the link between the lives that they left behind and the lives they rebuilt in England. But a particularly important source of information on aspects of migration should come from individual narratives as it gives a greater insight and scope. Gray argues that the term migration was often used in an abstract and very universal way describing the movements of peoples without researching the stories of these people.[52] In Gray's project on the Irish women who remained in Ireland, she argues that:

> *"In the 1950s, Ireland was experiencing the highest levels of emigration of the twentieth century. Yet, we know little about the impact of emigration on those who stayed. This project (which was part funded by the Higher Education Authority, Ireland) set out to capture living memories of Irish life in the 1950s by interviewing those who stayed in Ireland in a decade when so many were leaving."*[53]

She and her co-workers established an archive of 78 oral narratives and 12 text contributions of which fifty of the oral narratives are published on the web site. They form a basis where oral history can be collected and used for history purposes.

Another piece of research that demonstrates the complexity of family life on the family farms is the contemporary study of Shortall who examines the power relationships that affect women on Irish farms.[54] She stresses that women who cannot get together easily because of living on remote farms and working long hours have no forum. When women have no forums, they remain silent and silence might be seen as an agreement to the position of the dominant group thus perpetuating patriarchy. Women's lives as Shortall argues are closely connected to their social surroundings and the position they have in their own society and family, their identity from their rural background.

It also is important to note that due to the declining fortunes of the small family farm, female migration accelerated. Moser's research shows that in 1936 in Connacht 19,000 female relatives worked on the farms but that figure had gone down to 9,000 only fifteen years later.[55] This hints at the complexities involving the lives of these family farms and that it often meant for the daughters migration to the unknown.

Identity, Irish Catholic women and faith

For some, identity is related to the way in which we view ourselves and how we connect with ourselves. As Markus, Hazel, Kitayama and Shinobu describe, people in different cultures have strikingly different construals (perception) of the self and of others but also how these two interact. These construals can influence, and often also determine, the nature of individual experience, including emotion and motivation. Many Asian cultures for instance have distinct conceptions of individuality that insist on the fundamental relatedness of individuals to each other.[56] Irish women as examined in the interviews later on in chapter 5, were thought only ever to see themselves through relationship with others to which they performed a serving and inferior role. In their upbringing the Virgin Mary was instrumental to guide these girls into their sense of the self. They are therefore unable to see themselves as a self and independently of the others like in Asian cultures. The difference here is that her Irish male counterparts were encouraged to see themselves as strong and independent individuals, with perhaps the exception of the son's relationship towards his mother. With reference to the Virgin Mary Beale writes:

> *"This image of Mary contains the origin of the stereotype of the traditional Irish mother as a women over devoted to her sons, protecting them and serving, rearing them to believe that they are more important then she is."*[57]

When Irish women moved to England they maintained their Irish identity to some extent. This identity was closely connected to their Catholic identity in which women were at the heart of family life and supportive of others. In her study, Gray looks at women in Ireland and England and their relationship to Irishness.[58] What complicates their sense of self and identity is the suppressed position they held in Ireland, leading to their escape to England and the hostile reactions towards their Irish background by their new English neighbours. The racism that they encountered in England was difficult to research as Rossiter points out because race is not a biological construction but a social one that changes and reinvents itself.[59] Hickman stresses the gulf between the Irish and the English Catholics in England based on national identity and social-class background. She also argues that:

> *"The aim of the Church was to transform the Irish in Britain by strengthening their identity as Catholic at the expense of their Irishness."*[60]

The Catholic Irish children were not taught Irish history by their schools: what was taught instead was their Catholic identity. Hickman's work had resonance for my work in that she used local archives in London and Liverpool, hence highlighting the importance of using such sources of data in academic research. This thesis will be exploring how Irish identity was viewed by the Catholic Church in the locality of Romford, Essex. Another factor in the loss of Irish identity of the Irish women immigrants to England occurred because of marrying people from the host/indigenous communities. Whilst children do hold on to some of the traditions that parents pass on there is a chance that in mixed marriages there may be two quite distinct identities and cultural beliefs being transferred. It was indeed the case that Irish women often married outside their own community, particularly in the London area where more Irish single women migrated than men. King and O'Connor studied Irish women and their daily lives.[61] They interviewed women in Leicester researching the push and pull factors of migration but also compared those who married Irish men and those who married other men. The research also revealed that Irish men helped less with domestic chores at home than their English counterparts, falling back on traditional Irish family roles. This means that mixed marriages do then influence and change traditional patterns within the family. This was relevant because Irish women in the South East region also married outside their own community and mixed marriages emerged as an essential part of my thesis. But Hickman, Morgan and Walter's research demonstrates that in London more Irish women married Irish men than elsewhere.[62] The lack of information on Irish community in London emerged in a research project by Hickman, Morgan and Walter, commissioned by the Dion Committee. The report looked at needs of the Irish community and it found that:

> *"The authors were struck by the small amount of research on the needs of the Irish in Britain, and on the Irish in Britain in general, and on the Irish in London in particular, a major city of the Irish diaspora. The historiography of the Irish in London can be listed in one paragraph, in striking contrast to New York, for example, where a full-length book is needed simply to list research. This research gap points up the problematic and difficult position of the Irish in Britain."*[63]

There is research on communities in London in Walter's work that proved important to this thesis as it examines cases of women who settled in London. But also Walter's research on Irish diaspora explores the themes of displacement and the meaning of home for these women. She researched Irish women making comparisons possible for me and gave me insights into the way in which women settled but also how they looked at their own situation. Local area studies give a deeper understanding of women living and working in small communities, for example, local studies like that of Lambert in which she studies Irish women in Lancaster.[64]

Local studies can connect with broader studies like that of Delaney as this can achieve a balance between personal stories imbedded in local history and the broader economical and political arenas in which these lives are lived. And both sides need examining as they can highlight the obstacles involved and the complexities of the lives of immigrants. As Delaney points out:

> *"For the Irish, unlike the other migrants who arrived in Britain after the Second World War, adjusting did not involve overcoming the obstacles of mastering a new language or getting to grips with a completely alien culture. However, the widespread assumption that since the Irish no longer seemed so different to British eyes rapid assimilation occurred fails to take account of the complexities of adapting to a new life in a new country. May sought understandably to 'recreate the familiar whilst in the midst of change' to encounter the dislocation of emigration."*[65]

This is very relevant to this research and points at the problematic aspects of migration. It is the process of migration that remains complex and always means adapting and forging a new life for the migrant despite the fact that migrant communities in England had a framework established which was useful for the newcomer. New lives were in need of new community life and that was often very successfully established. A good example is the London Irish Centre that was opened in Camden Square in 1955 and had a predominantly social function. In chapter 4 of the thesis the more established social life in London will be explored and contrasted with the lack of social gatherings in Harold Hill. To the individual it often remained difficult to migrate and leave everything behind and newcomers were also required to find a place in this society for themselves even if much was already in place as was the case in London.

Delaney's work covers the political aspects of the dislocation of the Irish migrants and the response of the Catholic Church in Ireland and their desperate attempt to hold on to their Irish migrants in Protestant England. It highlights a church that understood how Irish migrants would build their communities even without a Catholic Church. The importance the Church placed on Catholic worship was closely connected with the safekeeping of this community away from home. This is highlighted by Delaney as he refers to the Catholic archbishop from Dublin John Charles McQuaid (from 1940 until the early 1970) who was much involved in the issue of Catholic welfare especially that of the women who he considered in more danger of various perils than the men.[66] What is missing in this informative work are the voices of the people who lived through it, how their faith influenced their life choices and how this was incorporated in their lives lived out in their community away from the farm and Irish life back home. But their views on the Catholic Church and their parish priest and other men religious and women are also important. This is missing in most work and there is very little research done into it as it is something people often do not talk about. It is also a very complex but important aspect of the way in which religion functions as Ryan, Rigby and King explain:

> *"In large part, specific religious beliefs are maintained through cultural transmission, in that they have continuity only through being passed on to new generations, the individual members of which must in turn adopt the transmitted beliefs and practices as their own. Put it differently, religions must be internalised by cultural members both to survive and to provide any functional value to adherents."*[67]

The Catholic Church expected laity to follow the Church's instructions and to look for guidance and explanation to the parish priest and to express it as a community, a parish. Faith is also a private and personal affair but in the case of Catholicism it is often misunderstood because Catholic worship is noted outwardly by the use of saints, statues and communal processions.

Therefore Irish Catholic worship was widely misunderstood in Protestant society and the Irish were seen as Delaney describes:

> *"Irish piety was recognised but Irish social graces and occupations looked down upon. The Irish were perceived holy, but lumpen, proletariat with inevitably, 'exceptions' among the priests and nuns, and friends."*[68]

In Werner's research on migrants in the Netherlands it proved difficult to encourage people to talk about their beliefs, particularly if the individual's beliefs differed from the rest of the 'host society'.[69] With reference to statues like the ornamented gods in the Hindu tradition; people rarely wish to talk about their significance or meaning.[70] As for the Catholics, Hornsby-Smith even refers to these beliefs as part of the working class Catholicism. Hornsby-Smith argues that Catholicism only matured during the latter part of the twentieth century when it became a more personally experienced faith and therefore more connected to the educated middle classes. He refers to rituals and numerous symbols of the mid twentieth century as part of the working class and a distinctive sub-culture.[71]

The lives and beliefs of Catholic women religious have been researched by McKenna who interviewed women religious who lived in convents in England and this research gives a great insight into their experience as Irish women and the complex position of the Irish nun in Catholic society.[72] It also examines this personal level in which faith operates. She argues the importance of these women in the history of migration, stating that:

> *"Indeed, such is the influence of Irish Catholic migration, it has been suggested that since the beginning of the nineteenth century the story of Catholicism in Britain is largely the story of Irish migration. However, one area remains almost entirely ignored: none of the studies on Irish Catholicism in or migration to Britain explore in any way the position, influence or experience of Irish women religious."*[73]

Missionary work was a very important feature in Irish Catholicism but as late as the 1930s and 1940s the government kept referring to all migrant women as domestics when the reality was that since the 1890s a growing number of women migrants had studied at university, many of whom were sisters.[74] As McCurtain explains, these women religious were prominent particularly in nursing, medicine and teaching.[75] In chapter 6 of the thesis the importance of women religious will be explored.

Irish women and their relationship with the Virgin Mary

In Catholic worship women were expected to become either women religious or mothers. But to both groups the mother of Christ was considered an icon and example. The Virgin Mary was influential in Catholic thinking and subsequently her cult dominated the way in which women were viewed. Marian devotion became more and more popular after Irish Independence as the Virgin became a symbol to all that was Catholic, and a nationalistic element of Irish Catholic identity. Irish identity was mainly Catholic, rural and closely connected to family values, all of which applied to Mary. Donnelly argues that after it became more established, with much help of the Church in the period 1850-1875, Marian devotion reached its peak in the period 1930-1960.[76] It was at the heart of Catholic worship and at the centre of family life with family prayers said with help of the rosary. Family was important to the Irish Free State and the holy family the ultimate example. Family life was seen as sacred and stable and a safe place away from the turmoil of society. But family life was much more than the cornerstone of society; it lay at the heart of Irish rural society. As Walter explains:

> *"All nations represent themselves as families, interconnected and united, but the trope is particularly resonant in Ireland."*[77]

To study Irish women in Harold Hill it was important to tackle two major themes that were connected in this research; the position of the Virgin Mary in the Catholic Church and the position of motherhood and how influential both themes were in the religious lives of the Irish women on the Harold Hill Estate. Motherhood had in the Virgin Mary the ultimate role model and Catholic women looked to her for guidance in their own relationships with her son and here the importance of Mary is directly connected to her relationship with her son but she was also seen as the Queen of Heaven. She was worshipped as a Queen but without a mortal throne and therefore was as powerful as humble. In the Irish tradition she was often referred to as Queen of Ireland supplanting the Queen of England.[78]

On the other hand expectations towards mothers connect with the model of Mary as a mother. Boss explains:

> *"Over time, devotion to the Virgin changed its emphasis in that it became less interested in Mary's authority and glory as Mother of God and more concerned with her spiritual role as mother of Christian and subsequently with her moral example as the recipient of God's word."*[79]

In this research women often referred to her as the ultimate mother or the mother to worship or even mimic. We needed therefore to look at research of the development of her role, her important place in the wider Catholic Church and whether this was different from the Irish Catholic Church. The role of mother in Catholic society can trace the origins of the ideals surrounding mothering back to her, as the psychologist Thurer describes in her research. Thurer traces traditions in mothering through the history of Western society and the emphasis in her research lies on how motherhood is viewed. According to Thurer, the problem with motherhood is:

> *"If every hope of fulfilment is bound to the one duty of childbearing, which is not universally fulfilling and frequently impossible to perform in the prescribed manner, motherhood is in danger of becoming an instrument of women's annulment as persons."*[80]

To model motherhood for ordinary mothers on Mary is not such a strange choice as she gives comfort to all. Thurer argues that Mary is far more powerful than most goddesses of earlier times because of the way in which she underpins motherhood that is central to her whole being:

> *"The Virgin Mary's popularity is not surprising. Who would not want such a martyr? Indeed, she is so abundantly gratifying as a concept, so responsive to suppressed human longings, that it is a wonder that she was not invented before. She is everything the great*

goddess, the Neolithic, Goddesses, and the Greek, Goddesses were not: merciful, trustworthy, overflowing with goodness. Imagine how soothing the contemplation of her must have been to hapless medieval women."[81]

It is therefore important to understand what this relationship is between women and the Virgin Mary within Catholicism. Mary is a powerful figure within Catholic teaching where her role as mother is connected with that of monarch and healer. To understand this relationship Warner made a striking impact with her research into the history of the Virgin and her influence in Catholic teaching throughout the history of the Church. This work was a completely new way of looking at the Virgin Mary and her influence. In her book *Alone of all her sex* Warner wrote how the Virgin Mary was able to rule over life and death, was able to strengthen life and heal but that despite her powers she could not empower women.[82]

Although women could connect with her by means of her gender it was her role as mother that was mostly idealised. This however did not raise women's own status in Catholic societies; they remained inferior to men. As Warner explains:

"Yet this veneration provokes no corresponding rise in status of women. On the contrary, the fertility ascribed to her reinforces the mythology that motherhood is the central point of a woman's life, where all the streams of her nature converge and prosper. For it is in Catholic countries above all, from Italy to Latin America, that women are subjected to the ideal of maternity."[83]

Warner argues that the history of Mary is very complex as she changed gradually from a position of powerful majesty to one of humble maiden. Mary emerged as a figure of importance in the Christian Church. Firstly the importance was placed on the virgin birth, as a sign of divine intervention. But the emphasis then shifted to the importance of her virginity. This emerged as the importance of original sin through the fall of Adam and in particular of Eve, created a renewed interest in the importance of the virginal status of Mary. The other daughters of Eve were considered corruptible and not as pure.[84] This shift had major implications for the position of women in society: it became the moral doctrine creating in Mary female subordination; virginal status became directly connected with humility and the position of a handmaiden. Subordination and servitude in Irish women centred round the kitchen and household chores were especially stressed in Irish teaching on Mary according to Warner:

> *"In Knock, now the most popular shrine of the Virgin in Ireland, the devotions focus on the hardships of Irish mothers in their family kitchens. One fast-selling holy picture at the shrine shows a wan, young mother in an apron stirring a bowl by a steaming stove. It is inscribed with the 'Kitchen Prayer'"*[85]

The concept of humility however was not strictly speaking a female quality in early Judean traditions. Warner does not explore the origins of humble and handmaiden, whereas the theologian Serra in *Magnificat Remembrance and Praise* does. He stresses the history of humility and the meaning that surrounds the word humble to early Judean traditions, highlighting that Mary was not unique in her role of humble servant carrying out the will of God the Father. The "humble servant" was also a male role in the Jewish tradition. According to Serra, unlike strong willed people, the faithful have the spirit of the poor; their whole way of living is a witness to God and obedience to his Covenant.[86] The Qumran writings mention poverty in the same way. This community considered themselves a community of the poor. A poor person relied on the Lord and his will, as was expressed in the Mosaic Law.[87] Humility in the Old Testament has a much wider implication and does not automatically connect with women per se. But in the Catholic teaching, humility became connected with the subordination of women and can be firmly placed at the feet of the Virgin.

When Warner researches the history of the images of Mary by the Church she does not reflect upon the effect this had on ordinary women, merely stating the development of her role, as Serra compared this with earlier Judean traditions. Only in the prologue do we get a glimpse of what the teachings on Mary had meant to Warner personally, when she writes of the impact it had on her as a child in the nineteen sixties. The feminist and philosopher Kristeva on the other hand, explores placing herself as a woman and mother within the story of Mary. She describes the joy of becoming a mother in *Stabat Mater* but does not research the suppressed self by externally enforced role patterns.[88] She highlights instead the joy she found in her relationship with her son and feels connected with the image of the Virgin Mary as she celebrates this recognition.

But what then connects Mary to women in their motherhood is their relationship to her son not her role as mother in general. Boss explores this relationship and how much the emphasis was shifting over the centuries from the 13th century towards her role as a mother at the cost of her role as the queen; ruler over life and death. She writes that in order to strengthen this development even further:

> *"In 1964, the Second Vatican Council published its decree on the Church, De Ecclesia. This includes a chapter on the Blessed Virgin Mary, in which it is written that 'the immaculate Virgin…was… exalted by the Lord as Queen of all things so that she might be more fully conformed to her Son, the Lord of Lords and victor over sin and death.'"*[89]

It does show the sense of importance for the Vatican to depict women only as mothers and the continuation of this trend.

The feminist and Catholic Spretnak however, argues that after the Second Vatican council of 1963 the Salve Regina was gradually removed from the Mass and in some places her statues as a central figure were removed from churches. She writes that the faithful continue to keep her beloved images alive and worship her in their homes. Spretnak argues that Mary's role as Queen of Heaven is more likely to empower women than her role as a mother serving her only son. She is not convinced that a more biblical Mary, one based on evidence of the mother of Jesus found in the Second Testament, would help women's issues in Catholic regions.[90] Spretnak refers here to the Catholic worshippers in general and makes references to Latin American nations and women today, her discussion is about the relationship women have in general with Mary as a role model.

Beale on the other hand specifically discusses the relationship of Irish women to Mary. She refers to the role of women in their family especially in relationship to their sons. This reminds us of the comment Boss made on the De Ecclesia. Irish women were important as mothers to their sons. We need to understand the relationship between Irish women and Mary and what they were taught when young. Beale argues:

> *"and as Mary was merciful, her son could not refuse his mother. A mother can manipulate the bond with her son to tie him to her and make him emotionally dependant on her, unable to free himself to love another woman."*[91]

Beale can explain the useful aspect of this worshipping of the mother Mary and in it mothers who mimic Mary would have a powerful hold over their sons later on in his life. But she argues that acting out Mary cannot be successful no matter how much she is committed because women were never equal to her. As Beale writes:

> *"The mother is Mary in her other aspect, as the mother who worshipped her son. As both mother and virgin, Mary represents the impossible ideal, the mother who bore a son but who was untainted by sex. And she reveals another aspect of the mother image – she is defined in relation to a male child, not a daughter. Mother is the woman who nurtures and services men."*[92]

The many shrines dedicated to the Virgin Mary demonstrate the importance of the mother of Christ in Ireland where her popularity increased after the Irish Free State was established as Donnelly explains:

> *"My general argument in all this will be that in its Marian aspect the Irish 'devotional revolution' which firmly established itself, according to Emmet Larkin at least, in the period 1850-75, reached its fullest flowering in the years 1930-1960, and that in this later period the Marian cult provided its central symbols, values, and devotional practices."*[93]

According to Donnelly in the Irish Free State Irish identity was closely linked with Catholicism. He argues that in Catholic worship Mother Mary meant a much sought after refuge for men and women. But Mary's role in worship also helped create a justification of a patriarchal society. The devotional practices are important to note as it was this devotion that Irish immigrants brought with them as they settled in England over the next two centuries and what can be found in the feelings expressed by Irish women interviewed in the research.

The influence of Irish Catholic migrants on the development of the Catholic Church in England

To try to understand Irish women's lives in Britain it is important to examine the influence the influx of the Irish migrants had on the English Catholic Church from the 19th century onwards. Irish migration to England slowed after 1880. During most of the 19th Century, Catholics were mainly situated in the rural areas such as Durham, Lancashire and Shropshire but this gradually changed. Hornsby-Smith produced several studies on the history of Catholic England and Catholic identity. In his study *Roman Catholic Beliefs in England,* he stresses how the Catholic communities from the 19th century onwards clustered mainly in urban society rather than in rural locations because of the increase in Irish immigrants.[94] This clustering of Irish immigrants changed the Church in England from a predominantly rural Church, from before the 19th century, into an urban phenomenon. Hornsby-Smith does believe that Irish worshippers lost their ethnic Irish identity and this allowed the erosion of the authority of the parish priest as the urban Catholics would not have given the parish priest the same authority over their community as rural Irish Catholics would have done. He questions the position of the parish priest in Irish Catholic migrant congregations:

> *"Thus concern about 'lapsation' rates of Irish Catholics was evident well before the end of the 19th century. Interview data and oral histories point to frequent and sometimes bitter conflict with priests over confession, birth control, marriage to a non-Catholic partner, and marital breakdown. A recurring theme in historical accounts is the authoritarianism of the parish priest in the Catholic community from the middle of the 19th century until the 1950s. Analysis of Charles Booth studies of religion in London at the turn of the century indicates that in some cases this resulted in an atmosphere*

> *of 'spiritual totalitarianism', and convocation led to a reaction against 'overbearing ministers' or 'benevolent tyrants' and revolt against coercive Catholic schools. There seems to be that ample evidence, then, for recognising that lay compliance to ecclesiastical authority always has been put partial and problematic."*[95]

Irish communities in England differed throughout the country and their relationship with their parish priest was different from the relationship that communities had with parish priests in rural Ireland. For instance the congregation would have not consisted of the same members: even in rural areas their numbers would have changed constantly, and that would have meant a less stable platform for priests to work from. Migrant workers could all too easily become an expendable commodity. Many Irish migrant workers who came to the English countryside in the 19th century were seasonal harvesters, who returned to their smallholdings in the winter having saved enough cash to pay the rent. Most of these itinerant workers were men, although in the 1870s women from Kerry were said to regularly migrate to the iron furnaces of South Wales. Irish seasonal and migrant workers were often a highly mobile and flexible workforce, vital to Britain's booming 19th-century economy.[96] Many Irish migrants survived in England by moving often from place to place seeking work. This contributed to a loosening of close ties and with it a reduction in the position of power for the priest. Hornsby-Smith's view over-simplifies what was happening and does not carefully compare the influence of a powerful Church connected with government powers in Ireland to the influence of a Catholic Church with no such connection in England over the Catholics.[97] It still leaves us with the question: during their years working and living in England did migrants lose their Irish ethnic identity, or as a result of their Irish Catholic identity, did they remain strongly committed to their faith and were therefore regular worshippers with great influence on their parishes in England? In this thesis will examine their ethnic make-up and in their Catholicism and if they influenced the places in which Catholics worshipped.

The Irish immigrants who came to Britain during the end of the 19th century moved from a predominantly Catholic country to overwhelmingly Protestant England. This did not mean an absence of a Catholic Church but, as described earlier, as a result of settlement patterns of Irish immigrants from 19th century onwards, Catholic parishes can be mainly found in the urban areas. Evidence of Irish Catholics in Romford can also be found from the early 19th century and from the influence that they had on local church and school building (see also chapters 5 and 6).[98] In the area around Brentwood in Essex a small number of Catholic gentry remained and financially supported the building of the first Catholic Church and Catholic hall in Romford during the mid 19-century. Because of the inflow of Irish Catholics by the late 19th century the number of Catholics in Britain had risen to one million, with most of them living in the urban areas. This had changed the whole picture of the Catholic Church from a small rural congregation to an overwhelmingly urban Irish working class congregation. The result was a decline of the influence of the Catholic gentry and an increase of power for the clergy, many of whom were Irish.[99] But as Hornsby-Smith explained their influence would not have been as great as that of their Irish brothers back home. The more traditional Catholics had hoped for a continuation of their 'English Catholicism' and were concerned about the arrival of large numbers of Irish Catholics.[100]

The increasing numbers of Irish regular church attendants on the one hand and the dwindling numbers of English Catholics created the need for a response from the English Church. But the lack of trust of Irish worshippers of mostly English parish priests made it a difficult process. As Hornsby Smith points out:

> *"What historical evidence there is, however, suggests that there never was a golden age when lay compliance to clerical authority was not contested, at least by some Catholics. Thus concern about 'lapsation' rates of Irish Catholics was evident well before the end of the 19th century."*[101]

In an attempt to bridge the gap the priests introduced Irish symbols, saints' names and Irish practices in their churches. Customs that had been used by Irish priests were taken over by others and near the end of the 19th century their use was widespread.[102] Irish priests themselves however were viewed with suspicion by the Church hierarchy and although there had been a shortage of priests even before the 1840s, Irish priests were not often introduced.

Although it is clear that 'English Catholics' were concerned about the arrival of Irish Catholics and their own traditions the Catholic Church of the late 19th century did experience a wider variety of beliefs and traditions and Heinmann argues that the Victorians were aware and to some extent tolerant to the wide scope of worshippers. Heinmann describes in her work *Catholic Devotion in Victorian England* the variations in devotional practices in the Catholic Church in the 19th century. She explains how earlier historians believed that ultramontanism triumphed over older styles of Catholic piety but also over liberalism. Heinmann questions this idea by researching statistics of church-based devotional activity.[103] What is important is that she demonstrates that the Irish Catholic immigrants in England greatly increased in numbers and with that their influence on devotional practices. She argues that:

> *"The difficulty assessing what exactly constitutes adherence to the Catholic Faith as opposed to superstitious beliefs or merely social habits has been further complicated by nationalist strain in much of the work on Irish Catholicism. Several of these working on Irish spirituality have stressed the loss of native or Gaelic spirituality and its replacement with European ultramontanism; this is Emmett Larkin's devotional revolution, seen as a handiwork of Cardinal Paul Cullen, who allegedly imposed an ultramontane brand of Faith on virtually (in the formal sense) unpractising people"*[104]

However she feels that she can rely on the words of Richard Simpson, a 19th century contemporary who describes the Church's broad appearance as follows:

> *"Catholicism is a fact, and not a theory, whatever schools of thought have their existence within the Church, they are not cast out from communion, are, ipso facto, shown to be consisted... with generous spirit of historical Catholicism, which is tolerant of differences in doubtful matters, provided that unity is not broken in the necessary points of Faith and morals."*[105]

There was already what he describes as a lateral Catholic Church in England that embraced many worshippers with many different ideas about their faith. Catholicism was more than a collection of the various schools of thought; instead it was a collection of many worshippers and therefore held a very broad community of Catholics. This broad community of English worshippers would of course have included Irish migrants. But it seems as if Heinmann is trying to play down the impact Irish immigrants had on the Church. Simpson argues that of course Victorian England had many Catholic worshippers, including a large number of Irish worshippers, but does not mention that this church was so much in decline before the inflow of Irish worshippers in the 19th century.

Dye examines the shortage of English priests as early as 1865 when he refers to a case in Liverpool:

> *"In August 1865, Liverpool's Catholic Bishop (1856-72), Alexander Goss, needed to find a priest. ...Goss intended to find an English priest to satisfy the local Catholic baronet Sir Robert Gerard, Goss lamented that "I have some difficulty in making arrangements to fill his place; for being myself a Lancashire man I can well understand your dislike to have one from a country (Ireland) where nationality seems to override every other feeling." Despite the region's expanding Irish population, the bishop sought to satisfy Gerard by recruiting an English priest. To Goss's frustration, however, most of the available priests were Irish."*[106]

This suggests the struggle to find English priests even when there was a preference for them. Because the congregations in Lancashire were swelling by the inflow of Irish worshippers, they brought with them Irish priests. This was a Church that on one hand was surviving because it had finally a lifeline in the newcomers but on the other hand it also feared the Irish sentiments on topics such as nationalism. The fact that the Bishop could not find an English priest clearly shows the lack of Catholics of English background.

This lack of priests did not stop the worshippers from setting out to build themselves parish churches and schools. Despite the lack of priests to organise and oversee such enterprises and despite the lack of funding the poor communities themselves were building many Catholic churches. The Irish made a huge contribution to the building program by donating and raising money and by providing the labour of builders.[107] However the number of school buildings available remained below the number of schools needed, particularly in London where some areas like Stratford had an expanded Catholic population. The importance of Catholic schools will be further discussed in chapter 6. For example from 1886, Stratford, Plaistow and West Ham village fell under the West Ham County Borough. The population counted 1500 Catholics in the 1870s.[108] In 1870 there were only three Catholic Schools in West Ham. The growing Catholic population during the 19th century meant that this segment of the population had grown in influence by the beginning of the 20th century.

Catholicism in England in the early 20th Century

The hierarchy of the Catholic Church was restored in 1850 which meant a political relationship between the Queen of England and her parliament and the Vatican.[109] That was particularly important to Rome during the early 20th century, as the British Empire was a powerful state to have dealings with. As Pollard points out:

> *"… that the Vatican could not afford poor relations with the British Empire, in whose various Dominions, protectorates and colonial territories there were very substantial numbers of Catholics. Moreover following the United States withdrawal from world affairs in 1920, Britain had become the world's superpower, extending its influence further as a result of colonial gains in the Versailles peace settlement."*[110]

The need to befriend Britain had consequences for the relationship between the Vatican and the Catholic majority in Ireland. The majority of the Irish ecclesiastical community were supportive of an independent Ireland and the mass emigration of Irish workers to Australia, New Zealand, Canada and the United States created support for the Irish cause there. The British government wanted a complete condemnation by the Pope of the violence of the Irish Nationalists. They had hoped that with use of threats the Pope would follow the policies of his predecessor Leo XIII (1878-1903), who had rejected the methods of warfare and boycotting of the British government in Ireland by Irish Catholics although Pope Leo XIII had approved such tactics by Catholics who opposed the Old Catholics in Prussia 13 years previously.[111] Instead Benedict XV published a letter in April 1921 to the Irish bishops appealing for peace.

Negotiations between the British government and the Irish Dail led unexpectedly to a deal in December 1921.[112] Benedict's response to the situation bore fruit in that it both left the reputation of Rome intact and the Catholic Church in England was now able to strengthen its contact with the congregation. Now it was time to for the Catholic Church to turn its attention to the large number of Irish working class Catholics and to find a way to incorporate them into the Church, which continued to stress their Catholic identity and by doing so masked their Irish identity. As Hickman writes:

> *"By the new century the 19th century immigrants had not been assimilated; however, their Irishness had become masked by Catholicism in the public sphere."*[113]

The Irish were viewed as a political threat before the recognition of the Irish Free State. As Hickman points out:

> *"...one consequence of the dominant position of Catholic institutions in Irish areas was that many Irish people maintained a low profile (outside Irish areas) about being Irish and about Irish national issues."*[114]

After the Irish Free State emerged out of the negotiations in 1921, the Irish immigrant community was for the first time concentrating on their own community in Britain. During this time large numbers of Irish priests left for Britain and became involved with their new communities. No longer was compliance expected of the Irish parish priest but rather his input into the parish. The hierarchy was no longer hostile to his presence as had been the case in the 19th century, but he still had to fight for respect and acceptance from his congregation. The fact that he was from the same nationality would not automatically mean he would be immediately accepted and respected by his congregation. The Irish priest came often from a middle class background and was not immediately trusted.

Many priests were actively involved building their parishes and were influential fundraisers who helped build their churches, particularly during the 1920s and 1930s but also in the 1950s as was the case in Harold Hill. Some priests who were seen as an example with their sober lifestyle and ceaseless effort to alleviate the poverty of their parishioners were often called 'Holy Men'.[115] After improvements in housing and wages and the introduction of the National Health Service, we tend to take faith as an abstract form of thinking, forgetting how much it was tied in with miseries that every day would bring. The consequence of poverty in the slum areas of the inner cities was a high death rate and the comfort from the parish priest was much needed, as he was both a family visitor on a par with the General Practitioner plus he was able to give comfort such as donations to his parishioners.

There continued to be a small Irish middle class in Britain throughout the 20th century that partook in the Catholic Church functions and societies just like the Irish working class. These activities helped the parish priest to stay in contact with the all of his parishioners, even those who were not regular church attendees and raised important funds. The regularity of mass attending was not as large as might be expected. The assumption is often made that lapsation and low mass attendance is a thing of today. But in South London in the 1930s only some 20% to 30% of the total Catholic population attended mass, and the majority were women.[116] What these figures prove was that the Church was in need of educating the young in order to keep its congregation.

The Importance of Schooling

The importance of commitment to the Catholic school and the fund raising for the school helped to construct a community out of the wider Catholic population in the parish area. Pope Leo XIII had urged parents to show responsibility for their children by their support of Catholic education. Where only state schools were available, he wrote in *Officio Sanctissimo*, the Catholics had to build establishments of their own.[117] Catholic Schools proved to be the greatest success of the English Catholic Church and their importance was backed up by the Popes of the 20th century. The schools would help ensure the Church retained the continuous grip on the lay, just as it had in the 19th century when primary education was intended to make good workers of the poor. Episcopal control over education was not to be missed as Pius XI wrote:

> *"The true Christian, product of Christian education" and "is the supernatural man who thinks, judges, and acts constantly and consistently in accordance with the right reason illuminated by the Supreme light of example and teaching of Christ; in other words, to use the common terms, the true and finished man of character."*[118]

At the beginning of the 20th century the Church of England and the Catholic Church campaigned for more aid for their schools and for minimum local control. The result was the 1902 Act, which abolished the 3,000 school boards and established the 328 Local Education Authorities (LEAs) formed along the lines of county boroughs. The LEAs were to supervise all the voluntary aided schools and levy rates in order to help them be financially independent. It meant more financial aid for the Catholic schools but there was still a large financial contribution that had to be paid by the Catholics themselves.[119] In 1944 it was decided that all schools had to provide religious education. The 1944 Education Act made R.E. compulsory and this enabled the churches to unite behind the Act and many schools of the various churches went over to state control with the Catholic Church as the exception: they could not accept a system that forced them to accept a reserve of teachers that were appointed by the local authorities to provide for religious instructions in the schools.[120] Because the Catholic Church rejected their lack of influence on the appointed teachers they were forced to opt, in accordance with the Pope's teachings, for voluntary status. The state was prepared under the new Act to pay for up to 50% of approved expenditure on repairs and 50% on necessary alterations that were needed now that the maximum age of school children was increased to 15.[121]

The large inflow of immigrants from Ireland changed the way the government handled the Catholic schooling problem. The Catholic Church, with help from the Labour MPs Wilson and Mellish, won a settlement in which the state promised to pay for up to 75% of an £80 million bill for the building of new schools needed to house the older children and the large input of new Irish immigrant children. The Labour Party proved throughout the 1950s and 1960s to be on the side of the Catholic working classes. Labour in a sense proved to be of more use to them than any other party. As the majority of Catholics belonged to the urban working classes it was ironically the non-denominational party that was to fight for the rights of Catholics.[122] This made the change in Catholic life possible from being concentrated on the parish and the school to expand to the broader community. Hornsby-Smith feels that:

> *"Up to the 1950s English Catholicism had been characterised by a distinctive subculture with an all embracing Catholic institutional life centred around parish and school and with its own norms, values and beliefs."*[123]

He refers to the proud Irish community with their own sense of identity. But as the work of Hickman shows it was not just the Vatican that had made the Catholics a segregated community. Much was also due to the Irish character of the poorer Catholics and strong hostilities that had accompanied their existence in England throughout the 19th and 20th centuries before the Second Vatican Council took place.

The English Church had brought the Irish worshipper into the fold because it needed to accept them as a lifeline to support declining numbers. Even in this research whenever I searched for Irish history in Harold Hill the influence of Irish priests and worshippers, even their Irish identity was played down by various English members of the clergy, but the area had known several Irish priests in its history and they had been of much influence in the parishes but their nationality was rarely mentioned. In the research I will explore attitudes towards Irish priests in Harold Hill to see what the situation was in this part of Essex in the mid 20th century.

In research of the Catholic Church in England the ethnic identity of the Catholic congregations are rarely mentioned. As Hickman discovered during her research in *Religion Class and Identity*. She argues that:

> *"The fact that Catholic elementary schools were full of Irish Catholics is not explored in great detail in these histories. For example, Beales (1946), in one of his many essays on Catholic education, mentions in passing that the Irish famines of the 1840s added to the ranks of the 'uneducated Catholic poor'. This obscures reality that most of the 'Catholic poor' already in the country were Irish or of Irish descent."*[124]

What she highlights is that the migration of Irish to England and their influence on the Catholic communities is much older than the time after the Irish Famines. What makes it more complex is this double denial of the Irish migrants' position here in England. But as research shows, Irish migrants were highly resourceful and capable of surviving and forming communities without help from the Catholic Church.

Despite the lapsation rate amongst Catholic Irish migrants being significant, Connolly puts it as 55%, and not all Irish Catholics actively worshipping, it still meant a huge increase in worshippers in a short period of time and this would have been very mobile communities taking their faith with them to the new areas in which they settled.[125] Therefore it could be argued that the success and survival of the Catholic Church in England was a direct result of Irish immigration. But the Irish Catholic had his/her own identity and his/her Irish display of devotion. It was this Irish Catholic identity that the Church continued to suppress, in order to enhance the Church's status it had to play down everything that could be perceived as working class and foreign.[126]

The foreign status of the Catholic Church was for Rome a delicate situation as the relations with England were improving. Riccards argues the Pope's position became highly personalised when he examines the re-establishment of Roman Catholic hierarchy in Britain from 1850 and the relationship between Rome and the Pope.[127] Another study by Coppa also looks at leadership and the relationship of Rome with the English Catholics.[128] He argues that there is definitely an active and popular Catholic Church uniting under the flag of Rome but the history of the Catholic Church in England is also connected with the humble immigrant who continued to worship in his/her own way.

At the beginning of the 20th century the Vatican continued to struggle to keep relations going with England, the Great British Empire, but also with its Irish worshippers. It was clear to the Vatican that with its colonial territories the British Empire had a substantial number of Catholics. That the Holy See wished to continue good relationships with Britain was obvious. Pollard refers to the difficulty the Holy See had with the Irish Question in 1920 when Sinn Fein pressed on for independence in the 1919-1921 Irish War of Independence. There was support for Irish Nationalism but:

> *"In May in a conversation with Carlo Monti, Gasparri made a very revealing statement: "The Holy See cannot afford to get on the wrong side of England which gives the broadest freedom to the Catholics: it would be the end of Catholicism in England."*[129]

Despite the Irish sympathies and Irish Diaspora into the United States and Australia, their influence in the New World was simply not as large as that of England. The best Pope Benedict could do was show his impartiality and his wish for peace.[130] This did nothing to improve the position of Irish immigrants in England and shows that despite the appreciation of the Irish Catholic Church in Rome, the Vatican did not wish to get involved in the whole debate surrounding Irish independence. Catholics in England might have been largely of Irish backgrounds but their future was tied up with England's colonial powers.

Only in the latter part of the twentieth century after the Second Vatican Council did the situation of the Catholics in England change and, according to Hornsby Smith, their identity of Irish Catholics assimilate into English Catholics. Hornsby Smith points out in *The Changing Identity of Catholics in England* that English Catholic identity shifts and that Irish identity which was largely working class shifts with it.

> *"In other words the answer to our initial question 'what do you mean when you say you are a Roman Catholic?' at the turn of the millennium is much more ambiguous and varied and individually selected than it was 50 years ago when it was still largely involuntarily and communally based in the distinctive Catholic subculture."*[131]

He believed Catholic culture of the 1950s period to be a culture based on Irish working class identity and disconnected from the rest of English society. He argues that overall Catholicism changed quite crucially after the Second World War: its identity especially changed visibly:

> *"There have been major transformations as a result of post war social changes, especially the impact of the 1944 Education Act, and post Vatican II religious changes, including the encouragement of new ecumenical approaches."[132]*

He argues that as a result of these changes the boundary wall that had previously defended what he considers a distinctive sub-culture was disappearing. If this was disappearing it was perhaps because many new comers in the fifties never felt really at home as Delaney explains:

> *"'Others' stressed on the difficulties of incorporating the newly arrived Irish into the established social life of an English parish, much of which was anathema to the average working-class migrant, and many ended up on the fringes of parish life. Even when migrants did attend, the physical location of the Irish at the back of the Church was symbolic of their marginal status."[133]*

If there is a noticeable shift in the makeup of the Catholics in England with its working class features disappearing then it needs to be examined where it shifted to and where this shift places the Irish migrants. Therefore a study of the newly built community in Harold Hill, just after the Second World War can give an insight in the beliefs of the Irish working classes in England.

Local context of Harold Hill: the history of its building and growth and its relationship to Irish settlements in London

Local history can be of great value to historians in researching Irish migrant women as different areas opened up different opportunities and would have meant different ways in which Irish communities settled. It can therefore help in understanding the culture of Irish Catholic women in certain areas and how resourceful these women were in rebuilding their lives after migrating.

Researchers have followed the movements of communities, for example Clapson who researches the Blitz and consequently the break-up of the working class East End of London, but they have not examined a large estate like Harold Hill in Romford Essex.[134] The mass exodus of Irish immigrants from the slums of East London to the new housing estates after the Second World War has not been researched. This well planned mass exodus from the East of London into Essex, relocating people on a large scale, was an enormous undertaking. How Abercrombie's Greater London Plan was proposed, and then carried out and the influence this had on the Irish community will be examined in chapter 4. It is important to note that the new estate contained a large inflow of Irish Catholics increasing its proportion of Catholic population, which had an impact on the area. Irish women on the estate were very much part of building this new community.

The government's belief in a better future is overwhelming here but the building of new housing estates to accommodate residents of slum areas was not a phenomenon unique to Britain, as Douchen demonstrates in her research on the high rise built outside Paris.[135] Abercrombie's Plan can be compared with the system of express highways and parkways and city building of the fifties in the United States. This was touched upon very briefly by the journalist Platt whilst examining the housing programs to the west of London surrounding some parts of the dual-carriageway the A40. He discussed the history of urban development plans and how influential Abercrombie became in Britain. He also showed big urban developments in the States that had influenced Abercrombie's plan of London.[136]

Humphries and Weightman also considered the expansion of Greater London in connection to its industry and they demonstrate the importance of the motor industry in Dagenham and its influence in the area. Dagenham lays in close proximity to Romford and held the Becontree estate, at the time the largest newly built estate of Britain. Whilst the Becontree estate was constructed in the period 1914-1939, i.e. before the building of the Harold Hill Estate in Romford, its construction was also based on the need for slum clearance and the work of Humphries and Weightman gave much insight in the history of a similarly large and locally situated estate. Although the Ford Factory in Dagenham, a few miles from East London, was connected to a smaller factory in Cork, Ireland, Humphries and Weightman never discussed the relevance of this connection.[137]

Picture no 01 aerial photo of the Becontree Housing Estate Dagenham 1966[138]

To examine the impact Irish migrants had on the Harold Hill Estate their impact on East London becomes important. Irish migrants had been part of an established Irish community in London which means that there were a substantial number of Irish Catholic people living in East London. The census of 1851 shows that already by then there were more Irish-born people in London than any other city in England and Wales: this figure even exceeded the number of people living in Dublin. In 1851 Irish immigrants comprised 4.6 % of the London population.[139] At least, that is what is recorded in the official numbers, but it can be a much larger percentage, as it is known that not all occupants were registered in the census. Irish immigrants were heavily concentrated in St Giles, Whitechapel and Southwark, both parts of East London. Poverty endured in this area which affected the Irish community in particular. It was partly the reason to build on a different area and the help clear the slums of East London after the Second World War as discussed by Abercrombie in his Greater London Plan[140] the influence of Abercrombie was great as Simmie explains:

> *A major source of demand for land is demographic change. Again it is shown that, during the post-war period, the population of inner London fell. This was in line with the Abercrombie intention of restricting growth in inner London and assisting it in the Outer Metropolitan Area.*[141]

Picture no 02: A map of Inner London including the twelve central boroughs plus the City of London which covers roughly the area that was built up before 1914 and formed the first metropolitan government under the jurisdiction of the London County Council [142]

As early as the 1890s Charles Booth started to research poverty in London. Booth in particular refers to the poverty in the area in East London in which many of the Irish population lived and worked, which was far more significant than in central London.[143] In 1884 he researched the census returns for the Lord Mayor of London's Relief Fund in which he questions the nature of the census and the lack of data that could be extracted from it. In 1885 Henry Hyndman published the results of an inquiry into poverty conducted by the Social Democratic Federation, which claimed that up to twenty-five percent of the population of London lived in extreme poverty.

In 1886 Booth, who visited researcher and sociologist Hyndman, started his own inquiry into the condition of workers in London. This resulted in work that would last until 1903 and resulted in the publication of three editions of the survey, the final edition of *Life and Labour of the People in London* running to seventeen volumes.[144] The survey shows Charles and Mary Booth's work as well as that of their dedicated team of social investigators including, at various times, Beatrice Webb. Booth researched the causes of poverty and found the connection between poverty and regularity of income. He demonstrated that a regular income played the largest role in determining poverty status. Booth discovered that, of the 4,076 poor individuals he studied, 62 percent were paid low or irregular wages; of these 23 percent had large families and a substantial number suffered from illness. About 15 percent of the individuals he studied refused work or showed signs of alcohol addiction.[145] The Booths' work does refer to the Irish slum dwellers and the extreme poverty in which they lived. The poverty remained in much of the early 20th century only to improve after the slum clearance from after the Second World War. MacAmlaigh wrote about his own experiences in *An Irish Navvy: The Diary of an Exile* in which he describes how the men were working as navvies helping to rebuild the London infrastructure after the war and how much they remained involved in Irish culture in particular in East London he refers to how their lives resembled the lives they lived back home in Ireland, as they attend Mass on a Sunday (even if it means rising early to get to work on time in the railway tunnel), and follow the Catholic tradition of fasting on Good Friday.[146] MacAmlaigh told the stories and background of the navvies and gives an insight into their lives.

Finding information on Irish Catholic communities specifically from East London prior to the clearance, to get a better picture as to who they were, proved very difficult. Porter, for instance, briefly mentions in his social history of London the concentration of Irish settlers in East London as well as St Giles-in-the-Fields. The Jewish settlers get several references, and so do the French Huguenots.[147] A local study by a group of researchers at West Ham does refer to Irish settlers in several of the papers and Widowson mentions the local Catholic Church, built in 1814, having no windows onto the main street as anti-Irish rioters were rife in the area. Widowson also comments on the fact that East Ham was the first Catholic parish of Essex in

1717.[148] It made a good comparison with Ward who as a local historian researched Brentwood and the area round it, which is only 5 miles or so away from Romford (see map no 04) and the Harold Hill Estate, in which she referred back to the presence of Catholics in the area but never really examined the Irish community there.[149]

Research has been conducted into development in London and the growth of the population in the region around London. In *A History of the County of Essex: Volume 5* an urban development is discussed from areas like Poplar further out into Stratford and onwards into West Ham. Here reference is made to the numerous substantial villages in South-west Essex, places like Barking, Epping, and Stratford and a fast developing urban area from 1851 to 1911 is described. (see maps picture no 03 and again map picture no 04 below)

Picture no 03: This is a map from just before 1850 showing the small hamlets and towns of Essex and urban developments[150]

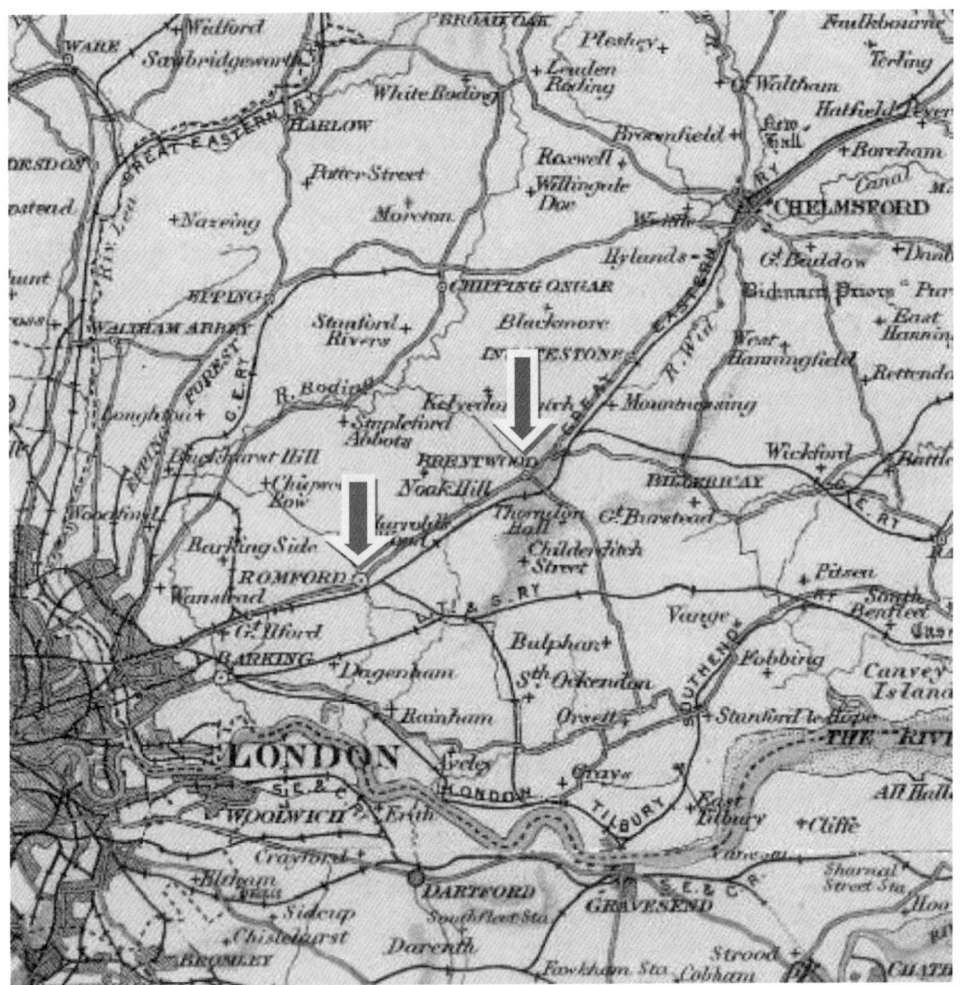

Picture no 04: This is a map from just before 1911 showing an increase in urban development and the spreading of London developments. Arrow showing Romford and Brentwood

London and its migrant community was instrumental in this development.

> *"Consideration of the birthplaces of the population resident in a rather larger area in 1911, when the growth of several of the Essex suburbs was nearly complete, indicates the continuance of a high level of immigration and confirms the importance of London as a source of population. All the large Essex suburbs had an unusually*

52

> *low proportion of native-born in their populations and, as might be expected, the more recent the period of rapid growth the smaller the proportion of natives".*[151]

However there was no mention of the Irish migrants in this process. In chapter 6 I shall explore findings from the register of the Romford Catholic church Edward the Confessor, which point towards a gradual process of moving further out into the Romford area from places such as East Ham from the late nineteenth century onwards. In 1903 the total attendance at Roman Catholic churches in West Ham was higher than that for any other borough in outer London and the percentage of Roman Catholic worshippers was also far above the average for the area: 11.8 compared with 6.2 for the whole of outer London. As research of the area shows these high proportions were due mainly to Irish immigration.[152]

Another good source which explores the Irish population in East London and Essex is *The Catholic Marriage Index* by Adolph, which covers some 30,000 marriages, chiefly for London and Essex from the mid-eighteenth century to approximately the 1870's and it is considered a particularly important source for Irish people in London.[153] It shows data of members of that community in which can be traced the origin and the size of this community which by its size can be concluded that it was influential in the area of London and Essex. How influential shall be examined in chapter 6.

Research has also been done on council housing or rather the lack of it in the area of East London and the rebuilding of East London after the Second World War. Hobnouse explores the complexities of the range of building programs in East London and makes it obvious why there was such a desperate need for further development outside London.[154] For instance in Poplar, as a result of the war, conditions in which families were living were considered so bad that it seemed as if the public housing initiatives of the 1930s had had no effect. It was initially estimated that 10,000 houses had been lost in Poplar as a result of war damage. The impact on working-class London, particularly the East End, of both enforced evacuation and the destruction of London by bombing, was researched in a paper by Clapson. He also focussed on the fragmentation of the dispersed working classes after the war and the urbanisation of London and the effects of the Second World

War on its population. However it focuses on the disappearing working classes and the changes of the area: it does not mention the exodus of the Irish community.[155]

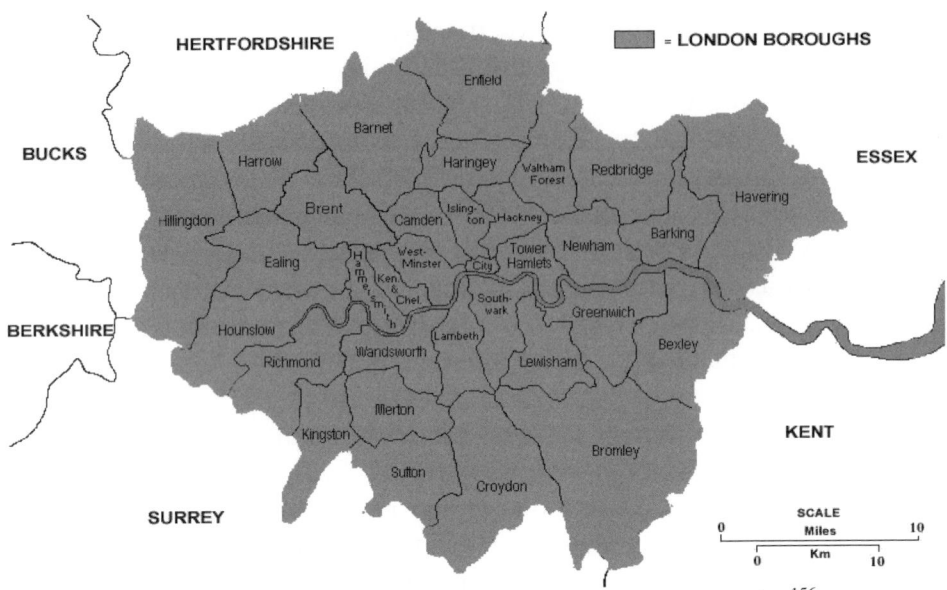

Picture no 05: Map of the London boroughs as they are known today[156]

The Irish community as a separate, or clearly identified, Irish immigrant community in London was also researched by Spinley in 1953 when she researched the poorest Irish communities, or as she describes them:

> *"The worst slums in London"*[157]

She felt that their impact on the area was notably bad and unlike Booth partially of their own consequence:

> *"The district is notorious in London for vice and delinquency; it is a major prostitution area and is considered by the Probation Service as the blackest spot in the city for juvenile delinquency. A large proportion of the inhabitants are Irish; social workers say: 'The Irish land here, and while the respectable soon all move away, the ignorant and shiftless stay.'"*[158]

It seems that her middle class English background compromised her research of the Irish community. She lacked an understanding of the Catholic practices around sexual intercourse, mistakenly believing that Irish men refused the use of sheaths (condoms) as they were considered too expensive. Catholics were not allowed any form of contraception except for the highly unreliable rhythm method.[159] She failed to understand therefore the reason behind the large families and the importance of family life within the Catholic tradition. Her research did not look at Irish migrants who had moved out of London as the focus of her study was on London. The move out of the slums and the subsequent effect this had on Irish families and how they rebuilt their lives was of interest to my study. But it was also important to note how much research had already been conducted examining the lives of the Irish community in East London.

The move after the Second World War from East London to a suburban estate had been recorded once before by Willmott and Young who researched the Bethnal Green area and moves to a newly built Becontree estate at Dagenham that they called Greenleigh (see pcture /map no1 an aerial photo and picture no 06 below).[160] What was interesting was how they discovered the closeness in the community between mothers and their daughters often living in close proximity to one another in East London. It gave a good insight into the communities of London and the new estate. It also highlighted the maternal influence on the daughters attending church and that women also went to church for a special service after confinement when they had their babies. But this Catholic tradition was not further researched and the ethnic origins of these Catholics were omitted. The researchers examined the differences between Greenleigh, which was the name they gave to the Dagenham Estate, and Bethnal Green and came to the conclusion that the community on the new estate was lacking community spirit as people felt more isolated from one another. As my research will demonstrate, Harold Hill had a large proportion of Catholics moving from East London after the slum clearance, like Greenleigh some years earlier, but the isolation was not as striking and the women were very active in making this community more cohesive. What the research of Greenleigh did not expose however were the problems women might have had leaving their mothers behind. But it did stress that mothers often had a great influence on their daughters who would have been very isolated in the new estate.

Research on the contacts between women and the lack of a mother nearby is important because of the significance of this relationship in the Catholic community. Not much was written about Romford in general, especially not in reference to the Harold Hill Estate built just outside its centre, or the Irish Catholic community. There is a reference to the Harold Hill housing estate and also to the Catholics in the town of Romford in the *History of the County of Essex* and they refer to the expansion of Romford itself but little about the occupants.[161]

Picture no 06 a photo of Dagenham Village from the church tower taken in 1954[162]

Another way to research the Catholic population of Harold Hill is to examine research that had been conducted by the Catholic Church itself in order to look at how active Catholics worshipped in England. The researcher Spencer carried out this research in several dioceses like Brentwood Diocese. To get a better understanding of the Catholics in the Brentwood Diocese, in the period researched for my thesis, it was important to look at the Spencer Research of 1961.[163] Spencer carried out this research on behalf of the Catholic Church in order to find out if Catholic communities were thriving and then to consider why this was the case. He found that in the Brentwood Diocese the communities were indeed socially thriving and the reason for more involved worshipping was given as the positive attitude within the faith that was preached by parish priests at the time. According to Spencer the emphasis therefore lay on the parish priest rather than the very large number of Irish immigrants that were used to an active worshipping and parish life. Spencer's survey will be examined further in chapter 6. As part of this survey the parish priest Connor conducted research in a parish of Liverpool.[164] That was part of an urban development and looked at the activities of the 'core laity' of the parish, as Hornsby-Smith describes them, and the unofficial activities of the parishioners.[165] Although a very different area it was interesting to see how Connor had conducted at this period a contemporary research and worked along the principles set up by the survey and what his finding were. The parishioners were often Irish, or of Irish descent. His survey research thus aimed to explore how parishes worked and the influence of laity on the parish was highlighted here. In the research he also refers to the newly built estate in which the community had to rebuild their Catholic network including the building of churches and schools. The geographer Walter also researched Irish immigrant women in London.[166] She explains:

> *"Within Irish neighbourhoods the work of women underpinned both formal and informal community institutions. But their visibility in named positions of leadership, except trade unions, has helped to hide this involvement. They also partook in street fights although there are only glimpses of this kind of activity in the surviving records."*[167]

To research Irish women and their experiences it is important to examine the oral accounts of their daily lives. Roberts, who focuses on women and their families and their domestic roles, highlights the importance of examining also the most mundane aspects of their stories. Only then can you piece together meaning and form an understanding of those lives. For chapter 5 her work was of interest as it follows women when they talk about the more mundane things in life but in doing so allowing Roberts to uncover import facts of family life: for instance about abuse and the position of mothers.[168] She writes on the importance of researching through oral history working class lives of women as they are otherwise not likely heard. She argues that neighbourhoods held an important place particularly in the lives of working class women in the 1940s and 1950s but what makes up a neighbourhood is not easily explained. She explains:

> *"It is not easy to define a neighbourhood at this time except in terms of its functions...although some people were well aware of living in a certain area, or on an estate, these larger groupings tended not to operate in any meaningful sense as a community. What was of primary importance was the street in which you lived and your immediate neighbours."*[169]

To Irish Catholic women who were new to the area, the parish became very much a focus point in the community as will be examined in the thesis in chapter 6. The research of Lambert's on Irish women in Lancaster included an entire chapter on Catholic worship and she was very thorough in her search for evidence of continued practices and changes in worship.[170] Her work was of importance because it explored the local communities and women's lives. She argues in an interview on the lives of Irish women:

> *"It had been assumed that because Irish women weren't visible in Britain, they had assimilated into British culture. I argued the opposite: that Irish women generally maintained strong cultural, familial and religious ties with Ireland after emigration."*[171]

The Irish population of London has been researched in another context; that of present day health and welfare, by Ryan in 2006, in which she examines the result of poorly planned migration and depression in Irish born people living in London, she highlights problems that also prevailed in the badly planned migrations of the women interviewed in this thesis.[172] It backs the findings in a nationally based study on suicide rates amongst Irish migrants by Aspinall in 2002.[173] Ryan's other study explores Irish female migration, and pays extra attention to how migrant women access and sustain social networks, both locally and spatially dispersed, over time. In it she examines Irish nurses in Britain, not just in London, and tries to achieve a better understanding of how migrant women access and utilize local ties post-migration. But it also shows how community spirited these women were and their choices of workplace in the healthcare sector which directly connects with some of the women in my sample.[174]

In other studies sociologists have examined immigrant women extensively but sociologists are rarely active in local research. The work of Ahrentzen for instance was helpful because she identified how the separation of home sphere and work sphere continue to permeate residential development and public policy, but both terms are in themselves socially constructed.[175] This was important because in the interview data it quickly became apparent that these home/work boundaries were viewed, by the Irish women, as superfluous or a false dichotomy. Ahrentzen highlights the importance of work and the social status that paid employment brings in communities and families to the individual. This shows how important the lack of paid work was on the Harold Hill Estate as shall be further explored. The lack of higher wages proved to make the women I interviewed more dependent on their husbands and it also made them less visible. Laws has studied the lack of access to knowledge in the case of women and therefore the lack of power in their own community and warns us that this limits their social role/status.[176] This will be examined in the thesis. According to Cortes and Cameron women have – because of their low social status due to low waged work – a need to express themselves.[177] They found that housewives were more focussed on expressing themselves better verbally than men. The interview data does highlight the ability of all women researched to communicate; much of parish work was based on communicating with others. But it also indicates that interviewing women would be useful resource data.

Working class women have been examined in the study of Todd who, using autobiographies from the 1918-1950 period, traces the complex interaction between class, gender, and the local areas that shaped young women's roles at work and home, indicating that paid work structured people's lives more profoundly than many social histories suggest.[178] This is an important study and although Todd's research is not a local study it highlights the influence of the local area in women's stories. It however does not highlight the significance of Irish working class women. The study of Giles deepens the research of women as it examines their apparent retreat to domesticity in 1950s England. This study connects with my research as it tries to rescue domestic lives from invisibility, much as my research highlights the women who worked as volunteers raising money for local schools and churches, founding a new community in the process.[179] But Giles' study doesn't address the position of working class Irish Catholic women.

In conclusion therefore a study on women in the locality of the Harold Hill Estate can broaden the information available as it deepens the understanding of the lives of Irish Catholic immigrant women in England and can draw on local history by means of archive material and interviews of the women themselves. The methods useful to this research need to be addressed and examined further in the next chapter.

Footnotes

[1] Kofman E., Phizacklea A., Raghuram P. and Sales R. (2000) *Gender and international migration in Europe. Employment, welfare and politics*, London 2000

[2] Guyot J., Padrun R., Dauphinet E., Jospa Y., E. Fischli, M.de Mestral, D. Giudici, C. Scheidecker (1978) *Migrant Women Speak*, London

[3] Hoffer C. *De dynamiek van cultuur en religie: volksgeloof onder moslims in Nederland.* (translated as; The dynamics of Culture and religion; popular beliefs under Muslims in the Netherlands) *NAK Magazine.* 13, najaar 2000:5-11. Utrecht, The Nederlands

[4] Jonkers M. (2003) *Een miskende revolutie. Het moederschap van Marokkaanse vrouwen*, (translation: a misunderstood revolution, motherhood of Moroccan Women) Amsterdam

[5] Hickman M. (1995), *Religion Class and Identity: The state, the Catholic Church and the Education of the Irish in Britain*, Aldershot, England p. 14

[6] Gray B. (2006) 'Changing Places: The Irish Migration, Race and Social Transformation', in: *Translocation Review* vol.1 Issue 1 autumn p.119

[7] Lyberaki, A. (2002) 'Social Capital Measurement in Greece', in: *Journal of migration vol. September*

7 Labrianidis L., Lyberaki A., Tinios P. and Hatziprokopiou P.(2004) 'Inflow of Migrants and Outflow of Investment: Aspects of Interdependence between Greece and the Balkans', in: *Journal of Ethic and migration studies (JEMS)* 30(6) p. 3

[9] Hickman M (1995) *Religion Class and Identity* p. 107

[10] Labrianidis L., Lyberaki A., Tinios P. and Hatziprokopiou P. (2004) *Inflow of Migrants and Outflow of Investment*, p. 2

[11] Walter B. and Hickman M. (1995) 'Deconstructing Whiteness; Irish women in Britain', in: *Feminist Review* no 50 pp. 5-19

[12] Walter B. (2001) *Outsiders inside; whitness, place and Irish women.* London

[13] Walter B. *Outsiders inside*, p. 209

[14] Hickman M. *Religion class and Identity*, p. 108

[15] Walter B. *Outsiders inside*, p. 118

[16] Walter B. *Outsiders inside*, chapters:
   textile workers in Scotland and north West England, p. 131
   domestic service workers in South East England, p. 143
   Irish women in post-war Britain: workplaces, p. 148

[17] Fitzpatrick D. (1986) 'A share of the Honeycomb: Education, Emigration and Irish Women', in: *Continuity and Change*, London

[18] Werner A. M*igrant communities and health care in the home, the influence of cultural, religious and migration factor*s. (Online), Available: http://buurtzorglive.com accessed May 2011 chapter 2, 15, 17

[19] McAdam M. (1994) 'Hidden From History: Women's Experience of Emigration', in: *Irish Reporter* vol.13

[20] Jackson P. (1987) *Women in 19th century Irish emigration* p. 1014

[21] Brown T. (1985) *Ireland a Social and cultural History, 1922 to the Present*, London p. 15

[22] McEvoy J. and Boyle M. (1998) 'Putting abortion in its social context: Northern Irish women's experiences of abortion in England', in: *Health an interdisciplinary journal for social study of health, illness and medicine* July 1998 vol. 2 no. 3 283-304 London

[23] Ryan L. (2006) 'Depression in Irish migrants living in London: case–control study', in: *The British Journal of Psychiatry*

[24] Tilki M. (2006) 'The Social Contexts of Drinking Among Irish Men in London: Evidence from a Qualitative Study', in: *Drugs: Education, Prevention and Policy*, 13(3) pp. 247-261

[25] Tilki M. (2006) *The Social Contexts of Drinking Among Irish Men in London*, 13(3) p. 247-261

[26] Tilki M, Taylor E, Pratt E, Mulligan E, Halley E. (2011) 'Older Irish people with dementia in England', in: *Advances in Mental Health, vol. 9(3)*, p. 221-232

[27] Owen D (1995) *Irish-Born People in Great Britain: Settlement Patterns and Socio-economic Circumstances*, Coventry

[28] Tilki, M. (2006) 'The social Contexts of Drinking Among Irish Men in London', in: *Drugs: Education, Prevention & Policy* vol. 13 no 3 June

Ryan L. (2007) 'Migrant Women, Social Networks and Motherhood: The Experiences of Irish Nurses', in: *Britain Sociology Journal* vol. April

[29] Lee J.J. (1978) 'Women and the Church Since the Famine'(eds.) Mac Curtain M. and O'Lorrain D., in: *Women in Irish society,* Dublin

[30] Mac Laughlin, J. (1997) 'The New Vanishing Irish', in: *Location and Dislocation in Contemporary Irish Society* Cork pp. 133-134

[31] Beale J. (1986) *Women in Ireland : Voices of Change* Dublin, p. 71

[32] O'Dowd, A. (1994) 'Women in Rural Ireland in the Nineteenth and Early Twentieth Centuries-how the Daughters and the Sisters of small Farmers and Landless Labourers Fared', in: *Rural History* 5.2 p. 175

[33] Bourke J. (1993) *Husbandry to Housewifery: Women, Economic Change and Housework in Ireland, 1890-1914*, Oxford

[34] Luddy M. (1995) *Women in Ireland 1800-1918: a Documentary History*, Cork

[35] Daly, M.E. (1995) 'Women in the Irish Free State, 1922-39: The Interaction Between Economics and Ideology' J.Hoff & M. Coulter (Eds), in: *Irish Women's Voices Past and Present*, Journal of Women's History, Winter/Spring, vol.6, no. 4 & vol. 7. no 1, 99-116.

[36] Daly M.E. (1995) 'Women in the Irish Free State 1922-1939. The Interaction Between Economies and Ideology', in: *Irish Women's Voices Past And Present*, Indianapolis, USA

[37] Brown T. *Ireland a Social and cultural History*, pp. 25-26

[38] Brown T. *Ireland a Social and cultural History*, chapt. 4

[39] Cairns D. and Richards S. (1988) *Writing Ireland, Colonialism, Nationalism and Culture*, Manchester

[40] Cairns D. and Richards S. *Writing Ireland* p. 76

[41] Brown T. *Ireland a Social and cultural History*

[42] Brown T. *Ireland a Social and cultural History*, p. 26

[43] Murphy B.P. (2005) *The Catholic Bulletin and Republican Ireland1898-1926*, Belfast

[44] Lee J.J. *Women and the Church Since the Famine*

[45] Valiutis M.G. (1995) 'Power, Gender, and Identity in the Irish Free State', J. Hoff and M. Coulter (eds), in: *Irish Women's Voices Past And Present* in Journal of Woman's History. vol.6. no.4

[46] McCullough, C. (1991) 'A Tie That Blinds: Family Ideology In Ireland', in: *Economic and Social Review* vol.22, London pp. 199-211

[47] Arensberg C. and Kimball S. (1968) *Family and Community in Ireland*, Cambridge

[48] Arensberg C. and Kimball S. 'Family and Community in Ireland', in: *A tie that blinds: Family and Ideology in Ireland* in *Economic and Social Review* vol 22, no3 (1991) pp 199-211

[49] Humphreys A.J. (1966) *New Dubliners: Urbanisation and the Irish Families*, London

[50] O'Dowd A. (1994) *Women in Rural Ireland in the Nineteenth and Early Twentieth Centuries* p. 172

[51] Nash C. (1993) 'Remapping and Renaming: New Cartographies of Identity, Gender and Landscape in Ireland. Women of the West: gender, nation and landscape in early 20th century Ireland', in: *Feminist Review* 44 pp. 39-57

[52] Gray B. (1996) 'Irishness – a global and gendered identity?', in: *Irish Studies Review* vol.16 autumn

[53] Gray B(online Available (online) website: http://migration.ucc.ie/oralarchive/testing/breaking/about.html (accessed May 2011) p. 1

[54] Shortall S.(1992) 'Power Analysis and Farm Wives: An Emperical Study of the power relationships Affecting Women on Irish farms', in: *Sociologia Ruralis* vol.32 pp. 431-451

[55] Moser P.(1993) 'Rural economy and female emigration in the West of Ireland 1936-1956', in: *Women's Studies Review* (1993)

[56] Markus H.R. and Kitayama S. (1991) 'Culture and the self: Implications for cognition, emotion, and motivation', in: *Psychological Review*, vol. 98(2), April, pp. 224-253.

[57] Beale J. (1987) *Women in Ireland: Voices of Change* p. 52

[58] Gray B. (1996) *Irishness – a global and gendered identity?*

[59] Rossiter A. (1992) 'Between the Devil and the Deep Blue Sea, Irish women, Catholicism and Colonialism', in: *Refusing Holy Orders, Women and Fundamentalism in Britain*, London

[60] M. Hickman *Religion Class and Identity*

[61] King R. and O'Connor H. (1996) 'Migration and Gender: Irish women', in: *Leicester Geography* 81.4 pp. 311-325

[62] Hickman M., Morgan S., Walter B.(1998) *Recent research into the needs of the Irish in Britain*, (Online) Available: http://ics.leeds.ac.uk/papers/vp01.cfm?outfit=ids&folder=112&paper=113 Accessed June 2011

[63] Hickman M., Morgan S., Walter B. *Recent research into the needs of the Irish in Britain*

[64] Lambert, S. (2004) 'Irish women's emigration, 1922-1960: the lengthening of family ties', in: *Irish women's history*, London, pp. 152-167

[65] Delaney E. (2007) *The Irish in Post War Britain*, Oxford p. 127

[66] Delaney E. (2007) *The Irish in Post War Britain*, Oxford p. 135

[67] Ryan R.M., Rigby S., King K. (1993) 'Two types of religious internalisation and their relations to religious Orientations and Mental Health', in: *Journal of Personality and Social Psychology* vol. 65 No3 p. 586
[68] Delaney E. (2007) *The Irish* p. 144
[69] Werner A. (2011) *The migrant community and healthcare at home*.
[70] Werner A. (2011). *The migrant community* chapt. 12
[71] Hornsby-Smith R.P. (2004) *The Changing Identity of Catholic in England in Religion, Identity and Change*, London p. 43
[72] McKenna Y.(2002) *Negotiating Identities: Irish Women Religious and Migrations* then still an unpublished PhD thesis for University of Warwick publ. in Warwick
[73] McKenna Y. (2002) p. 38
[74] McCurtain M. (1995) 'Late in the field: Catholic sisters in the Twentieth century Ireland and the New Religious History', Hoff J. and Voulter M. (eds), in: *Irish Women's voices: past and present* in *Journal of Women's History* 6.4, 7.1 pp. 49-63
[75] McCurtain M. *Late in the field*
[76] Donnelly J.S.(2000), *Piety and Power in Ireland 1760-1960* (eds) Brown S.J. and David W. Miller D.W. Indiana, USA
[77] Walter B. *Outsiders inside* p. 19
[78] Concannon H. (1997) 'The Queen of Ireland', in: Kenny M. *Goodbye to Catholic Ireland*, London p. 51
[79] Boss S. (2000) *Empress and Handmaid, On nature and Gender in the Cult of the Virgin Mary*, London p. 51
[80] Thurer S. (1994) *The Myths of Motherhood, How Culture Reinvents the Good Mother*, London p. 80
[81] Thurer S. *The Myths of Motherhood*, p. 82
[82] Warner M, *Alone of all her sex*
[83] Warner M, *Alone of all her sex*, p. 284
[84] Warner M, *Alone of all her sex*, p. 49
[85] Warner M, *Alone of all her sex*, p. 190
[86] Serra A.M. (1999) 'Magnificat; Remembrance and Praise', in: *Marian Studies Journal* vol. L
[87] Serra A. M. Magnificat 1999
[88] Kristeva J. (1977) 'Stabat Mater, The Heretic of Love', in: *Tel Quel* vol. 74 winter, Paris
[89] Boss S. *Empress and Handmaid*, p. 1
[90] Spretnak C. (2004) *Missing Mary: The Queen of Heaven and Her Re-Emergence in the Modern Era*, New York p. 280
[91] Beale J. *Women in Ireland: Voices of Change* p. 52
[92] Beale J. *Women in Ireland* p. 73
[93] Donnelly J.S.(2000) *The Peak of Marianism* p. 253
[94] Hornsby-Smith M.P. (1991) *Roman Catholic Beliefs in England. Customary Catholicism and Transformations of Religious Authority*, Cambridge (online) available: http://www.movinghere.org.uk/galleries/histories/irish/working_lives/working_lives.htm accessed May 2011
[95] Hornsby-Smith M.P. *Roman Catholic Beliefs in England* p. 165

[96] http://www.movinghere.org.uk/galleries/histories/irish/working_lives/working_lives.htm
[97] Brown T, *Ireland a Social and cultural History* chapt. 1
[98] Hickman M.J. *Religion Class and Identity:* p. 96
[99] Hickman M.J. *Religion Class* chapt. 3
[100] Hickman M.J. *Religion Class* pp. 101-102
[101] Hornsby-Smith M. P. *Roman Catholic Beliefs in England.*
[102] Hickman M.J. *Religion Class* p. 114
[103] Heimann M. (1995) *Catholic devotion in Victorian England,* Oxford
[104] Heimann M. *Catholic devotion in Victorian* p. 14
[105] Heimann M. *Catholic devotion in Victorian* p. 93 referring to R. Simpson in *Milner and his Times from Home and Foreign Review 1*863 p. 557
[106] Dye R. (2001) 'Catholic Protectionism or Irish Nationalism? Religion and Politics in Liverpool, 1829-1845', in: *The Journal of British Studies* vol. 40, no. 3 July, pp. 357-390
[107] Hickman M.J. *Religion Class* p. 172
[108] Hickman M.J. *Religion Class* p. 172
[109] Foster S.M. (1994) *A history of the Diocese of Brentwood 1917-1992,* Brentwood p. 1
[110] Pollard J.F. (1999) *The Unknown Pope Benedict XV (1914-1922) and the Pursuit of Peace,* London p. 152
[111] Schuck M.J. (1991) *That They Be One, the Social Teaching of the Papal Encyclicals 1740-1989,* Washington D.C. p. 50
[112] Pollard J.F. *The Unknown Pope* p. 154
[113] Hickman M.J. *Religion Class* p. 18
[114] Hickman M.J. *Religion Class* p. 230
[115] Patrick and Aoife (Greater London), 1999 (names altered), Interview 1, transcript
[116] Hickman M.J. *Religion Class* p. 232
[117] Schuck M.J. *That They Be One* p. 80
[118] Schuck M.J. *That They Be One* p. 72
[119] Hickman M.J. *Religion Class* pp. 195-196
[120] The Education Act 1944 changed the education system for secondary schools in England and Wales. This Act was named after the Conservative politician R.A. Butler. It introduced the Tripartite System of secondary education which made secondary education free for all pupils. This system consisted of three different types of secondary school: grammar schools, secondary technical schools and secondary modern schools. This created a system of direct grant schools, and a number of independent schools received a direct grant from the Ministry of Education exchange for accepting a number of pupils on "free places" see http://en.wikipedia.org/wiki/Education_Act_1944
[121] Hickman M.J. *Religion Class* pp. 196
[122] Hickman M.J. *Religion Class* pp. 241-242
[123] Hornsby-Smith M. P. *Roman Catholic Beliefs in England* p. 7
[124] Hickman M. *Religion, Class* p. 159
[125] Connolly, G (1985) 'Irish and Catholic: Myth or Reality? Another Sort of Irish and Renewal of the Clerical Profession among Catholics in England, 1971-1918', Swift, R. Amd Gilley, S. (eds), in: *The Irish in the Victorian City*, Kent.
[126] Hickman M. *Religion, Class*, chapt. 5

[127] Riccards M.P. (1998) *Vicars of Christ. Popes. Power, and Politics in the Modern World*, New York
[128] Coppa F. J.(1998) *The Modern Papacy Since 1789*, Harlow
[129] Pollard John *The Unknown Pope Benedict XV* p. 152
[130] Pollard John *The Unknown Pope Benedict XV* p. 154
[131] Hornsby Smith M.P. (2004*)* 'The changing Identity of Catholics in England', in: *Religion, Identity and Change: Perspectives on Global Transformations* p. 54
[132] Hornsby-Smith M.P (2004) *Religion Identity and Change; the changing identity of Catholics in England* p. 43
[133] Delaney E. (2007) *The Irish in Post War Britain*, Oxford p. 161
[134] Clapson M. (2010) *The Blitz and the 'Break-up' of Working Class London, 1939-1960* a paper presented London (University of Westminster) 13-October
[135] Douchen C. (1994) *Women's rights and Women's Lives in France 1944-1968*, London
[136] Platt E. (2000), *Leadville, A biography of the A40*, London
[137] Humphries S. and Weightman G. (1984) *The Making of Modern London 1914-1939*, London
[138] Picture no. 01 aerial photo Becontree Housing Estate Dagenham 1966 (online) Available http://www.20thcenturylondon.org.uk/server.php?show=nav.484 (accessed October 2011)
[139] (online) available: http://www.british-history.ac.uk/report. (accessed June 2011)
[140] Abercrombie P. (1944) *Greater London Plan*, London chapt. Foreword
[141] Simmie J. (2002) *The changing City: Population, employment and Land use change since the 1943 county of London plan*, Oxford
[142] Simmie J. (2002) *The changing City: Population, employment and Land use change*
[143] Booth C. (1889-91, 1892-97, 1902) *Life and Labour of people in London*, London 17 vol. (1889–91, 1892–97, 1902)
[144] Booth C.(1889-91, 1892-97, 1902) *Life and Labour of people in London*
[145] Booth C. *Life and Labour of people in London*
[146] MacAmlaigh D. (1964) *An Irish Navvy: The Diary of an Exile*, Dublin
[147] Porter R. (1994) *London, a social History*, London
[148] John Widowson (1986) *A Marsh and Gasworks: One Hundred Years of Life in West Ham*, London
[149] Ward G.A. (1980) *Victorian & Edwardian Brentwood: A Pictorial History*, Brentwood
[150] Picture no.03 map of Essex 1848 by Robert Creighton, engr. J.& C. Walker for Lewis' Topographical Dictionary (online) available http://freepages.genealogy.rootsweb.ancestry.com accessed Oct 2011
[151] 'The Growth of Population and the Built-up Area 1850–1919 of Metropolitan Essex since 1850: Population growth and the built-up area', in: *A History of the County of Essex: Volume 5* (1966), pp. 2-9
[152] Powell W.R. (1973) (eds.) 'West Ham: Roman Catholicism, Nonconformity and Judaism', in: *A History of the County of Essex:* vol.6 (online) available*: http://www.british-history.ac.uk/report.aspx?compid=42701 (*accessed June 2011) pp. 338-339
And Powell W.R. (1973) (eds.) Roman Catholicism' in *A History of the County of Essex: Volume 9: The Borough of Colchester* pp.123-141

[153] Adolph A. (1991) 'The Catholic Marriage Index in Family History', in: *Journal of the IHGS* vol. 16, np 129, NS 105. October

[154] Hobhouse H. (1994) 'Public Housing in Poplar: The 1940s to the early 1990s', in: *Survey of London: Poplar, Blackwall and Isle of Dogs*, vol. 43 and 44 pp. 37-54, London

[155] Clapson M. *The Blitz and the 'Break-up' of Working Class London, 1939-1960* a paper presented at the University of Westminster, 13-October 2010 London

[156] LCR Archive: Picture no 03: Map of the London boroughs as they are known today in LCR Archive

[157] Spinley B.M. (1953) *The Deprived and the Privileged*, London p. 39

[158] Spinley B.M. *The Deprived and the Privileged*, p. 40

[159] Spinley B.M. *The Deprived and the Privileged*, p. 44

[160] Young M. and Willmott P. (1957) *Family And Kinship in East London*, London

[161] O'Brian C. (2005) 'In Buildings of England, London 5: East', in: *Victoria County History, A History of the County of Essex:* vol.7, p. 19

[162] Picture no 06 Dagenham Village from the church tower, 1954 (Online) available http://photographs.barkingdagenhamlocalhistory.net/ accessed October 2011

[163] Spencer (1961) *The Demographic Survey*, London

[164] Connor K. (1961) *Priest & People- A study on the sociology of Religion*, Liverpool

[165] Hornsby-Smith M.P. *Roman Catholic Beliefs*, p. 63

[166] Walter B. (1989) *Irish Women in London, the Ealing Dimension*, London Borough of Ealing Women's Unit

[167] Walter B. *Irish Women in London*, p. 58

[168] Roberts E. (1995) *Women and Families: An Oral History*, Oxford pp. 140-170

[169] Roberts E. *Women and Families: An Oral History*, pp. 199-200

[170] Lambert S. (2002) *Irish women in Lancaster 1922-1960*, England

[171] Lambert S. (2011) Interview about her research (Online)Available: *http://www.virtual-ancaster.net/reviews/interviews/lambert.htm* (accessed May 2011)

[172] Ryan L. (2006) 'Depression in Irish migrants living in London: case–control study', in: *The British Journal of Psychiatry*, 188 pp. 560-566

[173] Aspinall P.J. (2002) 'Suicide amongst Irish Migrants in Britain: A Review of the Identity and Integration Hypothesis', in: *The International Journal of Social Psychiatry*, December vol. 48 no. 4 pp. 290-304

[174] Ryan L. (2007) 'Migrant Women, Social Networks and Motherhood: The Experiences of Irish Nurses', in: *Britain Sociology Journal*, vol. April 41: pp. 295-312

[175] Ahrentzen S. (1997) 'The Meaning Of Home Workplaces For Women', in: *Thresholds in Feminist Geography;Difference, Methodology, Representation*, Oxford

[176] Laws G. (1997) 'Women's Life Courses, Spatial Mobility, and State Politics Thresholds', in: *Feminist Geography*, Oxford

[177] Cortes J. and Cameron D. (1989) *Woman in their speech communities: New perspectives on Language and Sex*, London

[178] Todd S. (2005) *Young Women, Work, and Family in England 1918—1950*, Oxford

[179] Giles J. (2004) *The Parlour and the Suburb. Domestic Identities, Class, Femininity and Modernity*, Oxford

CHAPTER 3: METHODOLOGY

This research employs qualitative research methodology with an inductive approach to allow a process in which information from the data is generated. The research then draws on multidisciplinary approaches, including: cultural history, oral history, geography and sociology to situate the findings. The objectives of this research are to explore: the migration of Irish migrant women from East London to Harold Hill and the impact this had on their lives; the importance of the Virgin Mary in the lives of these women and their families, and finally how their voluntary work, paid work and church support linked them with the wider community. To achieve this, interviews were conducted to generate data and data has also been generated from the local archives; triangulating both sources to enrich, complicate, reinforce or contradict the interpretations.

In this chapter I will explore the theories behind the methods that can be used, and will discuss the correlation between oral history and psychoanalysis. I will discuss the position of the historian in the interview and the use of language. I will explain how immigrant women fit in with the methodology and explain the research design, the process of interviewing and the interview sample chosen. This will be followed by the interview analysis in which the tools of storytelling and the space of the interview will be discussed and the outcome explained. The archive sample and the diary source will then be described.

The Theories behind the method of oral history

In the 1970s Thompson highlighted the importance of oral history and the vast amount of information it can elicit. Women's lives and experiences were often not highlighted by mainstream history research and therefore oral history, almost from the start, has been able to include women's history[1]. Feminists like Alexander and Davin, by using such methods during the 1970s and 1980s were able to research the lives and experiences of women both within the labour movement as well as in their working class lives.[2] In more recent studies the tradition of oral history is employed to research the lives of migrants. For example, Ryan's work on Irish women in Britain and Villarreal's exploration of women in Spanish music industries in Mexican American communities. What oral methods bring therefore in research endeavours is the opportunity to research in-depth the lived experiences of women within their social background. This is seen in the work of American sociologists, Mauthner and Doucet, which allow the subjectivity of their interviewees and give women research space.[3]

Historians write narratives and with these narratives they reconstruct the past. The interviewee is in a sense a storyteller and will use techniques she or he is accustomed to; but it is also up to the researcher to reconstruct the past through the questions asked based on the information that the interviewee gives. Historians using interviews as data can have difficulty finding good interviewees with information. Oral data can be of great value; the need for clear guidelines about the processes of data collecting come from social researchers who have been exploring interviews as data for their own purposes. Sociologists grapple with all the complexities that surround this particular type of source. Within sociological research the feminist movement has been very influential. Feminist sociologists gradually moved away from quantitative research and moved more and more towards qualitative methods.[4] The aim of qualitative methods is to generate more in depth information from the respondents. Qualitative research methods can be of great importance too to the historian. In the first place it is important not only to find out what happened but also understand how this was perceived and valued by those who lived through it and who are now looking back at this particular time. Secondly it gives us scope to look at history at different angles as different interviewees show us different perspectives. The research that then develops can concentrate on the different layers of interpretation, of the variety of ways in which people experience their past. This is of particular interest to the oral historian.

How the past is experienced is connected with the aspect of memory; how do we remember our past? Ryan agrees with Thomson as he writes:

> *'We compose our memories to make sense of our past and present lives'.*[5]

He goes on to say:

> *'We "compose" memories which help us to feel relatively comfortable with our lives… We seek composure, an alignment of our past, present and future lives'.* [6]

We seem to create our sense of self by selectively holding on to some memories and recreating in a sense our own identity. Memories then make a person into a self / a whole unique other human being. In some ways the memories define who you are. Memories are instrumental in how we perceive ourselves; where we place ourselves in society. The historian Sangster, in her research into women's memories of a textile workers strike in 1937, highlighted that the way women remember was often linked with their role in society and how they viewed this.[7] Bornat and Diamond write in their paper that remembering in old age is demographically speaking a woman's experience and they explain that women of this age group are a rich source of information to feminists.[8]

For the researcher to understand the respondent's comments is not enough; she/he needs to use analytical research tools: for instance grounded theory and the importance of the theories that lie behind research have to be explored. Mauthner and Doucet realised that by looking again and again at the data that was collected during the interviews they conducted for their own social research.[9] It made them consider in more depth the data analysis process and the various assumptions that underpinned their approach. As they point out:

> *"For example, our understanding of how our data analysis methods were infused with epistemological and ontological assumptions that we were not fully aware of at the time has deepened as a result of progress in our thinking about epistemology and ontology."*[10]

Mauthner and Doucet argued further that their understanding of the their roles as researchers deepened because they considered more fundamental questions such as how the knowledge was acquired and how do researchers know what they know? They argued that a researcher is unable to be unconnected with the interviews as they themselves had a role to perform in the interviews and were an active party in that process and hence influenced the outcome. Indeed as Denzin argues:

"Social researchers we are integral to the social world we study."[11]

Therefore in order to analyse data about human beings a researcher is inevitably part of the social structure and is bound to be subjective in some way. Indeed a logical consequence of qualitative research philosophy is that any research endeavour will always be value-laden and never neutral.

After the interview, the researcher then goes on to use various methods of analysing data; transcribing and reading it through is also part of individual interpretation and therefore exposes our literary background in reading text. Mauthner and Doucet, whilst they advise that researchers should be aware of their own influence on the research data, do warn:

> *"Situating ourselves socially and emotionally in relation to respondents is an important element of reflexivity. However, too much has been made of the oft-repeated references made by feminist researchers to their positioning of gender, class, ethnicity, sexuality and geographical location. These locations are often 'deployed as badges', which are meant to represent 'one's respects to "difference"' but do not affect any aspect of the research or interpretative process."*[12]

This is a valued point; merely stating your background will not be sufficient, there is a need to understand the subject and the nature of subjectivity and also be aware that part of this could be exploring your own position in the research giving data its value. Feminist methodologies focus on what women talk about and how they express themselves in interviews. Although it is never a completely transparent text that the researcher has before her/him, she/he can with care and in time draw conclusions and learn from statements that have been made. As Mauthner and Doucet explain:

> *"We suggest that our subjects are reflexively constituted between the researcher and the researched, and that while they are therefore always completely unknown, it is possible to grasp something of their articulated experience and subjectivity through a research encounter."*[13]

We are then able to locate the researcher through what she/he says about her/his own position and the way in which she/he analyses the various texts and the researcher in turn is able to allow the subject some space within the text; that of the story teller. In oral history that is particularly important because we have already established the need for the interviewee to justify their actions in the past, as explained in the process of immigration, so as to make sense of their existence today but also to use it as an alignment of past, present and future.

Feminist approaches are able to look into the deeper layers of the text itself unlike the positivist approach commonly adopted by natural science and of great influence in earlier sociological research. The positivist approach has a theory as its starting point and the collecting of data to prove the hypothesis. The researchers' own values are considered of no importance and the data is on the whole quantitatively collected.[14] I believe that qualitative methods on the other hand work particularly well with psychoanalytical methods in which listening is the main way of collecting data from text (the interviews).[15] The disadvantage here for sociologists lies in the clinical background of psychoanalytical theories as they were developed by Freud, for and by listening to patients. The accounts of the interviewees that sociologists use for their data give more in the way of cultural background and individual reflections on their own social group, whereas psychoanalytical research centres on the malfunctioning interviewee.[16]

Analytical research methods are very thorough as the constant filtering through texts is a bit like peeling an onion. Researchers also critically evaluate all the stages of their research. This particular method, based on *grounded theory* can also help historians. The sociologist Parr explains:

> *"The strengths of grounded theory are the emphasis on an open-mindedness and a willingness to listen, hear and act on the results at all stages of the research process, grounding the analysis in the research data rather than trying to fit the data into an a prior framework. This is consistent with a feminist framework, which has rejected positivism, largely because of its emphasis on value freedom and objectivity. Rather, what is emphasised here is the importance of contextual factors regardless of whether qualitative or quantitative data collecting methods are used."*[17]

Her concerns are the strong emphasis on the value freedom and objectivity in positivist approaches, which could present an inaccurate picture.

To analyse the data then becomes an ongoing process that extends throughout the whole period of the research. Grounded theory allows the research to develop in order to find its core/its base, throughout the whole of its process. Speech in my opinion is essentially a social tool and the data is carefully examined because I believe it lies at the heart of sociology. But this is also where the problems lie for the historian. Meaning behind text is important and very complex, there are many different layers of meaning that are partly socially constructed, however a historian has to accept somewhere that this is the text given by the interviewee: this is how she/he translates the past and reflects on that past, because the historian makes a study of events that took place previously. To me the historian is not researching the functioning of a social group or society but searching for what has happened with the people in that group and how that was experienced. I have chosen to use insights from grounded theory for the process of data analysis. I have also drawn on psychoanalytical theory in terms of aiding the interview process as well as for the process of data analysis.

Oral history and psychoanalysis

The biggest problem for me was to overcome the fear of 'false' or 'inaccurate' accounts. How useful are interviewees' accounts when they might not be accurate? This is an interesting point because in court cases, witness accounts are sometimes the only evidence available. But what is accurate within history? Portelli says about accurate accounts that:

> *"The importance of the oral source may often lie not in this adherence to facts but rather its divergence from them, were imagination, symbolism, desire break in. So therefore there are no false oral sources."*[18]

It can be argued that if you want a story about migrants, you want the story to be told by migrants. Oral sources are not objective accounts of "hard facts" but of a respondent's life story. There is no such thing as objective history. It can never be taken without partiality because the interviewees took part in history and therefore have views, which will be reflected in the way they look back. But this in turn creates a great opportunity for insight for the historian.[19] For the historian, therefore, all accounts are important within reason and that allows the historian to be free in using the snowball method, letting the contact between people of the community snowball more sources when sampling data.[20] But how to work with the interviewees remains an important aspect in the whole validity of the data.

In the 1980s historians like Passerini, Portelli, Alexander and Figlio examined the use of psychoanalysis for their research.[21] Psychoanalysis gives an insight in the position of the historian in an interview and in her/his role as narrator, which I felt was very important. In an interview transference takes place; this is the redirecting of childhood emotions to a new object, the listener, who is involved in the process of remembering the past with the emotional baggage of that past. The historian as listener then enters the story and becomes partly involved by the process of understanding the information by means of searching through her/his own experience in order to latch onto and pick up the data. This process is referred to as counter-transference.[22] In one interview the interviewee Caitlin talked about a goat being chained to the church tower as part of the celebrations in her hometown in Ireland and immediately I connected it with a festival in a rural town I once visited with my family where a (fake) cow was traditionally tied up at the church tower. I was sure we witnessed the same experience until I transcribed the tape and discovered that she never said it was hung at the tower it was just tied to the tower. I latched on with different information, wrongly as it happened because her memory made me remember mine.[23]

Gearhart examines this in her work on the psychoanalyst Lacan.[24] According to Lacan it is this distortion or bias of the listener imposed on the theory that unlocks the interview-data. Lacan argues that the counter-transference is the negative phase of a dialectic process that leads to positive transference and is the key to all successful analysis and a coherent unified scientific theory.[25] You use bias and make sense of the data by your own bias, or your own personal and academic background. But you need to be aware of your background and place this within the study, then the data will be properly analysed.

In Passerini's research on Italian fascism she uses the method of psychoanalysis because she understands the interviewee to be internally slightly inconsistent and conflicted as she/he struggles to express long-term needs which cannot be reduced to simple logic.[26] The information should not collapse under the inconsistent interview data nor be seen as having a spontaneous nature. As in my data all the interviewees of the research were very conscious of the importance of their story, which is what should be the case. The place in time and space where the interview takes place feels almost like a place they break away from their cultural surroundings, trying to assess the past as they see it. This is a very important process. I have used these historians in my research as examples of where I can position myself as a researcher using psychoanalysis as a tool to understand the interview process and the analysis of the samples.

Position of the historian in the interview

Ryan begins her work with her own background and expresses her concern about the influence of the researcher's own background.[27] She sets about researching Irish migrant women who left for England in the 1930s whilst she herself left in the 1990s which was a very different time in Ireland as well as England. She warns that simple concepts as *home* have been given a completely different meaning over time. In a way my lack of understanding of the concept *Ireland as homeland* made it also easier because the interviewees were very aware that I, as a Dutch woman, knew nothing of their background and were very careful not to leave anything out. My own migrant background made them more determined to tell all. But this can also leave you with a gap, perhaps a feeling of an aesthetic form of understanding or closeness whilst the gap might still be difficult to overcome. As Alexander argues about the position of feminist historians:

> *"We use transference as the informant passes on the information to the historian. We feel more interested because we are women too."* [28]

Although we understand much we should not forget that there is a gap between those interviewed and ourselves. This is also true of the way the historian then transcribes the interview. Transcribing is necessary as oral sources are just that, oral, and the transcript needs to be made into literary text in order to allow research to take place.[29] Portelli believes that to replace the tape with the transcript is like doing art criticism on art productions or literary criticism on translations.[30] What he feels is more important is the fact that the oral sources are a great addition to other sources especially with working classes because the lack of literary sources, but what makes them so unique is that events are felt differently by the interviewee and have an all original plot structure.[31] This is because people witness events from different backgrounds, in our case as outsiders of English society. And whilst they tell their tale they try and make sense of their lives, not sense of the all the historical processes of that past. An interview itself can also be deconstructed as a social relationship into gender and cultural expressions and this will influence the relationship between the interviewer and interviewee and determine its outcome as Bornat and Diamond stress.[32]

Culture and the use of language

In oral research it is clear language is very important, just as it is in any other form of history. In the past historians believed themselves to be close to science by ignoring the importance of the narrative element in history. Writing on Barthes his work *Death of an Author*, Hawkes argues that during the 19th century in France, as in England, a writing style emerged that pretended to be innocent and devoid of any writer behind the text.[33] Hawkes warns that also during the 20th century as this style became well established, some historians failed to acknowledge their bourgeois background, i.e. the background of the colonialist and aggressor. This style of writing is also named zero writing or blanco style, which sold the belief that the world researched was black and white. This use of this white language was obstructive to the science of history. Barthes writes in *Death of an Author* that the author can no longer be regarded as an authoritative figure providing the reader with all the answers but that she/he comes with her or his cultural background and that it is the reader that should be the focus here.[34]

In cultural history the way in which historians write is very important. As White explains:

> *"In order to write history or any given scholarly discipline or even of a science, one most be prepared to ask questions about it of a sort that do not have to be asked in the practice of it.'* [35]

White criticises Frye who argues that all literature has a myth basis and that this myth is recognised as a theme or plot structure and that if a historian did well she/he would get rid of the plot structure and would only then write discursively.[36] Whereas White argues that it is the ability of the historian to make a story out of chronicles. He points out that all the historian can see are story elements. All historical events are neutral, just factual data and without narrative do not make history. The reader needs to understand what the historian is highlighting. White feels that historical narratives point in two directions: to events and the story type used. He calls the latter mythos.

This mythos helps the reader to familiarise himself with the complexity of the information in the story. Mythos is a style like a tragedy or comedy and so on. This is particularly important with oral history when you might lose the reader by directly passing on the information of the interviewee; instead it is set in a mythos. It is not possible to allow the story telling of the interviewees to be the mythos or style as they do not know what it is you as researcher are researching and how you need to present the information. White adds to this that history is not literature despite the use of narrative because its contents are actual and not possible and that we need to use plot-structure.[37] I will use plot structure to highlight importance of events and translating situations that I learned from my sources.

Lacan stresses that the role of language is a fundamental part of the symbolic. Thompson studies Lacan and explains the value of his understanding of language.[38] Lacan believes that the unconscious is structured like language; he understands that the whole acquisition of the sexual and personal identity to be a simultaneous process and that its foundations are the bedrock of language. It is when the infant enters language she/he learns about the complexities of that language. Language is a social and cultural structure, it does not exist outside a group or unit or family. The interviewee will use the language she/he was brought up with, the family of her/his kin, to explain historic events that happened to them.

Thompson argues that:

> *"Masculinity and femininity are therefore imposed on the infant's inner psyche, long before sex differences have immediate meaning, through the conscious cultural symbolism of gender embedded in language. And we can understand more of what is not said. Again it is not the specific theories of psychoanalysis which prove most useful, so much as the new sensibility, an ability to notice what might have been missed."*[39]

The family or group is very important to the understanding of the interview sample. It throws light on the underlying meaning of the language used. The oral historian Figlio was very interested in the group structure.[40] He found that by talking with the interviewee he also entered the story. You could argue that in a sense he entered language and therefore took a position in the group: the listener or the outsider. Figlio states:

> *"The story is told by people of a group who feel that they belong together; part of this belonging is socially constructed and give solidarity but this solidarity is partly the myth of the group structure."*[41]

People will identify themselves within the history of their family and their culture, making connections and identifications of the self within the group.

In *Family Matters* Ryan describes how family is right at the heart of most migration issues. Families are often transformed by migration and reconfigured through it. She highlights that migration stories are family stories of love, conflict and sacrifices for the purpose of the family needs against that of the individual.[42] Bornat and Diamond refer in their paper on 'Women's history and Oral history' to Chamberlain whose work on Caribbean immigrants in the UK has shown how the emigration narratives, despite the fact that she researched family histories, were underpinned by gender dynamics.[43] The migration from farms to mill villages in the South of the US during 1910-1930s, researched by Beyer-Sherwood showed the difference in adaptation to the new situation was also gender based because leisure and work as well as chores around the house were gendered and therefore even smaller moves meant huge changes in families redefining gender roles.[44]

This concept of language in group structure as part of culture gave rise to an interesting form of theatre. I believe that theatre is the form of cultural language where the silence is filled with speech. The Brazilian theatre director and play-writer, Boal, uses forum theatre by allowing the audience to stop the performance when it is watched a second time round allowing the lines to be changed by the audience.[45] The audience is introduced to daily situations that they recognise and then the unspeakable is given a platform. This form of theatre he calls *theatre of the oppressed* allowing the audience a voice, to partake and help act out their situation, their stories are given importance. In his theatre the real oppressed were often the young women from poor families.

In the same way with oral history you allow people to make an active contribution. They tell what is important for instance about work. As a historian you ask them what did they do during the day, what was their role or what did Mary mean to them, and as they fill the answers in they fill in the gap left in history by the Church and the English and Irish governing bodies alike: they fill in the story. Placing themselves in history playing the main part, history becomes a story about all they represent: working class, migrants, Catholics, outsiders, mothers and daughters. They also become critical of institutions like the Church in a way they might never have voiced otherwise. They convey their criticism because I am as a historian a storyteller and with me between the audience and them it became a safe place to tell their family play about conflicts and change.

In conclusion of the use of theory

Instead of examining the same text in depth like grounded theorist in sociology, psychoanalysis focuses on the conduct of interviews themselves. But both grounded theory and psychoanalysis can be used when oral history is taken as the main approach in the thesis allowing the text to be analysed in a multidisciplinary way. Text itself is subjective; the historian looking at the text is also subjective. I therefore place the cultural inventions behind the text, for instance Irish upbringing, and to place the historian's position in the research. The historian has to try to make sense of the past by allowing the oral data to add another dimension to previous research of that past. I am not writing as a sociologist and therefore do not strip away layers and layers of meaning embedded in the text as it is in language but I watch with the care of an oral historian aware of the place that language holds in oral accounts just like literary accounts do. But I am not concentrating on people's free flow of expressing their fantasy and turbulent inner life but I am carefully recording their story to use it for narrating a specific aspect of history. Themes will be covered with the questions, the answers will be carefully recorded and studied and then compared with others. Stories will be compared with information about the Catholic community that comes from archive data. This will give the research momentum and value to the texts researched. Therefore in this research no grounded theory was chosen, but an acute awareness of all the pitfalls, the complex nature of language and the stage that surrounds the social actors: my interviewees.

Irish immigrant women and methodology

The research focuses on Irish working class women, highlighting cultural differences. It is designed to allow them a voice in history as immigrant women partaking in the history of the Harold Hill estate. In a paper Villarreal argues that oral history can give new significance to local sites highlighting their development in a unique way:

> *"Places gather significance when an experience is attached, and embody a sense of communal or shared space."*[46]

The Irish immigrant women in the samples, which will be discussed in Research Design of this chapter, came mostly from very poor rural areas in Ireland and were employed in lower paid jobs. Although many had been educated above the level of their brothers, they were however not often highly trained or from an academic background, with a few exceptions.[47] Most of the women, as married Catholic women elsewhere, were expected to stay at home and look after the children. The daily routine of bringing up the children and working often in part time, poorly paid, menial jobs that had to complement their husband's wages, took most of their time. But they contributed to community work for their local church and school.

Qualitative research in feminist methodology can be used because it allows us to look at the day to day routine in the lives of women without pushing aside the more mundane. To come to grips with the impact Irish immigrant women had on their community, one has to look at all the aspects of their lives. Ribbens and Edwards warn us that;

> *'There is a danger that the voices of particular groups, or particular forms of knowledge, may be drowned out, systematically silenced or misunderstood as research and researchers engage with dominant academic and public concerns and discourses."* [48]

A problem in my research is the use of the concepts the public and private spheres. Ribbens and Edwards argue:

> *"we believe these concepts are crucial to an understanding of both men's and women's lives in industrialised Western societies."*[49]

In my samples the spheres were not so separate and women moved continuously from home to community making these transitions rather fluid. Irish communities in England were mainly based on their Irish inheritance of a rural society that had been colonised for many centuries. Within Irish Catholic communities we encounter not a great border between the two spheres and more fluid shift from one to the other. This differs from research findings on English urban pattern like that of Ribbens and Edwards, in the situation of Irish communities these concepts of private and public spheres often do not apply. [50]

Women would use their talents and tasks that they used at home in community work and their daily routines at home would spill over into their work for and with the community. For instance cleaning the church; organising church events; helping children at school or in the local children's home; or visiting the sick. Celebrations that involved whole communities were some way or another connected with the daily routines around the house. The position of 'mother' in England that Ribbens and Edwards wrote about and researched is different from the women I have interviewed. In their paper they discuss the isolation of mothers with young children in England. But the people I have interviewed were mothers before the Second World War and had neighbours which they were closely involved with and had been involved with in social events, school events and Church events because all these were part of parish life. Their role as mothers in their Irish Catholic community meant that they often had no paid work but all the same were heavily involved in skilled work and in organisational work that was often beneficial for their own communities and therefore were operating within the public sphere.

Another point I noticed was that the use of academic language was developed for an English reader, but the background of the Irish immigrant women differed in that they have their Catholic faith and their Irish ancestors were colonised by Britain. They are or rather were making a living in a society that was often racist towards them. What then becomes very important is the quality of the listener during the research. The historian has to be a capable narrator. This is in general important to researchers of women but especially of Irish people because their story has components of the colonial experience in it and the position of the often unwanted Irish immigrant making the discourse for an English reader more complex. Also the position of the researcher is a very difficult one that puts her in the role of narrator and translator of the stories. The researcher has to be aware that she has to find some kind of balance between explaining what is said and allowing it to be said unaltered. Thompson argues:

> *"This is why an oral historian will always feel a specially strong tension between biography and cross-analysis. But this is a tension which rests on the strength of oral history."*[51]

In cross-analysis Thompson uses the interview as a source of information from which he constructs an argument about behaviour patterns and reflects on events in the past.

Research design

The thesis seeks to explore the impact of Irish women of the Harold Hill Estate and I chose to use oral testimonies of women plus a written testimony, comparing them with four public local archives: the Brentwood Diocese Archive; the Ursuline Convent Archive; the Archive of St Edwards Church and the Central Public library of Romford Archive. The Central Romford Library contains minutes from the council meetings of this period and copies of the Romford Recorder local newspaper and of the Romford Times and the Brentwood Gazette. The interviewees are women from the Irish community of Harold Hill with the exception of one woman religious, who grew up in East London where she educated children of Irish descent who lived there before the slum clearance.

I also approached the Ursuline Sisters of Brentwood as they had been so instrumental in setting up and running the local primary school but when I asked the sisters if they were willing to have some interviews with me they politely declined. It was, according to their archivist, too painful to look back knowing that the community was in a sense dying out. I had come at a very sad time. I did persuade them to see it at as a celebration of all their achievements but their sense of modesty dismissed this idea. They were also aware that some interesting research had already been done with the sisters in Billericay so it was not that important for an academic to do this all over again in Brentwood; the sisters knew the drawback for an historian to be second in line with research ideas.

I interviewed 7 women in total, and the interviews were gathered over a period of several years because of the time it took to gain access to people's private stories. The first two interviews were conducted as part of a MA course in 1994 when I realised that much important material was not being used in the study and valuable information felt like it was being "wasted". I was able to look at the material again when I conducted further interviews for the thesis from 1997 until the end of 1999.

The interviewees had known me or known of me through my voluntary work for the local churches, school and as a mother of two girls attending the same school as their daughters. At first no one was keen to talk; it was only when parishioners began to know me as a member of the community that the majority of the interviewees accepted me. Permission to interview came gradually and it was not until I became involved with the cleaning of the church that the women felt more positive towards the idea of participating in the research. I gained trust from those who had themselves never been involved in work for the community that held status or required training.

Other interviewees knew me through the children as one of the mothers who helped out in school. One woman knew me through my work as a nurse and another agreed to be interviewed after the local parish priest introduced us. Once the trust was established I was given all the help and information I was asking for. However it took in some cases several years of approaching the subject before the interview was agreed to. I do not believe it would have been possible to conduct this research as an outsider. To that extent my sampling technique was very much one of opportunism and similar to the snowball effect the women also needed to be "connected" to the research aims.

Snowball sampling was chosen because it was difficult to find enough interviewees due to lack of trust. This technique makes use of people within the community who were willing to let me interview them and they would approach other possible candidates. At first I was making no headway and to start this process two gatekeepers were approached from the community: the local priest and the head of the primary school. This technique however has a disadvantage in that maybe no suitable candidates were coming forward, but as this was a close knit community it would be very unlikely that possible candidates were overlooked by the members of the community. Gatekeepers can mean that others will check for the right kind of interviewees who would perhaps scan them on suitability based on what stories the Catholic community would prefer not being spilled to a historian. But I was lucky with my gatekeepers and both did nothing to either interfere or push for the right kind of people.[52]

The first gatekeeper I approached was an Irish priest who was much loved by his parishioners. He came from Cork and was very proud of his origins and talked openly about the poverty of his childhood and this helped me greatly in finding interviewees. The second gatekeeper was the head of the primary school who also offered a neutral space to conduct the interviews; if needed she would lend me her office. She was a daughter of an Irish farmer who often used examples of her childhood in class. The gatekeepers proved very important to me because although I had special access to the community because of my status as a mother and active church member, living and working within the community, women were very determined not to talk to me.

When the priest left I was having difficulties finding more interviewees. The new parish priest (and that of the other parish) was also not Irish and it also takes a new priest some time to get the trust of his congregation. The other priest who had been there for a long time was concerned that the thesis was only about Irish women. It is very difficult to create that trust when authoritative figures are not interested in the ethnic background of the community. I realised early on that the sample was always going to be small but saw it as an advantage that a small sample could be studied in depth and left enough room to research archive work alongside it to view the themes from a different angle.

The research respondents

The nine interviewees were: Caitlin, Eileen, Patrick and Aoife, Deirdre, Edna, Christina, Shona and Siobhan. In brief their backgrounds are as follows, introduced in order of age:
Caitlin was born in 1907 started the interview with:

> "I am 93 years old and I still got the brain and I can talk",

justifying her place in the research. She had moved to Romford from County Kerry in 1938. She was a daughter of a greengrocer and one of seven siblings. She and her husband had five children who were all born before the Second World War broke out. She had moved to the road opposite to the Harold Hill estate and was therefore one of the first occupants. Caitlin, and later on her son, was very much involved with the fundraising for the new St Dominic's Church.

Second-generation Eileen was born in 1924 and was in her early seventies at the time of the interview. She was the daughter of an Irish immigrant mother, who came from Tipperary and an English father. Eileen herself was born in Greenwich, was one of eight and moved first to the Isle of Dogs and then in 1953 with her husband to the estate, where she and her husband had four children. She was much involved with the fundraising and church work in the parish of The Holy Redeemer.

Aoife was nearly seventy at the time of the interview and was born in 1931 in Limerick City, a daughter of a pork butcher and one of ten children. She and her husband Patrick, who was one year older, came over in 1954. Patrick had first lived alone, in Camden Town. As a couple they had moved to Rush Green, Romford. A series of moves followed and eventually she moved to Harold Hill. She could verify Caitlin's story of the mass that was said in the pub as she was by then part of this emerging Catholic community on the Hill.

Second-generation Christina was born in 1932 in Stratford as a daughter of an Irish General Practitioner and his Irish wife. She was one of two siblings and was very involved in the community of Stratford, firstly when assisting her father's practice and later on as a woman religious of the Holy Child Order as a teacher in her own community. During the interviews she was in her seventies.

Deirdre was born in 1938 in County Mayo and one of six. During the interview she was in her mid sixties. She moved when she was only one to Kildare then at the age of three she moved again to an orphanage in Dublin where she lived until her fifteenth birthday. At the age of fifteen she moved to England, to Russell Square in the heart of London. She met her husband and lived with him in the Docklands and moved to Harold Hill much later on in 1970. Her story was important because it highlights the complex situation for some children in Irish society and the desperation to move away from home. She had six children and was very involved in working with mentally disabled children and adults from orphaned backgrounds and was also later on in her life involved with parish work in the Holy Redeemer.

Edna was born in 1945 in County Kerry, a daughter of a farmer and one of ten siblings. After her emigration she had moved from Wales gradually eastwards towards London and her interview made it clear that the Ireland she grew up in was very similar to that of the older interviewees. The contrasts between rural Catholic Ireland and Greater London were very carefully recorded in this interview. She had finally moved to the estate in the early seventies. She was involved with parish work mainly with helping the school.

Second-generation Shona and Siobhan were both daughters of Irish immigrant parents. Shona was born in 1956 and one of three and Siobhan was born in 1958 and one of four. Both had grown up in East London and had moved to Romford after their marriages. Each had two children in the Catholic School of Harold Hill at the time of the interviews when they were both in their thirties and were much involved in parish work for the school.

None of the interviewees ever referred to their parents by their first name nor did they explain what their first names or surnames were. They always used 'my mother' and 'my father' in a respectful tone and I will therefore continue to refer to their parents in the same manner.

The process of interviewing

The interviews were based on a set of open questions, and I employed interactive interviewing techniques.[53] Rather than leave it completely up to the interviewee, the stories flowed more easily when people were asked questions. Questions also triggered memories that were not in their minds at that moment in time. As Thompson argues:

> *"The questions should always be as simple and as straight forward as possible. Never ask complex, double-barrelled questions - only half will usually be answered, and it usually will not be clear which half."*[54]

I asked clear open questions that I could refer back to if they wandered off in different directions but there was room for moving away from the original questions so that the interview would not become too rigid with the risk that the information would dry-up.[55] As broad categories, I used growing up, migration and/or moving to the Harold Hill estate, their experience as mothers and their relationship to the Virgin Mary and their mother's relationship to her. I would always start with the straightforward questions of where were they born and when were they born. That followed with questions about their childhood.

When Eileen right at the beginning of the interview tells when her family came over to London I asked her if her father who was at that time a soldier remained in the army. She then told me that he was invalided out with epilepsy and that he was unable to work. That, epilepsy, was the key to the trust. Her generation felt uneasy with this illness as little of it was understood and the whole episodes of men going into mental institutions after the war, it was shrouded in shame and embarrassment. My sympathetic prodding:

> *"That must have been difficult with the money?"*

She answers that it must have been hard, but I want to know all about her Irish mother:

"For your mother..."[56]

Eileen continues to talk throughout the interview about hardship like poverty and illness and feels she can talk now openly about the tough life of her mother and how tough she was for her children. With people like Caitlin who were very upbeat and clear in their answers it was important to let her talk about her children for a while and then ask what it was like to have her first child and to prod a little:

"You lived in Romford when you had him?"[57]

This allowed her to tell how she had to leave him behind in Ireland with her mother without ever telling me how she experienced motherhood. It did prod her to talk about being apart from her oldest boy. With asking questions it was important to get behind generalised stories and the stereotype Irish mother with her children.

All women were able to give one interview but were initially very reluctant. Only Caitlin allowed me to conduct another interview very shortly after the first one, but this did not seem to produce more data. I would have preferred to go back to some topics to see if I could find out more information. All interviews were about two hours long. The interviews were done in the house of the interviewee with the exception of Shona and Siobhan, as it was easier for them to visit me. The use of school for an interview was declined by all perhaps because school was such a public and central place in the community. The interviews took place in their own home because they were more at ease there and their homes gave me more information about themselves and allowed me to see them in their own setting. Often walls were decked with photos of the past and in their own comfortable chair the women were more relaxed in talking to me. The photos were often talked about in length before the interview took place but none took out albums to show me more, I was clearly a visitor but that also meant that they gave me lots of cups of tea and biscuits.

Siobhan and Shona, who knew each other from school offered to visit me in my home as this was close to the primary school. They really used one another to trigger off memories but also for support, in case I would pressure them in anything they rather wanted not to talk about. Joint interviews can help people overcome their fear of talking but it can also make it harder to talk about something that others did not experience and when a researcher is asking too painful questions the interviewees can act as a united front blocking the questions. Christine offered to have the interview in the college where she worked which was a very fitting place for a sister who had dedicated her life to teaching and this was in many ways her home. All the participants were informed about the research and were therefore able to give an informed consent to taking part. Throughout the interviews I was sensitive to their feelings and did not push them to talk about uncomfortable issues. They were given pseudonyms to protect their anonymity.

The selection of the sample

It proved difficult to choose my sample; I had to accept that only some people were eventually prepared to be interviewed. The research population was the Irish immigrant female population in the Harold Hill community and therefore the criteria for the sample was that they all had to be Irish women or second-generation Irish women with close connection to the school and parishes. Seven women were a sufficient number because they all spread out over the whole period that was covered by the research. It was a unique sample that would have never been collected by an outsider. To ensure that there was enough information covered, the interviews would be part of research that also covered the archive material. The women were all connected with the parishes of Harold Hill and the Catholic school on the estate except for Christina, a nun, who was the daughter of a General Practitioner from East London and had been a teacher there. She could tell something of the background of the lives that people lived there before they came to Harold Hill. All women were still practising Catholics at the time of the interviews. All interviewees were mentally and emotionally able to talk about their lives.

The diary as a source

I had also been kindly lent a diary written by Ciara, by her daughter Colleen, who had kept it in her memory. Colleen did not wish to be interviewed but I was welcome to the dairy of her mother Ciara. Ciara was born on Canvey Island and was the daughter of Irish immigrants. She started her diary in 1938 when still in her early teens; the exact date is not known. Her diary gives an insight into the poems and the subjects girls were being taught at that time. Reading the diary the whole subject matters and language use allows us to step back into time.

When Ciara's diary entered the research as a source I was not certain as to how useful it was going to be, because the writer had since died and could not be interviewed which meant no further information could be added to the source. But what it did do was allow me an insight into the days of a young girl and later on young woman's thoughts and activities at the moment they occurred. I could place this diary as a form of information between archive material, which were more official documents meant for the public or as conformation of what took place (as in the convent's case) and the personal accounts as remembered at a later date in the interviews.
Ciara enters her diary for the first time on the 25-01-1938 and continues to record the dates of entry until the last date of 28-06-1941. After this the entries hold no dates but she continues to copy out religious poems about a mother's role in life and family life and also about the war. There was no mention of her age in the diary entries. I knew from her daughter that she was very young when she started her diary but unfortunately I never asked about her date of birth and I lost touch with her daughter. It still remained a good amount of material written and collected by this young girl and proved valuable to my research.

A diary's use often lies in the fact that diaries often have a self-analytical side to them allowing the writer to clear her mind.[58] Thompson refers to the work by Bohman who stresses that memoirs and interviews are very alike particularly what subject matter they are dealing with, but differ where the memoirs often use a more public abstract language.[59] The diary of Ciara was on the other hand a child's way of expressing herself and talking to herself as an outlet at the end of events that had happened. Her diary remained the personal sphere connecting collections of poems and the daydreams with day-to-day events.

The interview analysis: the tools of the story teller

The interviews were transcribed and the answers were grouped and checked for similarities and differences. Because questions were asked in a semi-structured way it was possible to compare responses. The text was then transcribed as spoken leaving it as oral text merely putting down on paper. The problem with oral text is that we believe we understand the way we use written text so well. Everything other than written text is viewed as less capable or simply less efficient. When we use written text we are aware that all the information we can gather is from the text and written text therefore has to be very precise. The mistake we make is to assume that the oral text is on the other hand less precise.

But oral text has its own techniques and what might look like a clumsy piece of oral text can in fact be a tool of storytelling. A good example is the transfer from one word to another. It gives you at first glance the impression that people are not concentrating well enough or are insecure or clumsy speakers. For a good example we can look at Edna's case. When examining the next sample she says:

> "*she would have been old enough to be in with the rest of them. [Kathy her sister a young teenager] But it is just coming from such a small place. Really they had no television or anything- People from rural areas coming in to bigger, bigger places. You have this problem, didn't they, on the whole.*"[60]

She uses the word *you* and transfers it to the word *they*. This is not a mistake but a clever technique she is using. By using *you* she is addressing the audience. *You* is here common ground: *us* or *you* and *me*: *Me* the storyteller and *you* the listener. *You* is here the general term of *us* human beings. Then she transfers it to *they* the people who came here, the people of the past. With her use of *you* she has raised both her and the listener onto this platform on which we both belong. After her appeal to *you (you* and *me us* people) it enables her to place her community in a safe position and now she can introduce the word *they*. But *they* is also Edna herself, as she too came over here. She too was viewed as different. But here she is still careful and by distancing herself from *they* she will hold on to the common ground that she created for herself and the listener.[61]

Another technique in which a storyteller makes a transfer is in times when stories are very painful and not easily told. A good example was the story of Caitlin. She told me about a bombardment of Romford during the Second World War. She described the morning after:

> *"We were walking down to Romford we saw a dead horse laying there, he'd been hit you see. Oh I thought that was awful that upset me no ends, you know; the horse."*[62]

They way she spoke and her tone of voice underlined the distress she said she had felt.

Much later on during the research I talked to her children and grandchildren and they told me that during this time she lost her sons: two small twin boys to illness. The family had to bury them in a mass grave, as there were so many people dead that there was no longer time or room to bury them in separate graves. Many years later the family tried to locate the graves of the boys to no avail. Too many casualties from bombing meant that there had been no time to write down the names of people in the mass graves. The boys were never mentioned in any of her stories all of which were about her family life. This was particularly strange, as she mentioned that some of her sons were altar boys. Her twins were also active in church services and well remembered by the rest of the Irish community.

Caitlin expresses the senseless deaths well by referring to the dead horse. For a country girl the dead horse stands for innocent lives lost and is the perfect metaphor. Caitlin manages to demonstrate the upset felt by the community by so many deaths without actually opening up painful wounds to a stranger. This is not bad memory but a carefully constructed way in which pain is translated.

Space to tell a tale

Another important factor when dealing with the interviewees is the amount of time and space they need to tell their story. Stories are often not told in a linear fashion. People may not come straight to the point. They had no time to prepare themselves for the questions I asked and their stories can ramble a little until they reach an interesting point. It is important to be careful when you steer an interviewee because she might have something important to say after not saying much at all. Our train of thought tends to run like this: we remember something that we associate with something else and that can lead to another point all together. A good example is Caitlin when I asked her about helping out with fundraising. She then moved on to say that:

> *"the money was for the church or what ever."*

Whatever is then highlighted by her casual comment:

> *"Because we had nothing."* [63]

Catholic women like Caitlin were forever helping out with fundraising; this was very much at the heart of their church, including charities and raising money for all sorts of projects.

After this little comment, at the moment I expected her to go on to talk about the fundraising, Caitlin remembered the lack of a church on the estate and then she went on to describe how priests used to say mass at the local pub. Earlier on she had told how she used to walk all the way to the town centre to go to mass and I could not have known that she also went to mass in the pub. She then turns out to have been responsible to prepare the place for mass and had instigated this service at the pub. What then follows is this great thing: when you allow people to talk about the mundane and ordinary things in life you suddenly get the extraordinary and unusual:

> *"I'll tell you this, I was, I was with all this young [her children] and on my own you see, and I thought; "O well, we got the Plough [public house], so that's alright. I go down there, ask the manager. This very very nice man, very good. And every Sunday I go down*

> *there. I help with the congregation, lay the tables out and the chairs you know. For the priests, different priests, we had a different priest, I never met so many priests. There must have been, I suppose the war being a, they came from France Germany, behind the Iron Curtain, Spain, oh what have you. I met so many different priests, there was…You would not have the same one every Sunday."*[64]

I found nothing about the many European priests that were working in the area in the local papers or the minutes of council meetings or the archives in Brentwood dioceses. Nor does anyone mention this in other documents. But Caitlin tells me very clearly that there were many priests from Europe and she suggests that that was because of the war. This makes a lot of sense but never came up before. It shows how little is documented of that time because this information connects to local history and was at the time not important to the Catholic Church and certainly not to English society and therefore after the war these priests gradually disappear from the scene. But it highlighted to me the scale of the exodus of Catholic Priests from occupied Europe and how they were used in Romford, especially in this little pub in Harold Hill. Their presence meant that the church services were able to continue and the parish was in a sense being born.

Another important example was the story told by Aoife and her husband Patrick. We were talking about the problem of raising children. I worked my way back to the subject I wanted to move on to, the Irish community, by commenting that they must have had some help from their close knit community with raising children. They were not isolated here. They had already told me about their social club. Then Aoife said:

> *"and they were mostly Irish, you know and you knew about all that was going on, mostly Cork mind you. Very, very few that were living from near us"*[65]

It was clear as in Christina's story that Cork was thought to be very different from Limerick and other areas and I had made the mistake to put all Irish men and women in a box without any other social or geographical labelling.

What then happened was very significant. As I was beginning to worry how far we had moved away from our estate and thinking of a way to move back on track, Patrick commented:

> "There were five, there were five clubs in Dagenham, Irish clubs, five." [66]

This was rather a large number and nobody in Dagenham ever told me about this great number of Irish social clubs. As Aoife talks on about their social life at the various clubs Patrick then reveals the reason behind all the clubs:

> "Fords was, Fords was all Irish back then, there were very few English men then."

And then his wife adds:

> "But didn't they call Cork, Cork it was, little Ireland wasn't it, so many Irish people from hmm Cork...in hmm Dagenham, that they called it little Cork." [67]

In the whole of the research of '*Family and Kinship*' there was no mention of the Irish past of the Catholics in East London but then as they moved to the new estate and the researchers Young and Willmott looked again at the community this time in Dagenham, they never noticed nor talked about the new influx of Irish men and women with a majority coming from Cork.[68] I conclude from this that the influence and Irish background of the working class in Dagenham had been completely overlooked in their research.

To let people talk and learn to listen is at the heart of oral research. To listen carefully in the interview and find out the information makes you review certain ideas you had and the whole of the research is now a process of developing an insight by allowing the people from the community to talk at their own pace. The strength of interviews lay in the strength of listening; perhaps it is therefore right to say that the researcher becomes in turn the storyteller by careful listening and mapping other people's stories.

Dirty linen and alcohol: the outcome

What occupied me the most and worried me throughout the interview sessions were the questions I had to ask. I was not from the Irish community and did not want to appear rude by asking painful or uncomfortable questions. The Irish community would not look kindly upon such research and would perhaps be annoyed that their own women would talk openly to me about problems with which they struggled.

What made it more difficult was that the women I interviewed were women who knew me well as I was part of their parish and was welcomed as a relative newcomer. Most women were nervous about the part they were to play in my research. Throughout the whole process they kept looking for something positive to say and it felt like it was difficult for a minority ethnic community to "hang their dirty washing out to dry". This is an ethnical issue and the intent behind the research was explained to the interviewees and the gatekeepers. The protection of their privacy in any material that was used for this university research was also explained to them, and they were also assured that their anonymity and privacy was safeguarded and I explained what the research was in aid of.

The biggest problem that had come back in previous private conversations was alcohol abuse. But was this a major problem in the Irish community or was it something that created more concern amongst the Irish women than for instance their British counterparts? It would have made a big impact on the lives of women if alcohol abuse did occur or had occurred in their lives. Alcohol is the most complex of hidden problems families face and makes a big impact on whole communities and is therefore important to explore. Research by Tilki explores this issue in semi-structured interviews, explaining the social and economic background of alcohol use amongst Irish men in London in 1960s and 1970s. The findings highlight the economic role of the pub and how alcohol and pub life protected the men from homesickness and gave them a sense of belonging. The paper also explores the ambivalent culture of alcohol in Ireland.[69]

The women in my research who had lived in Ireland were the most open about alcohol problems in their community. They also felt more hostile towards alcohol abuse and were more matter of fact about it. What Siobhan and Shona were suggesting was that the alcohol abuse often started in Britain. As second-generation Irish immigrants they saw no problems back in Ireland on their visits and blamed the harsh reality of the immigration process on the drinking problems amongst the Irish in Britain. What happened was that the second-generation Irish women in Britain were well acquainted with the problems of migration which sometimes resulted in alcohol abuse as they had witnessed these problems themselves but Ireland was very much viewed through the eyes of the holidaymaker. Their visits to Ireland were brief and their stay a pleasurable one.

Christina was the most direct about alcohol abuse. She did witness problems back home but also connected a difficult life in England with alcoholism as was the case with her uncle who had been a surgeon working during the war in the bowels of a big ship.[70] Deirdre was very realistic about the consequence of her father's alcoholism: it had put her and her sisters in the orphanage; a drunken widower was in no position to look after the children. It consequently spit the whole family up.

The issues that surrounded alcohol abuse were important to the lives of the women interviewed and most encountered abuse within the family. They proved important issues to discuss and it took time before people, very bravely, were able to talk about it. The older generation was more condemning towards the alcoholics whereas the younger generation was giving reasons behind the drinking. But even in casual answers about other matters alcohol always popped up in the interviews.

Translating hostilities

Memories can be very painful and they filter their way into our present. They become part of us today. What is interesting is that all interviewees expressed pain differently and translated it differently. I tried for instance to find out if they had encountered discrimination, something they normally never talked about but was still noticeable in English society during the interviews. It was bit like asking; "Is the Pope a Catholic?" But what was interesting was that some said they did not encounter hostilities at all. For instance Aoife and Patrick said they had never experienced any but had heard from Patrick's uncle back in the nineteen-thirties that they were not welcome.[71] In those early days it was harder according to Patrick and some of this could be explained by the recession, this is explored further in their interview. But what was noticeable was that Aoife and Patrick never ventured out of their Catholic clubs and neighbourhood and so would have been protected from English hostility. Edna explained the hostilities as a gap between rural and town communities when for instance her sister was treated as stupid by her teacher in England. In the case of Caitlin she started talking without prodding on hatred for Catholic children and I asked if she encountered a lot of people who did not like Catholics but his was quickly and firmly denied despite her previous story.

Racism then or hostilities towards a community are difficult to discuss and appear far more complex than the problems women encountered with alcohol abuse. Shona and Siobhan gave rather detailed information on racism during the seventies, a decade that all others had carefully left out of their story. This will be referred to later on in chapters 4, 5 and 6.

Archival and related source materials

The local archives contain much information about the area and the people that are being examined in the thesis. They are therefore good examples of information of what happened to the newcomers on the Harold Hill estate in Romford and how they were viewed by the local authorities, including the Romford County Council and the Catholic Bishop in Brentwood and the clergy. But also informative accounts on various events that took place on the estate can be further examined by the use of local archives. The most detailed sources were found in archives of the Catholic Church and archives belonging to the Public Central Library of Romford. They help illustrate how great the impact was of the Irish immigrant moving to the area, how they were settling in and what the consequences of such a large inflow of Irish Catholics were for the area. The data from the interviews needed to supplement the data derived from the oral sources by looking at local archives in order to get access to information and archive material covering the period and the area. I knew that if I wanted to map people's stories more information was needed and local archives could contextualise the experiences described in the interviews, providing more general information on the history of the development of Romford. I then discovered a vast amount of material highlighting different aspects of the themes that I wanted to cover.

For the research, four public local archives were used: the archive of the Central Library of Romford (CLR); 'Brentwood Diocesan Archives, Cathedral House Brentwood' (BDA); the Ursuline Convent Archive (UCA), and St Edwards Church Archive (ECA). The material of the local archives was divided into subjects covering population development and building developments, attitudes towards the dwellers of the new estate and response of the Catholic hierarchy to the growing Catholic population in the Diocese.

The CLR had all the copies of the local papers and very detailed minutes of the council meetings actually bound and well kept which reflects the effect the building of the Harold Hill estate had on the town. The papers examined were the weekly *Romford Recorder*, the weekly *Brentwood Gazette* and *Recorder*, and the weekly *Romford Times*. They recorded fetes and other public celebrations of the Catholic community but also informed on the attitudes of local people towards the newcomers. These three publications were all the papers of the area at the time. The minutes of the Borough of Romford Council at CLR that were used were from the period 1944 to 1960. These sources provided the much needed information on how the estate came to be and what problems occurred whilst the estate was being built. The newspapers were from the same period as the archive material from the BDA.

The BDA had several boxes filed by date, full of information on education and the growing number of Catholics moving to the area. These also contained examples of sermons, and information on the position of mothers and fathers in families as well as the distributed leaflets to parents that were available in the parishes at the time. They held correspondence with the Bishop, records of meetings by the Catholic Education Council and various documents which proved of much use to the research as it was informative about this growing new Catholic community.

As they were responsible for the setting up of the school, the archive of the Ursuline Convent of Brentwood, founded in 1900, had much information about the primary school on the estate and the day-to-day running of the school, showing all the financial decisions as well as the names of children on the school register in several boxes with much material placed together in order of subject matter of schools. The UCA also gave me information about the early years of the convent in Brentwood and the school there from

1903. Also included was the *Fair View Chronicle,* the religious periodical written and printed by the Ursuline sisters, which highlighted local news of the convent and her schools. To explore if there had been evidence of Irish settlers into the area of Romford prior to the building of the estate I looked at the ECA to investigate evidence of Irish surnames in St Edward's Church records and I went back to the earliest date of 1867, which were their earliest records of baptism. There were Irish names present which was expected with the building programs of many roads and the railway in the area in the nineteenth century but the number of Irish surnames of the period prior to the research data was not examined as it was of no consequence to the outcome of the research.

It was very difficult to get hold of other archive information. The Catholic Education Council (CEC) in Edgar Square London, which is managed by the Catholic Bishops' Conference of England and Wales, for instance was unable to help me with archive material on education in the 1950s as lack of space forced them to throw all of it out. Unfortunately this was the case with many Catholic organisations and the local churches because their first priority is the Catholic community, not the preservation of the past. The only other archive that was available to me was that of Cathedral House in Brentwood.

Archive material is a great asset to this type of research because it allows a glimpse in what can be interpreted as a major topic at the time. Also ideas that were expressed in writing and were stored in local archives can be traced unaltered by time unlike interview material. People clearly thought differently about their lives and lived differently from the present time and it feels like getting into a time capsule uncovering ordinary day-to-day things that nobody would have thought of looking at since. It does however not answer all questions research might bring up, but it gives a picture that is not changed by memory or time and that makes it a valid contribution along with oral data.

There was a good quantity of archive material in the community of the Ursuline Sisters. They were very hospitable and trusted me with all their information. After the initial meeting with the archivist, I felt I was completely trusted and was often struck by the warmth and kindness that they bestowed upon me. The community was going through a difficult time with one of the sisters being terminally ill and the sad prospects of no longer receiving young blood into the 'Family', as new members are in decline. Perhaps with this in mind they were very keen that something was written down before the final end of this successful house. They had set up a well-organised archive containing a wide range of historic data about the schools that they ran and the convent itself from school rotas to the financial administration. It was put together with love and attention by the sisters and many records and work of the former pupils of either of the three schools, that they had set up and had run and funded for many years, was carefully kept and preserved.

To research the archive material of the BDA proved more difficult. It took much persuasion to be allowed a search through their documentation. A sister who was aware of the importance of all the information collected over the years by the diocese had set up the archive some years before the research date. Thanks to her hard work it is possible to look at some aspects of the past of the Diocese of Brentwood. I examined weekly Church leaflets, brochures of various Catholic organisations like the pamphlets of the *Catholic Truth Society*, minutes of Diocese meetings and correspondence between other bishops and the bishop of Brentwood and copies of sermons. There were many letters; in 1967 for instance one was by a commission of Cardinals on the New Catechism discussing the position of the Church regarding the new Dutch catechism and the Cardinals' stand on it. Official letters such as these demonstrated the important debates on Church policies on various issues. The files ranged therefore on subjects of educational purposes to official letters from the Holy See to the Diocese and were all put together in the period order of ten years. I used the 1950 to 1960 files and 1960 to 1970 files checking everything whether it connected with the themes I was looking for, leaflet-by-leaflet, paper-by-paper, letter-by-letter.

Initially, the request to research the archive was rejected but I managed to persuade them with help from a sister who was active in instructing schools on the Catholic Religious Education Program. The archivist there was enthusiastic and made certain that there was always a secretary available to help me settle in, in her absence.

Conclusion

As a historian, rather than stripping away layers of meaning embedded in the text, I examine information given in the interviews. The oral historian is aware of the place that language holds in oral accounts just like in literary accounts. But in this research I am not concentrating on people's free flow of expression, examining their fantasies and turbulent inner life. History is a careful recording of the information of the past, in order to use it for narrating a special aspect of history. As a historian I have to remain aware of all the pitfalls; the complex nature of language and the stage or backdrop that surrounds the social actors: my interviewees. [72]

The use of oral data therefore adds a different dimension to the archive data in this research to ensure that the picture that emerges is informative and only then can it give an insight into the lives of the Irish immigrant women on the Harold Hill estate. The archive data looks from a completely different angle at the same themes that run through the research. It highlights the growing Irish population and the work done in the two parishes by laywomen and the Ursuline sisters as well as the Diocese of Brentwood. It is like opening a time capsule where none of the recordings are altered or changed through time, all is just as it was written in the period the interviewees covered with their stories. The archives highlight how the Irish community was perceived and what town community they moved into. It also showed what the area had to offer and how it was changed by their settlement.

The findings of the interview and archive data can be placed into the categories that should run like a thread through the research: The role model of the Virgin Mary and how this influenced these women; the Irish traditions and beliefs that they were brought up with; their migration stories and the importance that education held in their lives. Also the reasons for emigrating and the places that they moved to and eventually the place that they settled after the slum clearance of East London which brought them into Romford on the Harold Hill Estate shall be examined.

Footnotes

What is such a pity in these places is that against this friendliness I also met with deep suspicion from some of the priests who neither knew me nor were interested in finding out, but were very critical of this foreign lay woman who walked around the place as if she was entitled to be there. This despite the written request for researching the archive which they had received well before I started my work there. On one visit I was stopped by a priest in the corridor, not being allowed to move either forward or backwards. I introduced myself and my reason for being there and referred to one of my supervisors to enable the priest to phone him and check my story out but to no avail. Only when a secretary came to my rescue explaining that I was neither a liar nor an intruder was I allowed to go about my business. It is sad that people in these positions are so very wary and seem unable to trust lay Catholics, making it appear to me as if the Church had something to hide. If that was the case of the Brentwood Diocese I can only say that I haven't found it.

[1] Thompson, P. (1975) *The Edwardians: The Remaking of British Society,* London
[2] Alexander S. and Davin A. (1979) 'Labouring Women: A reply to Eric Hobsbawm', in: *History Workshop Journal no. 8* (1) pp. 174-182
[3] Mauthner N. and Doucet A. (2003) 'Reflexive Accounts and Accounts of Reflexivity', in: *Qualitative Data in Sociology* Vol. 37(3), London
[4] Mauthner N. and Doucet A. (2003) *Reflexive Accounts and Accounts*
[5] Ryan L. (2002) 'I'm Going to England. Women's narratives of leaving Ireland in the 1930s', in: *Oral History Workshop Journa*l Spring p. 44
[6] Ryan L. (2002) 'I'm Going to England. Women's Narratives of Leaving Ireland in the 1930s', in: *Oral History Workshop Journa*l Spring p. 44
[7] Sangster J. (1994) 'Telling Our Stories: Feminists Debates and the Use of Oral history', in: *Women's History Review* vol 32 p. 22
[8] Bornat J. and Diamond H. (2007) 'Women's History and Oral History: Developments and Debates', in: *Women's History Review* vol 16 p. 30
[9] Mauthner N. and Doucet A. (2003) *Reflexive Accounts*
[10] Mauthner N. and Doucet A. (2003) *Reflexive Accounts* p. 415
[11] Mauthner N. and Doucet A. (2003) *Reflexive Accounts* p. 415
[12] Mauthner N. and Doucet A. (2003) *Reflexive Accounts* p. 419
[13] Mauthner N. and Doucet A. (2003) *Reflexive Accounts* p. 423
[14] Oliver P. (2004) *Writing Your Thesis,* London p. 28
[15] Freud, S. (1953) *Case Histories I,* London
[16] Horney, K. (1950) *Are you considering psychoanalysis?,* Amsterdam
[17] Parr J. (1998) 'Theoretical Voices and Women's Own Voices. The Stories of Mature Women Students', in: *Feminist Dilemas in Quality Research,* London p. 90
[18] Portelli A. (1981) 'The peculiarities of Oral history', in: *History Workshop Journal,* 12 autumn p. 100
[19] Humphries S. (1995) *Hooligans or rebels,* Oxford p. 27

[20] Oliver P. (2004) *Writing Your Thesis* p. 129
[21] Passerini L. (1979) 'Work ideology and consensus under Italian Fascism', in: *History Workshop Journal* 8 autumn
　Portelli A. (1981) 'The Peculiarities of Oral history', in: *History Workshop Journal 12* autumn
　Alexander S. (1994) *Becoming a Woman*, London
　Figlio K. (1987) 'Oral history and the Unconscious in Psychoanalysis', in: *History Workshop Journal*
[22] Gearhart S. (1979) 'The Scene of Psychoanalysis: The unanswered Questions of Dora', in: *Diacritics* spring pp. 114-126
[23] Caitlin (Greater London, 1999; name altered), Interview 2, transcript p. 1
[24] Gearhart S. (1979) 'The Scene of Psychoanalysis: The unanswered Questions', in: *Diacritics* Spring (1979) pp. 105-127
[25] Gearhart S. (1979) *The Scene of Psychoanalysis*, pp. 105
[26] Passerini L. (1979) 'Work ideology and consensus under Italian Fascism', in: *History Workshop Journal*, 8 autumn
[27] Ryan L. (2002) 'I'm Going to England. Women's narratives of leaving Ireland in the 1930s', in: *Oral History* spring
[28] Alexander S. (1994) *Becoming a Woman*, London pp. 234-235
[29] Thompson (1988) *Voices of the Past*, London p. 260
[30] Portelli A. (1981) *The peculiarities of Oral history*
[31] Portelli A. (1981) *The peculiarities of Oral history*, p. 100
[32] Bornat J. Diamond H. (2007) 'Women's History and Oral history: Developments and Debates', in: *Women's History Review* Vol. 6 No. 1 February p. 27
[33] Hawkes T. (1983) *Structuralism and semiotics*, London
[34] Barthes R. (1992) 'Death of an Author', in: *Art: Context and Value* (ed) Sim S., London
[35] White H. (1978) *Tropics of discourse: Essays in Cultural Criticism*, London p. 81
[36] White H. (1978) *Tropics of discourse*, p. 81
[37] White H. (1978) *Tropics of discourse*, p. 88
[38] Thompson (1988) *Voices of the Past*, p. 155
[39] Thompson (1988) *Voices of the Past*, p. 155
[40] Figlio K. (1987) 'Oral history and the unconscious', in: *History Workshop Journal*
[41] Figlio K. (1987) 'Oral history and the unconscious', in: *History Workshop Journal*, p. 130
[42] Ryan L. (2004) 'Family Matters: (e) Migration, Familial Networks and Irish women in Britain', in: *Sociological Review*
[43] Bornat J. Diamond H. (2007) *Women's History and Oral history*, p. 31
[44] Beyer-Sherwood (2006) 'From Farm to Factory: Transition in Work, Gender, and Leisure at Banning Mill, 1910-1930', in: *Oral History Review* Vol. 33 Issue 2
[45] Boal A. (1992) *Games for Actors and Non-Actors*, London
[46] Villarreal M. A. (2006) 'Finding Our Place: Reconstructing Community Through Oral history', in: *Oral History Review* Vol. 33 Issue2 p. 45
[47] Fitzpatrick D. (1986) 'A share of the Honeycomb: education, emigration and Irish women', in: *Continuity and Change*, London

[48] Ribbens J. and Edwards R. (1998) 'Living on the Edges. Public Knowledge, Private Lives, Personal Experience', in: *Feminist Dilemmas,* London p. 2
[49] Ribbens J.Edwards R. (1998) 'Introducing Our Voices', in: *Feminist Dilemmas,* p. 8
[50] Ribbens J.Edwards R. (1998) *Introducing Our Voices,* p. 8
[51] Thompson, P. (1988) *Voices of the Past,* London p. 272
[52] Oliver, P. (2004) *Writing Your Thesis,* p. 126
[53] Thompson, P. (1988) *Voices of the Past,* p. 228
[54] Thompson, P. (1988) *Voices of the Past,* p. 228
[55] see appendix I interviews question list
[56] Eileen (Greater London, 1995; name altered), Interview 5, transcript p. 1
[57] Caitlin Interview 2, transcript p. 6
[58] Thompson, P. (1988) *Voices of the Past,* p. 183
[59] Thompson, P. (1988) *Voices of the Past,* p. 278
[60] Edna interview, p. 3
[61] Thompson, P. (1988) *Voices of the Past,* chapt. 5
[62] Caitlin Patrick (Greater London), 1999 (names altered), Interview 2, transcript p. 6
[63] Caitlin Interview 2, transcript p. 4
[64] Caitlin interview 2, p. 5
[65] Aoife and Patrick (Greater London), 1999 (names altered), Interview 1, transcript p. 6
[66] Aoife and Patrick interview 1, p. 6
[67] Aoife and Patrick interview 1, p. 7
[68] Young M and Willmott P. (1957) *Family And Kinship in East London,* London
[69] Tilki, M. (2006) 'The social Contexts of Drinking Among Irish Men in London', in: *Drugs: Education, Prevention & Policy* vol. 13 no 3 June pp. 247-261
[70] Christina (Greater London, 1999; name altered), Interview 4, transcript p. 7
[71] Aoife and Patrick interview 1, p. 5
[72] Thompson, P. (1988) *Voices of the Past,* London p. 151

CHAPTER 4: FROM EAST LONDON TO HAROLD HILL

This chapter will discuss the situation of the Catholic Church in England and the influence of the Irish Catholics from the 19th century and the position of Irish immigrants in the Catholic Church in the early 20th century. Within this, the influence of the large influx of Irish Catholics in the Catholic Church in England will be considered. This chapter also looks in particular at the movement from East London to Harold Hill by Irish immigrants, and how they influenced the newly built estate and will consider their impact on the Catholic Church in the Diocese of Brentwood. It examines the mass exodus of people from the slums of East London to the new housing estates after the Second World War, which included Irish immigrants. It discusses the importance of housing and neighbourhoods through the impact they made on the Irish women and their families. The chapter will make reference to the Catholic Diocese of Brentwood and the congregation of Romford in particular. The chapter will end with a discussion on the reality of a new life on the estate.

The Irish community in East London

The mass exodus of Irish immigrants from the slums of the East End to the new housing estates after the Second World War has never been studied. This is despite the fact that the government of the time planned a total of a million people to move in the immediate aftermath of the Second World War with a further quarter of a million who would join them in the following decade. Nor has research been conducted into the origins and background of the East Enders who were the largest group of Londoners that were involved in the move to the new estates.[1] The Greater London Plan of Professor Abercrombie and how it made its mark on the people involved is explored here.

The Irish immigrants, like English migrants who had moved away from the poverty of the countryside, were often found in the poorest areas. All housing conditions in the poorer areas were cramped, as many families shared one family home, and were forced to share the same kitchen facilities. Families of multiple homes often shared outdoor toilets. Many people lived in very small apartments and cellars were often used as living accommodation.[2] The water from sewers would often penetrate through the walls of the apartments near the river. Some 100,000 people were still living in cellars in the beginning of the nineteen-fifties. The overcrowding was a real threat to the health of the population of London.[3]

The research interview data covers the experiences of some of the interviewed women during their time in East London. The parents of Christina, one of the women interviewed, moved to London during this period. This makes her an important eyewitness growing up in East London during the 1930s and 1940s. Christina was born in 1932 in Stratford East London. She was the daughter of Irish immigrants and the first of two children. Her parents married in 1931 and her father was a General Practitioner who had already moved to his new practice, his bride joined him soon after the wedding.

> *"I believe that he would have gone to the East End about 1929-1930. My parents were married in 1931 and I was born in 1932. And where we lived we had a surgery at the side of the road."*[4]

The reasons for their migration were in her father's past. He had been training as a priest but left the seminary early as Christina explains:

> *"His scenario was really, quite interesting actually. He was the only son of a farmer and he started to study for the priesthood at Maynooth, which is quite a well known Irish seminary, **the** Irish seminary. And then something happened, we don't know what but we think it was very small, misdemeanour. Like going to the pub or being late or something. Some disciplinary thing happened and he and his friend were sent home in disgrace, it was nothing very big. But my mother never, never, never knew what it was, but we know it was something disciplinary."*[5]

Her father never told her the details it was all too much of a disgrace and was never to be mentioned again. The whole episode was shrouded in shame:

> *"He never told, he just kept quiet about it because to go home when you went off to be a priest was they called it being a spoiled priest because, you know, they didn't like you coming back and father*

didn't like coming back. So instead of inheriting a farm he went off to study medicine that was the next best thing as it were. But the greatest thing in the family would be to have a son as priest."[6]

In Ireland it was considered a sign of respectability to have a son as a priest and gave the family much in the form of status within their own community and can help explain why so many chose a religious life for their children. Much of Irish life revolved around the Catholic faith and the Church and Irish families did steer their children into religious life as it was such an important part of everything in society. Back in Ireland throughout the 1930s until the late 1950s, both government and Church believed that it was possible to apply Catholic principles to every aspect of secular social life and in doing so create a thoroughly Christian society. It is impossible to ignore the fact that the majority of the Irish population was deeply pious and that this had a huge impact on how society was run.[7] It also shows that economic pressure was not the only reason for leaving. In this tightly Catholic controlled Irish society shame or escaping expectations were also great motivators to emigrate. Christina's father no longer held a social status in this society:

> *"Yes, and the next best thing would be to do medicine, so his father sacrificed him, he was badly needed at home because he only had two sisters. But his father was young enough to go on (working on the farm) so my father went to Cork University and he studied during the time of Troubles, during the time of the Black and Tans and the struggle of Irish independence in 1921."*[8]

The move to London had been gradual but the choice of working abroad was made the moment her father left the seminary. The evidence in the interviews suggests that for many Irish workers Wales was the first port of call. And this gradual moving further and further away from the Irish Sea towards the East was often repeated by migrant women in the sample of this research:

> *"In the twenties like many people he went to Wales first. He got his first job in Swansea or Cardiff or thereabouts where he was in a rural practice. (But) he worked in a hospital first and then in a rural practice in Wales."*[9]

Christina knows that he finished his training in Wales and moved as a qualified doctor to London:

> *"I know that he went to London about 1929 and he would have been qualified then, somewhere between 1925 and 1929. He, he was thirty when he married and he would have been twenty five or twenty six when he qualified as a General Practitioner. So in those first four years he would have spent time in Cardiff. In a very rough rural practice and also in a hospital."*[10]

To find work was not that difficult as there were General Practitioners looking for Irish colleagues often working in an Irish community:

> *"I don't know much about that period; certainly the man who was in practice the chief doctor was an Irishman as well so probably he advertised [in Irish papers]."*[11]

The areas in Wales where he worked would have included many Irish settlers who preferred an Irish General Practitioner. The trust in your local doctor was a very important part of the practice and the faith of the doctors was important to confide in and trust them and in important health decisions Catholics were required to follow the rules laid down by the Vatican. Women were expected to reproduce even if this meant a risk to their own health. Therefore Catholic doctors and midwives were very experienced in delivering and looking after women at risk in their own community, as the autobiography of Worth describes.[12]

Christina's father left Wales behind and moved to London where he again set to work amongst the poorest families in the local area. This time he took over a practice in East London in Stratford but it meant hard work and often little or no income:

> *"I remember we were [poor], this was before National Health you see. So my father didn't get paid so we didn't have much income and he struggled away for a long time."*[13]

Many of his patients were also Irish migrants and some received financial aid from the state to cover their health bills but it was never enough:

> *"They got a little bit of help from the State, they [the poorest] were mostly the Irish immigrants, people living near the surgery, the area of my father as a doctor. They, [the patients], would have been what was known as panel-patients or poor patients. They had some sort of very minimum income."*[14]

The reason to move to London was not because the predecessor was Irish but, as she remembers many of the patients were:

> *"How he came to London I don't know, but the man before him wasn't Irish. Dr Goodson was his name, he was English and he was a very distinguished old gentleman who used to go round in a carriage-and-horses until quite recently. We knew because in our house in Leytonstone road where we lived, the garage was in fact an old stable as often in London the old surgeries had stables."*[15]

The stables and the house itself were unusual and would have stood out in the local area:

> *"Now people round our area had very poor houses, but we actually had stables and a small garden."*[16]

At first both the doctors worked together to help the old practitioner with his heavy workload as he worked towards his retirement and also to introduce the young doctor to his new patients and the community:

> *"As children we used to imagine the horses and in this place but of course we had cars. But my father's predecessor used to have to go and visit people in the East End in his carriage, his horse and carriage. So that was continuity. And my father worked with him for a little while and then he the old doctor retired and my father was alone in his practice. Nowadays you work very rarely alone."*[17]

When the old doctor retired her father was to work all hours by himself:

> *"But when he was alone in practice, he could really hardly ever leave it because he was afraid that if he didn't answer a call, he would lose a patient. And of course he had to go out often at night time and it was tough, tough work, building up a practice on his own in the East End."*[18]

The move to East London was not an easy one as she recalls and to be accepted by the East Enders was even more difficult:

> *"We took a long time to be accepted as really local but then he was very accepted and hmm he struggled from 1930 until he retired in 1964-ish something like that and he was very well known and loved. He was very much the Catholic doctor. He went to church, to the Franciscan church and the Franciscans knew a lot about him."*[19]

Although the previous doctor was not Irish many of the other local doctors were and most of them knew each other from before the move to England:

> *"My uncle was another Irish doctor down the road. And my godfather was another Irish doctor further down the road, so there was a whole cluster of friends who came from Cork University and settled in East London. Now there are Pakistani doctors who are doing it. Very often there is a cluster of immigrants."*[20]

The large influx of educated medical graduates from Cork University has not been often referred to but Cork had an outstanding reputation on training for the health sector, particularly in medicine. Shepard whose study focused on Irish journalists has recently focussed on the role of Irish universities played in producing graduates for imperial service but also at the Irish intellectual/professional diaspora during this period, especially the training and migration of Irish medical doctors during the nineteenth century.[21] Christina's mother met her husband when she attended Cork University as a student. The families accepted the necessity of emigration especially for educated women, but the importance that it held for the women themselves was often ignored. Gray argued that for women, who were able to do well in Britain unlike Ireland and had made it their home, were almost seen as temporarily displaced by the community back home. She describes:

> *"While Aine might be living, working and indeed feeling more at home in London than in Ireland, as far as her parents are concerned she can only ever belong in Ireland. This denial of Aine's actual life in London enables her parents to believe that she will return and live in Ireland, 'where she rightly belongs'."*[22]

Although it is not clear from her interview whether Christina's mother's family felt the same way about their daughter's stay in England, her interview did however describe that both her parents tried to move back to Ireland. They always believed it to be the logical development of their migration pattern: the need to return to Ireland and the expectation to return was consistent in their story. The friendships Christina's parents struck up at university made a strong bond and they supported each other in this new life. In fact their friendship was instrumental to their success in London as they helped each other to set up as practitioners as Christina explains:

> *"In his day...you had to buy your practice before, because it wasn't on the National Health. And then when the National Health came in 1948 they bought the practice from the doctors, they gave them compensation, not very much. But those days the practice was personal and you bought the good will. And in the early days my uncle came and helped my father and he got himself a practice down the road and married. In Leytonstone Road my memory is that my godfather was (based) at the top-end, my uncle in the middle and my father down the end road. So in a way they could say 'could you look after my practice tonight' to get away. Often, we had to ring up if we went out for the day, to find out if there was a patient on call. And my father would stop the holiday and we had to drive back to see them but they would cover each others' practice."*[23]

Picture 07 Map of East London, in 1950[24]

And she recalls chemists that were very much part of the group of friends of her family. The time before the emergence of the National Health Service made areas like East London with so much poverty automatically a heavy workload and the lack of income meant that English doctors were rarely interested in setting up a practice there. This also applied for chemists who played more and more an important part in heath care, they were also part of this group of friends of Christina's father and they assisted each other but also kept each other in business:

> *"We were great friends with Desmond's the chemist also an Irish family with another whole history and they owned a chemist around Ilford and they were great friends comrades they had one or two chemist shops I think. So the doctor and the chemist worked very close together."*[25]

A doctor's practice in East London

Communities often had their own doctor from a similar background particularly where their faith or religion was concerned. For instance there were Jewish doctors for mostly Jewish patients although also English cockneys visited them. But Jews and Irish even in the same profession did not mingle as Christina remembers and they never befriended the Irish doctors, but this was a religious issue:

> *"There were stories, they were very anti Jewish, which is an interesting [story]. My father would talk about those Jew-boys these doctors down the road who had set-up, who weren't Catholic and so on. Nowadays we laugh at the fact that these very good (caring) Irish Catholics were so anti Semitic."*[26]

As Walter discusses Catholics were often involved in Jewish prejudice:

> *"Catholics have been at the forefront of anti-Jewish attitudes and behaviour – many older people can recall hearing and using the label 'Christ-killers' in taunts against Jews."*[27]

There was contact with English families but this was fraught with difficulty. The parents of Christina did mingle with English people of the local community but at parties always kept them separate from their Irish friends:

> *"We didn't mix our friends put it like that or if we did it was a disaster. So my father made often very good friends but he was very careful at a Christmas party not to invite the people who occasionally started an Irish/English sort of argie bargie".*[28]

It could be little things that would flair up out of all proportions:

> *"Once my mother stuck stamps on the bills, she managed it to stick the queen's head upside down and caused a riot. And the patients were absolutely furious and thought that these Irish people deliberately demeaned the queen and it was just a mistake. So you couldn't afford to make mistakes like that."*[29]

This puts into question Hornsby-Smith's idea that the Irish were almost like a sub society controlled by the Catholic Church so much so that they did not even wish to venture out. Christina's story sheds new light on this period and shows that although her parents were well connected with the English families in the area there were people who viewed them with some suspicion and were very much underlining the differences between Irish and English not based on faith but politics and the emergence of the Irish Free State.

The family practice in East London made up much of Cristina's childhood memories and made her aware of the poverty and sickness that played such a big part in her father's work:

> *"As a child before the war and after the war I loved to go round with my father in the car. And I would say to him 'what is the matter with this family, what is the matter with that family'. And there would be all these straight houses in these old fashioned streets and many of them there, the old fashioned streets with the lavatory out of the back."*[30]

The memories of the Irish community were often of the poorest families. As the earlier studies of Booth explored many of the poor of East London were of Irish background. But Christina feels that little of this life is remembered in East London especially the lives there lived by this large Irish community:

> *"I took a strong interest in the Irish in New York I was there in the summer and saw the old St Patrick's Cathedral. We had monuments on the Irish in the basements and so on. I though this is stupid, this happened in London too you know. When people came they were seen as very different and once in England they integrated more."*[31]

Poverty and the lack of chances to improve upon their situation made a mark on young Christina as she was well informed about her father's practice:

> *"That to me is the most vivid because being a doctor's family we were aware and I am grateful I grew up in the East End and was*

> *made aware of these bitter problems because my father wasn't a rich practitioner. And the needy...ah terrible stories usual[ly] a doctor would have to [deal with]."*[32]

But some stories stood out more than others:

> *"One funny story was when a well-known robber in those days was amongst his patients; Jim White, his name was, but he was dying. So my father went in and he said 'Now Jim you have to put your affairs right, you haven't got long you know. Both knew he was dying. And the fellow opened one eye and he said 'I know doctor' he said"*[33]

Her father as a religious man believed that this patient needed to give back what he had stolen which was perhaps still in his possession especially as he was going to face God, but the man said:

> *"It is the people like you who have to make the provisions for dying (but) I don't have to tell anybody anything my grief"*[34]

Christina continued:

> *"He got his goods, they were his goods."*[35]

As her father could not help the man out financially he explained his own situation:

> *"And then my father said 'O well I hope you know I haven't got any goods too with my (poor practice)...' and the man answered 'O yes I know that doctor I cased your joint' he had been round the house, he had been in. And it was a well known criminal and his intentions were clear to anybody"*[36]

For her mother, life in Stratford was connected with her husband's practice. Before her marriage she had been a teacher but as a mother she was expected to raise her family:

> *"When she married she didn't teach because she was then fulltime mother and also she had a role in the practice she was virtually my*

> *father's secretary unpaid secretary and lots of other roles as well. And she had to look after everything. We also dispensed our medicine from early on we had a dispenser in the surgery we dispensed our own medicine"*[37]

The work also included small laboratory work on urine, stool or blood samples taken or brought in by the patients:

> *"My mother once gave urine back out, they (a patient) sent in a urine sample and she thought it was the medicine and sent back (instead of the medicine) the same parcel which had the urine in"*[38]

It became more and more common practice to work with the local chemist and eventually the surgery lost this work to the chemist:

> *"And then gradually we hmm we hmm gave up with the dispensary. I suppose with the (introduction of the) National Health Service."*[39]

Her mother was happy as a doctor's wife with all her responsibilities. Unfortunately her work has been overlooked by researchers as this was not paid work and therefore the importance of the input of a doctor's wife as an assistant and chemist are not well known, unlike the work of nurses and midwives (see Walter and Hickman).[40] But Christina remembers her mother's presence in the surgery and her charm:

> *"She enjoyed (it) because she was a very gregarious person too, and she enjoyed meeting the patients and keeping the registers and supporting him and of course she had two children and so on."*[41]

Christina's story is important to research as it gives a detailed account of the lives of the Irish medical profession and their personal lives in East London. It allows us a glimpse of the lives lived behind closed doors of the Irish doctor and his family.

Socialising, the Church involvement and the Irish highly educated community members

Little is known about the highly educated Irish immigrants in East London although they had a very strong social life and were closely connected with social clubs with the Catholic Church. They were part of a social life in which mainly the men would participate by being members of the various clubs. Catholic Clubs, as Delaney explored, were often also set up in English cities as an initiative of the Irish Catholic Church.[42] As Christina remembers:

> *"There was a St Anthony's Club in Forest Gate, after twelve o'clock mass most of the men went to the twelve o'clock mass and the women were absolutely worn out because their men never came home for Sunday lunch. They were in this watering hole.*
> *And hmm St Anthony's club was forever been rung up 'is my husband there'...'Yes' 'no', a lie or whatever. A great hole, it was more for the men, I think it was only for the men St Anthony's club famous club in Forest Gate, it was hmm a great source of after twelve o'clock mass hmm.*
> *Also if you had a party the night before, nobody got up early for early morning mass, but they all went to either twelve o'clock mass at Forest Gate or twelve o'clock mass at Walthamstow. And you see all the party looking bleary eyed, but never miss mass, never ever, ever miss mass but they managed to get in late at the last minute to justify."*[43]

Some of these clubs were connected with their professions and this meant close ties between the various members of the club and support where needed as Christina explains:

> *"They were also for my father they would have been professional clubs because he was a professional. The important one in their lives was Catenian's, it was called Catenian: It is still there. It is a sort of rosary-club for Catholic professional people. They held annual dinners and they helped you if you were in financial difficulties, a sort of club."*[44]

The Catenian Association was funded by Casartelli, who became Bishop of Salford in 1903. He felt that there was a need for the emerging Irish Catholic urban middle class to mingle and support one another. It would also help raise their position in society. The bishop wanted the laity to play their role:

> "...in matters social, municipal, philanthropic, educational, artistic, literary in which we may use the powers we enjoy".[45].

The club still operates today and has members worldwide and still focuses on highly educated professionals and still has a site in Radnor Road Chelsea. The name is taken from 'Catena' the Latin for chain.

Her father was a member of another club which was not based on members sharing the same profession but was still very much part of the Irish community:

> "But the other one was more for not quite professional people. There was a second club and they belonged to both. And my brother was also a member, he wouldn't join the Catenians', he was fed up with them, they served as the old medieval guild thing the club. But the Catenians' had a club in London."[46]

They served also as a backup in case members became ill or had fallen on hard times:

> "When my mother died and my father said he couldn't manage with his heart he went to live in the Catenian club, so that was an important thing."[47]

The other club based its origins on the prayers said with use of the rosary. But it was also very much a social club with outings and parties. As MacAmlaigh wrote as late as the 1960s that many clubs and dance halls were set up by the Irish communities and people had a very social life in their own community if they wished to Christina continues:

> "There was also another Catholic body, a sort of rosary-club. This was a professional club where you pay a subscription and you had

> *social events like dinner dances and you meet like with like and was sure that all the boys and friends were there. The club consisted of two levels, one was more for professionals, you had to be a doctor or a teacher or something, the other was more for Catholic business men, the name of the second one escapes me, but my father belonged to both."*[48]

Social events and outings were an important break from the difficult lives of a general practitioner in East *London* and this social aspect of the club was much appreciated by the members who were all of Irish nationality:

> *"And I suppose the most important event for our professional level was the Irish dinner dance up in London in Groven House. It was a sort of dinner dance for Irish people. It was the event of the year and you bought tickets for this dinner dance. And in my generation, not the old people, but when we grew up at the beginning when we were eighteen to twenty, we go with them. We were all pleased to go and we had a few tables for supper and a dance floor and so on. And hmm but we were young. So the next generation was invited to go to this dinner and dance and another social event was when the Irish ambassador came and, lots of well-known Irish doctors and also other Irish people in London came and somebody might give speeches."*[49]

The wives and older children of the members also visited these social events:

> *"We had lots of social days like that and my mother would go on about this for the whole year. And then of course we came back from this dinner dance and had a party at home and we took it in turns which house to have it in. So yes there was great enjoyment and lots of Christmas parties. After midnight mass we always had a do back in our house. But it was always entirely professional friends."*[50]

The contact with the Irish friends was often connected with families back home and the ties stayed strong:

> *"We also had a network of [other professional-] Irish friends who lived in the area. For example my brother who is a doctor in the South of England: One of my father's patients went to register with my brother and he went down as being the last uncle, grand-uncle to the family. So the links were very strong ... I know their story like anything. But again they [other Irish immigrants] moved out of London when he retired, the East End did not hold them all."*[51]

Religious life in East London

That Catholic religious life was thriving was clear to Christina because of the number of Irish priests that were based in the Stratford area and were visiting her family's surgery:

> *"That is why I thought that there was a (large) Catholic community in Stratford because I knew the [Irish] names of the priests, because all those priests went to my father as a doctor."*[52]

The priests were not always seen as welcome guests by the whole of the household as they required special treatment and special time was set aside for them, as Christina remembered:

> *"We were worn out when they came to see him because they came to see him privately and they didn't go to the surgery because they didn't want to go the surgery, so my father I think over a jar of whiskey saw most of these priests and he also had some position in the property of the Franciscans they had a lay person who looked normally after their property and do something like that."*[53]

East London also had communities of sisters working amongst the poor Irish of East London and they were very influential in the area:

> *"The sisters they are a big story. The (Ursuline) sisters in Forest Gate yes, they are the same as the sisters in Ilford. The Brentwood Ursuline sisters were a different branch."*[54]

The influence of the Ursuline sisters was primarily on education and the importance of education for the poor:

> *"Forest Gate was [came] first and Ilford was done later, was a later foundation. The Forest Gate foundation the actual buildings go back to the 19th century."*[55]

The order Christine later became a member of, the Holy Child Order, focussed mainly on primary education and their schools for the poor were made possible after the Second World War because of the new Education Act:

> *"Mostly we got started teaching in our schools at the end of the war, naturally. And they [the Ursuline Sisters] would have been more in the secondary education. But some of their sisters were also working in elementary schools. They would have stories about the Catholic families. And some sisters were evacuated. But what you need to know is that the present system before 1944 was not compulsory and the system was different"*[56]

The impact that the Second World War had on the Irish community of East London

The lives of the families were interrupted by the outbreak of the Second World War because Christina, her brother and their mother went back to stay in Ireland, as it was safer for them. They were able to move to their plot of land that her father had purchased earlier on. She explains:

> *"He bought some land for us in Ireland because he thought if he would have to lose all his money, he would be safe on the land, this is typical Irish instinct. But my mother hated it, because she was not a farmer's daughter she was a city woman."*[57]

This need for land back home has been repeated throughout the history of migration as many migrants came and still come from rural areas where land means either status or belonging but at any rate always means crop or dairy produce and therefore survival in hard times.[58]

The enforced time spent back in Ireland during the war made her mother feel more settled in London on her return as Christina explains:

> *"I think the war was a great break for her. They all found when they went back to Ireland they didn't really want to live there anymore. It is an interesting factor my father thought about shall I retire back to Ireland or shall I not. And he didn't, he spent a lot of time back with his sisters for holidays but they all knew they had become too used to the English way of doing things. Legally you know and all these waiting and all these, a little bit hmm the Irish way, easy going not so business like then, now it is different. So they really adopted to it the country and we were over here so long. So like so many people they considered going back to Ireland. Just at the very end, they both died in Ireland but hmm that was because they were on holiday. They both happened to die quite close to each other. On holiday in Ireland. So he really became very fond of the way of the English. And also what knit my father in the community was staying with the people during the war."*[59]

Coming back had been difficult for the family as they found their surgery and home in rubble:

> *"Our house was at the very last year of the war bombed. We had a Doodle-bug on the house next door which demolished our house."*[60]

Some of the house remained intact and had to continue to function as a home and a surgery but they were one of the many in the Stratford area to have been hit this way:

> *"They hit many houses during the war. So we were living in the basement, we had the kitchen, our dining room and the surgery and we had to sleep in the surgery now. Which my mother was terrified of germs she used to scrub all out every night."*[61]

After the war the rebuilding of the country began and part of that rebuilding was the change in the law for education. The importance of education was not lost on the doctor whose family were for the time being living in Ireland for at least some part of the Second World War:

> *"Then in 1944 England had a new Education Act. The end of the war was part of a new social change and socialists in power. There was a very good Education Act where everybody up to sixteen had to go to school and so on. And then the arrangements for children were much, much better, very sound and the basis of modern education. And my father said we had to come back from Ireland and go into the new education system."*[62]

But being educated in Stratford proved difficult:

> *"[Because of the bombing of the house] we had to go to boarding school because they really could only put us up for few weeks over Christmas. So for those eighteen months I stayed at boarding school down in St Leonards-on-Sea East Sussex, which was run by a religious order 'the Order of the Holy Child'."*[63]

The order was well known to Christina and her family as she explains:

> *"This order has also nuns down in the East End, so I was taught by the Ursuline Sisters in the first place and the Holy Child in the second place."*[64]

The war had done enormous damage to the area and made the living conditions even worse but for Christina and her family it also meant that they were able to move to a better area. This move out of the surgery's annexed family home was also part of a bigger plan to gain more social status:

> *"Because our house was partially bombed, the house next door was flattened and our house partially damaged... And so after the war my father wanted us, then in our teens, to grow up in a better area, than the side of the road in Stratford. So only his work was in Stratford. And we then bought a house in Woodford in other words, we did the same thing (as others do), you want your children to move up-market. This was all so that we could live in a nicer place and my father coming in every single day. But their group of friends, [remained] almost entirely of the Irish community in Stratford."*[65]

As it was very much a family practice they all helped out as the need arose after their move to Woodford, but extra help was again found in the Irish community:

> "Well we then had to go sometimes into the surgery to help out, to be on guard or whatever. And then gradually we got an Irish man, a husband and his wife to live there as caretakers in the surgery."[66]

Her Irish identity remained with her throughout her life although she felt that she had also an English identity and was critical of the Irish way in which they sometimes held on to their roots. She explains:

> "As for nostalgia I think some of the nostalgia was reinforced by the old songs and my family used to laugh at them. My father never took it seriously because memories are preserved in singsong. But those old songs were very important especially the story of this Irish boy. It is an old song about how a young boy went to confession and the confessor wasn't a priest but a British soldier and so he was found out through his confessions that he fought for the Irish. He, this became a song about this boy it was the sad story I am sure you have heard the story. It was a very famous story, even I feel terribly sad about the whole thing that that boy went to confession but it wasn't a priest. And the robes came off and there he was: a British soldier and he was condemned by what he had said in confession, it outraged the seal of confession the whole of Catholicism, betrayal, I don't know. Went down as a terribly sad story."[67]

Although believed to be true she feels that it was also used to remain resentful of the English as Christina explains:

> "But your anti-British feelings were reinforced by sometimes nostalgic songs about the moonlight in Ireland."[68]

Another interviewee, Eileen, had not been brought up with the same Irish nostalgic songs as Christina. She was born in East London during the nineteen twenties and had an Irish mother but an English father. Eileen had no sense of Irish nostalgia as she never spent any of her childhood years in Ireland, but visited it once she was an adult. Her parents had met in Ireland:

> *"She met my father when he was stationed in Ireland in the British Army, because he was English and my mother was Irish and they married and came over to England two years after they were married.*
> *I suppose this was roughly in 1919 after the war. It was roughly around that time. She already had one child and she had seven children after that and we all lived in London."*[69]

The Second World War had been a difficult time for Eileen, as she never left during the bombing campaign:

> *"I still went to work, but I mean, sometimes it was very difficult, because of the bombs and everything, but... I managed to carry on working in London, doing dressmaking."*[70]

After the war she married her husband Pete and as there was a shortage of housing she moved in with his family:

> *"But then it was very difficult to get... somewhere to live, because there was a lot of bombing during the war, a lot of the houses were bombed. So, the thing was when... couples were married they just... you just used to live with their parents when they first got married, because they didn't have anywhere, you couldn't... Well you didn't have any money to buy a place, and there were little or no places to rent so the majority of times they lived with their parents until the council which was by that time the war was over they were beginning to start the building. Because during the war, all that came to a stop, you see. No houses or anything like it. And then when they took all the houses that were bombed, that was all those places that were habitable, that meant that there wasn't that many to go round, so we waited four years."*[71]

It did mean moving out of her own community for Eileen:

> *"Well, we got married after the war, we got married in 1947, and I was living with John and my mother-in-law for four years... They lived on the other side of the river to us. Because we lived in Greenwich, the River Thames comes there, and right opposite the river, is what they called the Isle of Dogs. Which comes under East London, and that's where John lived, so really I was sort of just across the river. But... I wasn't really happy there"*[72]

Eileen hated the Isle of Dogs and was desperate to move out of the over-cramped housing conditions at her mother-in-law's. There was no real married life for the couple. Pete came from a large family of only boys and Eileen used hate the pressure that life brought.

Edna came over from Ireland after she quit the college that she had been attending in County Kerry. She went to Wales after her father got a job for her:

> *"I had gone to College and then, been there for a year and a half. Then I left there, I went to trek for three months and you know obviously I couldn't settle anywhere and drove my mum mad, and then I came over here. (It was) ...; Housekeeping with two children, my Dad got that for me."*[73]

When they never managed to cope financially her mother decided that they all had to move to England:

> *"Yes everybody moved, my mother eventually came over with the last hmm two."*[74]

Eileen moved from various jobs in various areas before she settled on a job in Camden in London:

> *"I don't know how long I was there. And then I went to Kempton Middlesex. My dad again got me this other job, and then I gone in, in the bar. I gone in the bar which was, you know...quite nice, more social. But they had to put me down as older, because I wasn't old enough. But probably they accepted there, but I wasn't eighteen anyway, because you had to be eighteen, I wasn't old enough. I

remember he put me down as older. But hmm that's quite good. And then I went to work in London, I was doing the office work you know; filing, the work, and stock control."[75]

The importance of the information these women gave was that before the Second World War there was a large Irish community and many members of this community later moved out to places like Harold Hill in Romford. Moving into the new estates became an important part of their history.

New Housing Programs

The many immigrants in London tried to move out from the city centre into better accommodation elsewhere after they got settled there. Areas further out of the centre such as West Ham and East Ham were already too densely populated even before the Second World War and could not be considered for further development. (See map; picture 08 on following page)

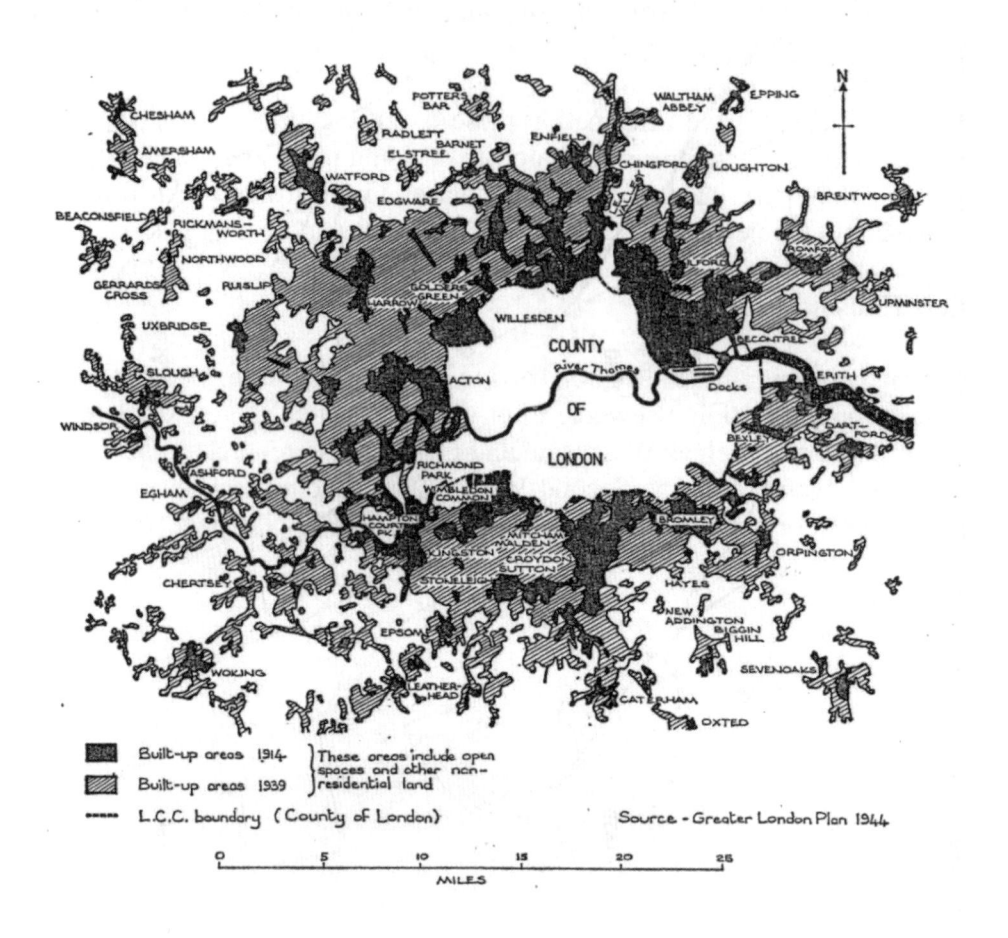

Picture no 08: Map from the Greater London Plan of 1944, showing the growth of London between 1914 & 1939[76]

Small parts of London that were not built up were either not suitable for housing or left for recreation. On the one hand there was a need to house the working classes and to build in the poorer parts of London which did occur during the years between the wars, but on the other hand there were also a growing number of middle class families who were looking for better accommodation away from the exorbitant rents set by private landlords. These occupants were looking for small affordable housing that they would

130

be able to own. This created a contrast between the public provisions made for the masses of the worst slums and the private builders catering for home ownership. According to Humphries and Weightman from the 700,000 houses built between the wars about 75% were privately built for homeowners.[77] The London County Council (L.C.C.) had been active in suburbia since 1900 when it had helped erect 'cottage' like estates at Norbury and Tottenham but it was very much a small-scale development. The L.C.C. was able to build more substantial estates after the Minister of Health initiated an Act (the Addison Act of 1919, named after the Minister of Health, which would enable local councils to build new housing estates with government funding). Backed by the funding provided through the Addison Act, the L.C.C. began their large building projects in Roehampton in South West London, Bellingham near Catford in South London and their biggest project was a large piece of land they bought in the marshes near the East of London and near the tiny village of Dagenham. This is where they built the Becontree Cottage Estate, at the time, the single largest council development in the world. Ford was the only real industrial development that was built on the estate, the rest of the new industry developed on the West side of London, forcing more and more workers who were moving to the east onto the new estates to travel on the 8 o'clock train with a cheap workman's ticket.[78] With the continuous pull of the British population to London, the relatively late timing of the government's grants and the lack of capital for the industries, the amount of good quality housing was far from adequate. The Second World War and in particular the German bombing campaign would increase the problem.

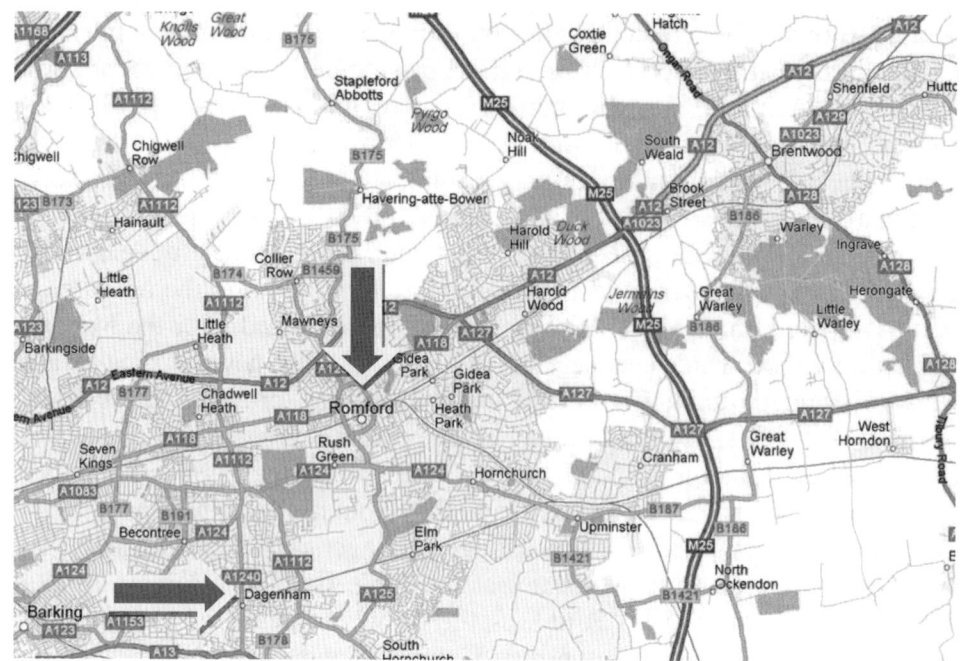

Picture no. 09. Map shows the area and where Romford lays in relation to Dagenham[79]

The total population of Great Britain increased by 5 million between 1919 and 1939. In 1919 Greater London contained about 11% of the population of England and Wales, in 1939 that had increased to 15%.[80] There was also a decrease in the numbers of people emigrating to the colonies overseas. Lack of job opportunities there, as well as in the rural areas, meant a large increase of people seeking their fortune in London from all other parts of the country. Of all the new jobs created in Great Britain, up to two thirds were created in Greater London and there were 900 new firms employing 25 people or over set-up in the London area between 1932 and 1938.[81] Between the First and Second World Wars 1,883,000 people moved in to Greater London and unlike before, most of them stayed.

After the First World War, the trends of industrial development continued to pull homes and workplace apart: the London County Council was building enormous 'cottage' council estates in places like Becontree in the London borough of Barking and Dagenham, East London to re-house slum dwellers.

But the large housing programs also functioned as a way of creating homes for men returning from the War.

The Greater London Plan

In previous years, as people were moving into London, others were moving out, usually just outside the Greater London Area. What this meant was that once their situation improved people moved out of the inner city, but those who were in desperately poor situations kept moving in to the area, which continually reinforced the large slum areas of the very low wage working classes. What increased the urgency this time was the damage the bombing campaign had done to the East End of London. Abercrombie's plan to relocate communities was very well laid out in his report; it shows clearly how the Harold Hill estate was to be built and how ambitious the government was in slum clearance.[82] The government's belief in a better future is overwhelming here but the building of new housing. The Ministry of Town and Country Planning commissioned Professor Patrick Abercrombie of Town Planning at the University of London to deal with the situation. Abercrombie had published the Dublin Town Plan in 1942. In his report "Greater London Plan" Abercrombie wrote in 1943:

> *"What we now find before us is the combined result of two opposing trends. There has been an exodus of the London workers from the centre, people moving out in process over voluntary decentralisation of homes, if not work, and at the same time, the pull of London has caused an immigration from various parts of the country."*[83]

Slough was given as an example; on the outskirts of London there was a settlement formed between the old inhabitants of Slough and the immigrants from urban areas of Greater London and South Wales. Abercrombie referred in his claim to the records of the Census Tables from 1921 and onwards. He also expressed concern that the reverse movement, of people leaving London, had slowed down dramatically in the thirties, which meant that permanent housing was needed to accommodate the increase in the population of London. They might be trying to leave the Centre of London but they did not leave the area and many remained relatively poor.

The main reasons the Government gave for the overall increase in the London population were fivefold: the pre-war stagnation of rural life; bad working conditions; the lack of work in rural areas and the smaller towns; the over-centralisation of the government, and the loss of markets abroad which had created an impoverished working class. This resulted in rapid overcrowding and the failure to provide enough good housing. It also resulted in an increase in land value in Greater London, which made further housing developments impossible.[84]

Ward explained that throughout the late Victorian times to the late 1920s much building took place on a local scale; filling in small vacant areas. London was the only city in Britain where the building of housing had been large-scale throughout the late 19th Century. In most other cities and towns the additions to the built-up areas were often limited and very patchy in set-up. But housing booms did exist in the past.[85]

According to Abercrombie, in the beginning of the 20th century, the fast expanding housing areas round London were based upon the anticipation that the metropolis would continue sucking in an all together undue proportion of the country's population growth.[86] The Becontree Estate near Dagenham was built between the mid twenties and the mid thirties. It moved thousands of East Enders from very poor housing accommodation. The Ford car manufacturer, which opened a plant in Manchester in 1911 and a small one in Cork needed to expand. The Manchester plant was moved to Dagenham to be re-opened in 1931. Becontree became the first large council estate to be built entirely round one factory, the Ford Dagenham Plant.[87]

The funding for the housing boom was connected with the lack of investment opportunities abroad. It therefore fluctuated in accordance with the economy abroad and not necessarily when new houses were mostly needed. Building would occur sometimes in the wrong areas and the new houses sometimes remained empty, as was the case in Leeds therefore the slums remained.[88] There was also another problem that Abercrombie referred to in the case of London; there were 143 local authorities representing the various London Boroughs outside the City; the metropolitan area. They each tried solving the housing problems relating to their own borough. The only substantial council with a large area under its supervision was the L.C.C. All the individual companies and authorities like the Gas Company, the Electricity Company and the builders had to be pulled together under different schemes with different boroughs. The multiplicity of the local administrative units contrasted sharply with the compact unity of the City as 2,599 square miles were divided up between the 143 authorities.

In his Greater London Plan, Abercrombie adopted the concentric rings, which can be measured in terms of housing density.[89] The central and overcrowded urban mass of London was not confined within, but in places overlapped the L.C.C. boundaries. Outside this density in population were the fully developed suburbs. Some lay within the city of London, but most were placed outside it. Immediately after this zone lay the outer ring of London. It had sufficient amount of open space that attempts had been made to create a Green Belt, a zone in which the communities could continue to maintain some of their distinct individualities. Behind this Green Belt open space, he referred to an outer zone of mostly old communities with an agricultural background. Greater London was then considered by the L.C.C. to have a boundary of roughly 30 miles from the centre of London: this included Brentwood. This faint structure of change in density of urban development and population was the beginning point of Abercrombie's Greater London Plan. Abercrombie explains how law protected the Green Belt after the London Society had suggested the idea in 1938.[90]

1944 Abercrombie Park System

Picture no 10: Map also shown in the Greater London Plan as a way to keep green areas like parks working for the population of London[91]

The plan was to decentralise one million people in the first stage, and to persuade them to move out but also encourage businesses to become interested and make room for the first move of industry. This stage was to be completed in ten years time after the interregnum. He stated clearly that this was only to be achieved if the war-time powers behind the plan were to continue to put in all their effort and all the local authorities, contractors, house-builders and other companies involved, were to continue to give it their full support. In the second and final stage, a further quarter of a million people would be moved and the program would be completed with the final detail of added building work. The second stage would be carried out under the new powers, as the war period measures would have by then lapsed. [92]

In addition to overpopulation of London, the war had caused the destruction of large areas, particularly in the centre, and had forced the evacuation of a large proportion of the population. Their situation and the stop on building projects during the war had exacerbated the lack of housing that had existed prior to the war.

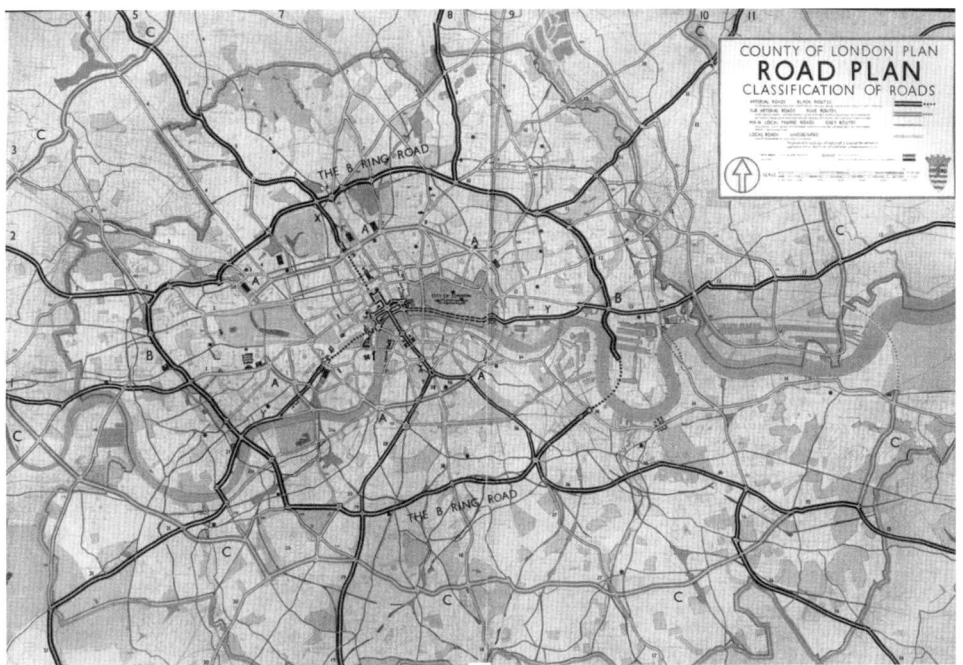

Picture no 11: Map also shown in the greater London Plan, with the classification of the arterial roads exploring accessibility of various sites based on the old road system with additional new roads added[93]

The War had also created much upheaval in the industries due to war production so that when the initial pre-manufactured houses or the pre-fabs, were ordered, the British companies couldn't make enough as the war effort had taken all their resources and an order was sent to the United States for aluminium pre-fab houses. The people of London were so used to the constant evacuation that Abercrombie argued that they had become quite accustomed to it and if given the choice of good housing would move again. He wrote:

> *"There is now a chance - and a similar one may not occur again - of getting the main features of this program of redistributing population and work carried through rapidly and effectively, thereby reducing overcrowding and gaining local industry in conjunction"*.[94]

He believed that if you gave:

> *"The man and his wife a first-rate house, a community, and occupation of various kinds reasonably near at hand, within the regional framework which enables them to move more freely and safely about, to see their friends and enjoy the advantages of London; add to these wide freedom of choice, and they will not crumble in the years immediately following the war."*[95]

And the industrialist when offered a choice of sites with modern facilities, a licence to build and enough labour provided would jump at the chance. The Government believed if trading estates were already laid out for rent, they would quickly fill with small enterprises, which would create coherent new communities.[96]

New Communities

What was going to be achieved was the building of self-sufficient communities. Abercrombie included the advice from sociologists before the execution of his plan he wrote:

> *"The conception of community.*
>
> *Sociologists and others have studied the effects of housing and planning policy between the wars and put some main arguments in a negative way: Unanimous conclusion is that general welfare has not been appreciably improved, and indeed, has often been harmed by what is commonly called suburban development. Excessively large areas of housing occupied by people of one income group, with little provision for other related buildings (schools recreation, hospitals and shops)."*[97]

They all concluded that the general welfare had not been improved and in some cases even harmed by so-called suburban development. What was suggested was the creation of neighbourhoods: villages:[98]

> *"It is an essential recommendation of our scheme that the slabs of housing should be welded into real communities, their ragged edges rounded off, social and shopping centres popularly planned, and local green belt provided."*[99]

A variety of dwellings were to be arranged to provide for 100 to 300 families. Each group would have its own distinctive character.[100]

The maximum floor space standard for the houses was set at 20,000 square feet per net residential acre. That is the equivalent to 20 three-bed-houses, 5 persons each, per net residential acre.[101] An important point that the author of the Greater London Plan made was that the advised and preferred level of building was a density of 100 persons per acre. But a density of 136 persons per acre had to be adopted, because it was feared that more people were needed to fill the industries and had to be encouraged to move to the outskirts of London.[102]

The inner ring that urgently needed depopulating was to have a maximum net population density of between 75 and 100 persons per acre for the different parts of this zone. The building of the new neighbourhoods would solve the problem of 'strap hanging', in which people only lived in overcrowded areas as the factory in which they worked was based there. The new estates needed to be connected by means of new roads with the other zones, and these 'arterial roads' with the new roads in the newly created areas would mean an ease of congestion in the centre and no money was needed on expensive widening of the existing roads.[103] The importance of picking the right area to build was well examined by Abercrombie. This is when they turned to Romford as one of the possible sites to build new housing.

Choosing a Site

The planners wanted to choose sites throughout the region which could be used without over balancing existing suburban communities. Romford had a large farming area just on its outskirts that was considered suitable. In previous large scale housing booms there had been an almost unlimited choice of sites but this was no longer to continue as the area needed to be better planned for the new residents and better incorporated with existing communities. There were also areas considered for recreation and to be preserved, as was the case at Romford with Noak Hill and the village of Havering Atte-Bower, in and just outside the Green Belt.[104] They looked at places that had a certain number of industries already on location. Romford, also inside the Green Belt, was mentioned as a place with industry, a market and a railway link. It was also noted that it was situated on the old Roman road from London to Chelmsford and therefore already in possession of an arterial road. It was therefore one of the first chosen locations where the building began.[105] The site at Harold Hill had been a farming community from early recordings of the Domesday Book of 1086 up to 1947 with agriculture being the main industry. The land had belonged from the middle ages to the manors of Dagnam and Gooshays.

The Ministry of Agriculture provided the plan with much information about the soil in the areas around London. The Thames plains (which included Romford) were considered the most suitable for building as the soil contained gravel and fine sand. This was a result of the faster running of the river in these areas in older times. The important thing was that this was not marshland, as was the case in Dagenham. The land would be easier to build on and the air was less damp and therefore better for the health of the population. The importance of the plains was acknowledged in the Greater London Plan, and that the plains stretched all the way to Romford.[106]

The plains had been of importance throughout time. From an agricultural point of view the fertile soil needed little labour and the area had known a long-standing agricultural tradition. The farmers at Romford were unhappy with the fixed price the L.C.C. offered to them for the land needed for the development of the estate. They expressed their opposition in the council meetings and remained opposed to the building of the new estate. The Neave family that owned a large part of the land had been willing to give up their share for the need of the desperate situation of many Londoners. This had made it more difficult for the farmers as the landowners were now no longer united in their attempts to avoid selling.[107]

Romford had also been bombed during the war and lacked sufficient accommodation. But even before the Second World War Romford struggled with a shortage of housing, as did many other towns. Caitlin, an Irish immigrant who had moved to Romford with her husband in 1938 remembered in her interview:

> *"...we didn't have a lot of room, we had the top part of the house, and I wanted out. Still a country girl, I wanted to get out of that..."*[108]

During the war the situation had grown worse and at one point a family had even refused to leave the bomb-shelter as they had been evicted from their home and no other accommodation was available to them. [109]

On the 19th of September 1945 the Romford Times broke the news with the headline:

> *"L.C.C. to build 10,000 Housing Estate in Romford".*

It continued:

> *"Under a huge housing scheme, details of which are now being discussed by the L.C.C. something like 50,000 of East-London's population will within the next few years be 'decanted' into Romford."*

The Government had ignored the request of the Council not to inform the papers until they had some time to organise themselves. The council was furious to have to read all about it in the local paper for themselves.[110] The Greater London Plan had appeared earlier in the Times in December 1944. But much of the details of location had been kept quiet. The total of the housing development would almost double the population of Romford of 63,000.

One major concern was the responsibility of Romford for these people. The L.C.C. was no longer responsible for the hospital treatment for the new inhabitants of the Estate. They would automatically fall under the care of the council who did not have a large budget. The National Health scheme was set up in June 1948 and up until that time the local authorities paid for those who could not afford prescriptions, or fees for healthcare treatment. As most of the newcomers were known to be poor, it was feared that this group of non-payers would increase by 27,000 people. Applicants for re-housing who had a family member with a poor bill of health were at top of the list with the L.C.C.[111] Many of the girls of the Quarles Girls School on the Harold Hill Estate, when asked in 1959 to write an essay about the reasons behind their move to the estate mentioned bad health of other siblings or parents.[112] It was also mentioned in the papers that of the new occupants, one in seven were Irish born. [113]

That Abercrombie's plan would solve the problem of poverty and overcrowding was not something everyone agreed on. The Romford Recorder newspaper reported that:

> *"The council had expressed horror that people were to be moved around like a flock of sheep to live in these horrible places built for their incarceration, rather than stay in the town where they were born or certainly where they choose to live."*[114]

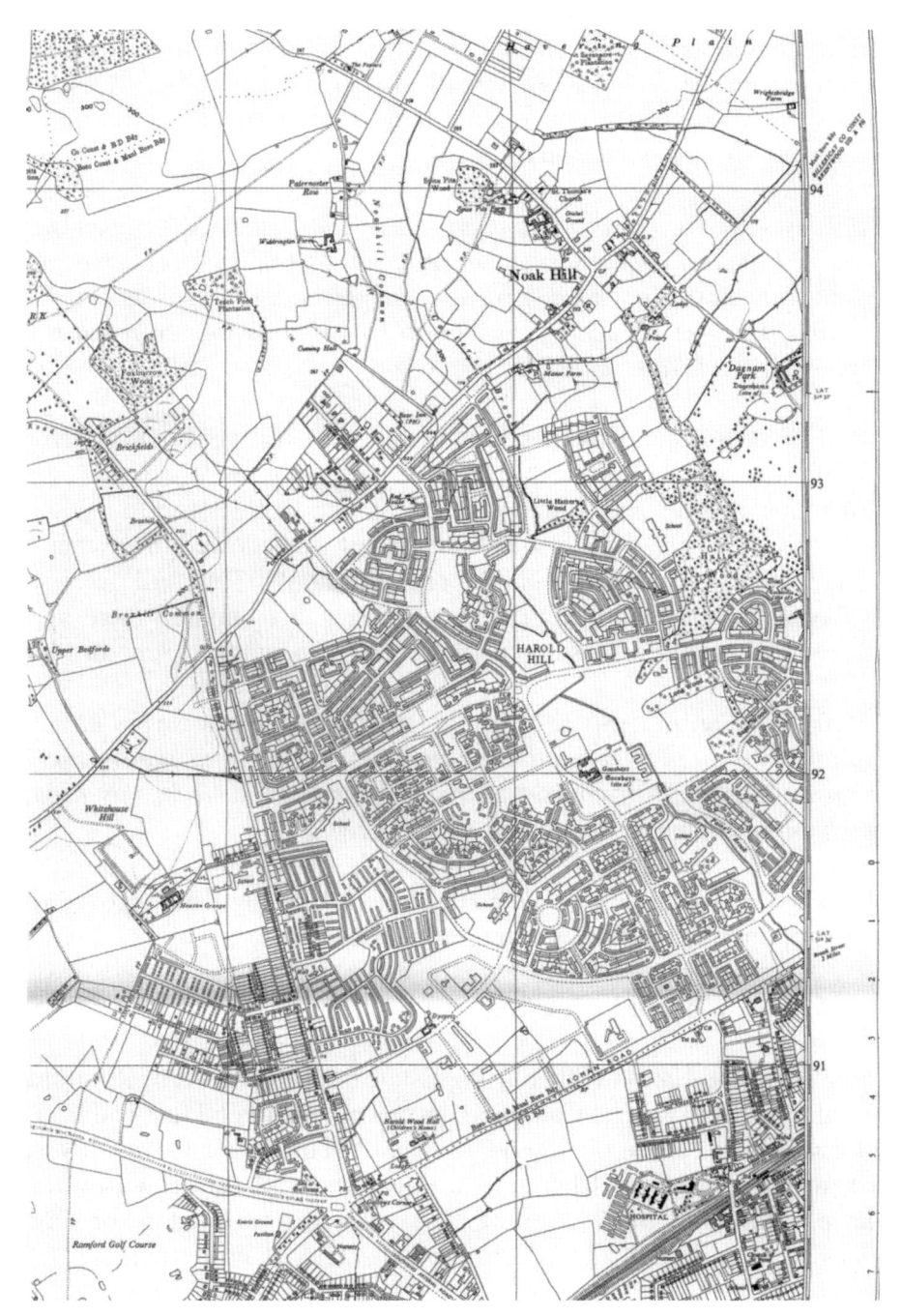

Picture no 12: Map of Harold Hill here shows what it looked like just after most of the building was finished in 1960 [115]

The prefab houses were also very damp as they were made completely of aluminium - even the drawers in the wall-to-wall kitchen units.[116] Despite the negative reactions of the council and their concern for the newcomers, Eileen enjoyed her new home and the area:

> *"They gave us a two bedroomed house and it seemed so open out here, I mean London seemed so built up, lots of buildings, but out here you have got more fresh air, we never had a garden, and... (John) He likes gardening, and so do I - although we never had not much time when the children were young."*[117]

Eileen had little time and was mostly too busy with her family to want for more. There was not much else other than the prefab houses. There was also a lack of shops, schools and churches. The Catholic families had to use the local pub, "The Plough" for worship as the priest was allowed to say mass there. They also had to send their children to the school in Romford that was run by the Sisters of Mercy. Caitlin too had sent her children there and remembered the way the sisters organised the travel to and from school:

> *"Mother Gerard...was her name; Gerard... Ah, she was very nice, - But they went to the bus all nicely to go together, as far she see them on the bus. And of course the children then came from this area, which was being turned (into)... Harold Hill."*[118]

Catholic schooling for children on the Harold Hill Housing Estate proved to play an important part in the new emerging parishes.

Diocese of Brentwood and schooling

The Catholics of the Harold Hill Housing Estate on the outskirts of Romford were to fall under the Roman Catholic Diocese of Brentwood that had been newly formed in 1917 (see picture no 12 map of Harold Hill above). It was established by the Catholic Church as a direct result of the growth in the Catholic population in those parts of Essex adjacent to London (or East London as it is now called) and its urbanised character as Foster writes:

> *"With regard to Essex, Bourne realised that the Church would benefit from having a bishop resident in the county, yet he attached certain conditions to any such development."*[119]

Abercrombie stresses in his report the importance of churches in the new communities.[120] He suggested that:

> *"It is estimated that church provision should be made for about 10% of the population"*[121]

The Diocese still has the original boundaries of the county of Essex. In this area there had always been a strong link with Catholicism as a few of the noble families like the Petre family and Countess Tasker of Middleton Hall, who held a title dating back to the Holy Roman Empire, had done much to revive Catholicism in the area. The 11th Lord Petre, William Henry Francis, gave a plot of ground by the Ingrave Road, Brentwood in 1834 so that the chapel St Helen could be built: the land on which it stood was consecrated in 1837.[122]

By the time the Church of The Sacred Heart & St Helen was built, the chapel St Helen became a school in 1861. The new church was built with much financial aid of William Bernard the 12th Lord Petre. The church opened in 1861 and was consecrated in 1869. When the new Roman Catholic diocese was formed in 1917, the Church of The Sacred Heart & St Helen became the cathedral. The Catholics had some strong supporters in the district, notably the Willmott and the Lescher families. The Lescher family from Great Warley was responsible for the founding of the Church of the Holy Cross in Warley that opened in 1881.

Brentwood Diocese was known for its large number of schools for rich and poor children and the Catholic Church had contributed to the founding of schools since the nineteenth century. According to Ward sometime after 1869 the Sisters of Mercy of the convent in Chelsea founded a Convent in Brentwood, and they also built an orphanage for the poor Catholic children of Brentwood.[123] The Sister's aim was to educate the underprivileged. Many of the teachers at the Catholic schools belonged to religious orders like the Irish Christian Brothers and were often of Irish descent. The St Ursuline Sisters opened the first High School for girls in Brentwood in 1900. St

Ursuline's were originally two schools, one for the traders' daughters and one for the aristocrats. In October 1953 Bishop Beck of Brentwood had been asked by Mother Clare of the St Ursuline Sisters to request a Catholic school on the Harold Hill estate. Again, Abercrombie advised in his plan the exact amount of schools for the new communities but does not mention their denomination.

Bishop Beck approached the local committee of education in October 1953. He suggested that the school would originally start in the newly built church hall in Petersfield Avenue on the Harold Hill estate, Romford. The Authorities agreed provided that the school would be the responsibility of the Ursuline Sisters and provided they would find the funding for the building and would be responsible for the running of the school. The hall could accommodate two classes of infant children pending the completion of a new school in Straight Road, also in Harold Hill. During this time the local school in the town centre was considered by the town planners as the other option but Catholic parents objected as it was considered too far to travel from some parts of the new estate. There were no bus routes from these parts to the centre and children had to walk a long distance. This created so much upset with the parents that in the winter of 1949 the local paper reported that on 9th December 1949 mothers kept their children home as a form of protest. The mothers demanded a bus route for their children to bring them to the school in Romford from the Harold Hill estate.[124]

The Minister of Education objected to the two classes in the church hall. He ruled in June 1954 that he could not recognise the church hall as a school, and therefore the children were not to benefit from the school meal service on the normal terms. The ministry could supply dinners but at the full cost. Also milk was not to be handed out unless the full price was paid. He argued that there were perfectly good C. of E. schools nearby.[125] The Romford Council and Education Committee wrote that they found the ruling harsh.[126] These poor families had been part of Abercrombie's scheme to improve their living standards and were the reason behind the plan for free milk and meals at schools in the first place.[127]

The Council launched an official protest with no result. As the new school was going to open in Easter 1955, it was decided to wait for the new school with its own canteen. A van was made available to drive the school meals from the new canteen to the temporarily set-up classes. The hall was still in use as part of the school in October 1957.

The battle for a school was only one aspect of life on the new estate; families experienced huge changes in their lives on the new estate. But not changes were a result of their new surroundings and not all considered difficult as Eileen explains:

> *"There were a lot of differences, but I think when you're young, and you're bringing up your family... You don't have a lot of time, or an interest in things like that, you know?"*[128]

The new estate also brought much more space for the young families as Eileen tells:

> *"It seemed so open out here, I mean London seemed so built up, lots of buildings, but out here you have got more fresh air"*[129]

A new life

The new estates did not always create a comfortable life for the women involved. The shops were few and far between and it was much more expensive to buy from the shopkeepers than to visit the many markets that the old East End held. As Wilmott and Young explained in East London for most of the families, relatives had lived only a few doors away, often in the same road, which meant help and moral support for mothers.[130] They were removed from their old neighbourhoods and new jobs for the women on the just established estate, when needed, were hard to come by, unlike central London. That the move of industry was not a huge success became clear when the local papers started to advertise jobs in London for men on the estate. An example is the British Ply Wood Manufacturers Ltd, Wharf Road, Ponders End advertisement, which read:

> *"Of special interest to the residents of Harold Hill Estate: transport available, morning and evenings to and from Ponders End for male Unskilled Labour in the Plywood factory."*[131]

The local papers advertised for months work for unskilled labour with their ads targeting the new inhabitants of the estate. The ads even included the offer of organised transport bringing people back to the jobs in the old docks of East London. But for women no job advertisements appeared. It certainly was not all abundance and comfort for the newcomers either, for example the papers referred to a case in which a young boy of the estate was reported to have stolen £2 because of the poverty his parents lived in.[132] There were many such cases reported in the local papers but no mention of the religious or ethnic background of the families involved.

Another example mentioned in the Romford Recorder was that of family Smith who had also moved to Harold Hill. Mrs E Smith could no longer afford the expense of her four children. It was true that their health had improved but that had meant that they had developed a bigger appetite and grew out of their clothes more quickly. This had led her husband, despite his job, to resort to theft, as they could no longer afford the bills. Mr Smith subsequently received a sentence of six months imprisonment although the mitigation was accepted.[133] This is a good example of how the court and the paper understood the problem behind the case. The cases of inner-city children suffering from rickets and lacking strong frames were well known by the members of the public.

Several members of the Romford community remarked upon the relationship between poverty and theft on the new estate. Important people with respectable social status were often reported in the local papers. People like a local QC, and Chairman at the Essex Quarter Sessions commented that there were:

"undesirable people relocating into the Romford area".[134]

The attitude to the 'undesirables' was not completely disconnected from the resentment felt for the former East Enders. Another important member of the community of Romford, the Matron of Victoria Hospital was quoted in 1955 saying Harold Hill was:

"ugly and part of the East End of London."

These people were most likely to see the less fortunate members of the new community; the physically weak and the petty criminals. These comments came often after the papers mentioned something about the prefab houses or the large amount of East Enders living there. Many Harold Hill residents reacted angrily in the papers highlighting that they were sent there for their bad health and that it had not been a matter of choice. They had expected some sympathy from a matron.[135]

Another incident that occurred shows the irritation at times of the local population towards the new residents. The L.C.C. decided that in order to maintain the estate they had to help the residents to cultivate their gardens. The former East Enders had not had the luxury of gardens before and "gardening" was unheard of in areas like the Docklands and Poplar. The whole idea of owning a space outside the front or back door was new, as Eileen who had lived in the Docklands explained earlier, when asked if she liked gardening she said:

> "yes, so did John. Yes, we never had a garden, and... He likes gardening, and so do I"

This was new to them but also would help people enjoy their new place. It was therefore decided that the new estate dwellers should be given some incentive. Gardening societies were set up as an initiative, as was the case in many other newly built estates in the fifties and prize money could be won for the best kept garden. The Romford Recorder reported on 22 July 1949:

> "Harold Hill show was resounding success. The LCC had suggested a year ago to give advice on the inhabitant's gardens. Most had never had a garden before. The Harold Hill Horticultural Society held its first Flower and Veg show."

It was a great success. Money was also made available to fence off gardens so that everyone could view that little patch of land as their own. This was not a luxury as it was often reported that local horses and cows were strolling into the gardens and destroying the washing lines on the estate. But this initiative created some irritation among the Gidea Park residents, who were situated next to the Harold Hill Estate. They too had gardens, were experienced gardeners and lay great value on their little plots of land.

Unfortunately they had to find their own funding for fencing off their gardens. Romford council, which was responsible for the council houses in Gidea Park had less money available to spend in that area. The complaints were voiced in various meetings of residents of Gidea Park, but it really came to a head when the L.C.C. decided that the wooden fences were now to be painted white at the residents' expense.[136] In the reports of the meeting where Romford Council tried to placate angry Gidea Park residents, a sense of fear emerged that although the East Enders were entitled to re-housing, there would be the danger that they were treated with more care than they deserved.

The area that had been used for the Harold Hill Estate was situated on farmland near the old London Road. In fact so many were heading towards the Harold Hill estate that as early as December 1949 Romford received a Circular from the Ministry of Town and Planning; to respond to the density of the residential area in Green Belt and the over-spill of population and industry.[137] They (the council) had to move people on, as there were already too many heading to the borough. Romford, it was suggested, should see itself as an "Exporting Authority", exporting people and industry to Basildon, Harlow, Billericay and Thurrock. The Council's concern over the wisdom of the government proposals on such a large project to transplant large amounts of the people of East London had not been without ground.

Conclusion

This chapter discussed the influence Irish migrants had on the Catholic Church and how they urbanised that Church, changing its congregation predominantly into working class and Irish. It also discussed the influence of the migrants in the south East and particular in the Brentwood diocese and showed the impact this Catholic community had on the local Diocese of Brentwood by dramatically increasing the numbers of Catholics that lived in the area. But it also highlights the importance of housing and neighbourhoods especially for the Irish women.

It researched the importance of the exodus from the East End during the aftermath of the Second World War to Harold Hill and explored how the building projects of this particular estate were planned and how it fitted in with the major project of re-housing. It explores the Irish immigrants that were affected by the change to living on the new estate and the response of the local community. The lives of the Irish immigrant women in their homes and how they rebuild their lives and raised their children on the new estate shall be explored in the next chapter.

Footnotes

[1] Abercrombie P. (1944) *Greater London Plan*
[2] Worth J. (2002) *Tales from a midwife. True stories in the East End in the 1950s,* p. 68
[3] Lingham B.F. (1969) *Harold Hill and Noak Hill* in LCR Archive
[4] Christina (Greater London, 1999; name altered), Interview 4, transcript p. 1.
[5] Christina Interview 4, transcript p. 3
[6] Christina Interview 4, transcript p. 3
[7] McCullough, C. (2010) *A Tie That Blinds: Family Ideology In Ireland - Economic and Social Review* 22, pp. 199-211
[8] Christina Interview 4, transcript p. 3
[9] Christina Interview 4, transcript p. 3
[10] Christina Interview 4, transcript p. 3
[11] Christina Interview 4, transcript p. 3
[12] Worth J. *Tales from a midwife* p. 68
[13] Christina Interview 4, transcript p. 1
[14] Christina Interview 4, transcript p. 1
[15] Christina Interview 4, transcript p. 3
[16] Christina Interview 4, transcript p. 3
[17] Christina Interview 4, transcript p. 6
[18] Christina Interview 4, transcript p. 4
[19] Christina Interview 4, transcript p. 4
[20] Christina Interview 4, transcript p. 7
[21] Shepard C. (2010) 'Irish journalists in the intellectual diaspora: Edward Alexander Morphy and Henry David O'Shea and in the Far East', in: *New Hibernia Review*, vol. 14, no. 3 (Autumn 2010), pp. 75-90.
[22] Gray B. (1997) 'Unmasking Irishness, Irish women, the Irish Nation and the Irish Diaspora', in: *Location and Dislocation in Contemporary Irish Society,* Cork, p. 216
[23] Christina Interview 4, transcript p. 4
[24] Picture 07 map of East London Online available www.oldemaps.co.uk accessed May 2010
[25] Christina Interview 4, transcript p. 6
[26] Christina Interview 4, transcript p. 4
[27] Walter B. (2010) 'Irish/Jewish diasporic intersections in the East End of London: paradoxes and shared locations', in: M. Prum (ed) *La place de l'autre* Paris: L'Harmattan Press, pp. 53-67
[28] Christina Interview 4, transcript p. 7
[29] Christina Interview 4, transcript p. 7
[30] Christina Interview 4, transcript p. 5
[31] Christina Interview 4, transcript p. 20
[32] Christina Interview 4, transcript p. 16
[33] Christina Interview 4, transcript p. 16
[34] Christina Interview 4, transcript p. 16
[35] Christina Interview 4, transcript p. 16
[36] Christina Interview 4, transcript p. 16

[37] Christina Interview 4, transcript p. 18
[38] Christina Interview 4, transcript p. 6
[39] Christina Interview 4, transcript p. 6
[40] Walter B. and Hickman M. (1995) 'Deconstructing Whiteness; Irish women in Britain', in: *Feminist Review no. 50*
[41] Christina Interview 4, transcript p. 7
[42] Delaney E. (2007) *The Irish in post war Britain cultures of adjustment*, p. 135
[43] Christina Interview 4, transcript p. 9
[44] Christina Interview 4, transcript p. 9
[45] http://www.thecatenians.com/pages/history_organisation/default.aspx
[46] Christina Interview 4, transcript p. 9
[47] Christina Interview 4, transcript p. 9
[48] Christina Interview 4, transcript p. 9
[49] Christina Interview 4, transcript p. 9
[50] Christina Interview 4, transcript p. 10
[51] Christina Interview 4, transcript p. 10
[52] Christina Interview 4, transcript p. 5
[53] Christina Interview 4, transcript p. 5
[54] Christina Interview 4, transcript p. 19
[55] Christina Interview 4, transcript p. 19
[56] Christina Interview 4, transcript p. 19
[57] Christina Interview 4, transcript p. 5
[58] Werner A. (2011) *The migrant communities and health care at home* on *Buurtzorg Life Web*
[59] Christina Interview 4, transcript p. 7
[60] Christina Interview 4, transcript p. 6
[61] Christina Interview 4, transcript p. 6
[62] Christina Interview 4, transcript p. 6
[63] Christina Interview 4, transcript p. 6
[64] Christina Interview 4, transcript p. 7
[65] Christina Interview 4, transcript p. 1
[66] Christina Interview 4, transcript p. 7
[67] Christina Interview 4, transcript p. 21
[68] Christina Interview 4, transcript p. 21
[69] Eileen (Greater London, 1995; name altered), Interview 5, transcript p.1. "Eileen might have mixed up the First World War at the time that English soldiers fought during the 1916 Rising. As Ireland was regarded as *home* no medals were awarded for any action these soldiers took part in and therefore little is known about those who were stationed there"
[70] Eileen Interview 5, transcript p. 14
[71] Eileen Interview 5, transcript p. 3
[72] Eileen Interview 5, transcript p. 3
[73] Edna (Greater London, 1999; name altered), Interview 3, transcript p. 3
[74] Edna Interview 3, transcript p. 3
[75] Edna Interview 3, transcript p. 10

[76] *Picture no 08: Map from the Greater London Plan of 1944, showing the growth of London between 1914 & 1939 LCR Archive*
[77] Humphries, S. and Weightman G. (1984) *The Making Of Modern London 1914-1939*, London, p. 100
[78] Humphries, S. and Weightman G. (1984) *The Making of Modern London*, p. 74
[79] Picture no. 09: Map shows the area and where Romford lays in relation to Dagenham (online) available http://maps.google.co.uk/ accessed September 2011
[80] Abercrombie P. *Greater London Plan*
[81] Humphries, S. and Weightman G. *The Making Of Modern London*, p. 49
[82] Booth C. (1902) *Life and Labour of people in London* 17 vol. (1889–91, 1892–97, 1902)
[83] Abercrombie P. *Greater London Plan*, p. 4
[84] Abercrombie P. *Greater London Plan*, p. 2
[85] Ward D. (1992) *Essays in Comparative History - A Comparative Historical Geography of Streetcar Suburbs in Boston, Massachusetts and Leeds, England: 1850-1920*, Buckingham
[86] Abercrombie P. *Greater London Plan*, p. 19
[87] Humphries, S. and Weightman G. *The Making of Modern London*, pp. 68-69
[88] Ward, D. *A Comparative Historical Geography*, p. 242
[89] Abercrombie P. *Greater London Plan*, pp. 4 - 7
[90] Abercrombie P. *Greater London Plan*, p. 4
[91] LCR Archive: Picture no 10: Map also shown in the greater London Plan as a way to keep green areas like parks working for the population of London
[92] Abercrombie P. *Greater London Plan*, Foreword I
[93] Picture no 11: Map also shown in the greater London Plan, with the classification of the arterial roads exploring accessibility of various sites based on the old road system with additional new roads added in LCR
[94] Abercrombie P. *Greater London Plan*, p. V (Foreword)
[95] Abercrombie P. *Greater London Plan*, p. V (Foreword)
[96] Abercrombie P. *Greater London Plan*, p. VI (Foreword)
[97] Abercrombie P. *Greater London Plan*, p. 111
[98] Abercrombie P. *Greater London Plan*, p. 111
[99] Abercrombie P. *Greater London Plan*, p. 13
[100] Abercrombie P. *Greater London Plan*, pp. 111 & 174
[101] Abercrombie P. *Greater London Plan*, p. 115
[102] Abercrombie P. *Greater London Plan*, p. 31
[103] Abercrombie P. *Greater London Plan*, p. 7
[104] Abercrombie P. *Greater London Plan*, chapt. 7
[105] Abercrombie P. *Greater London Plan*, p. 135
[106] Abercrombie P. *Greater London Plan*, p. 87
[107] LCR Archive: Minutes of the council meeting of the Borough of Romford Nov. 1945
[108] Interview Caitlin p. 2
[109] LCR Archive: Minutes of the council meeting of the Borough of Romford Nov. 1944 shelter dwellers

[110] LCR Archive: *The Hornchurch, Dagenham, Brentwood and Romford Times* newspaper 19th September, 1945

[111] LCR Archive: Housing, etc., Committee, Romford Council meeting minutes 27th March, 1945

[112] LCR Archive: Coffin R. (1986) 'Moving Out To Harold Hill', in: *Romford Record Journal*, London, p. 24

[113] LCR Archive: Lingham B.F. (1969) *Harold Hill and Noak Hill*, London

[114] LRC Archive: *Romford Times* newspaper 'North Romford Housing Inquiry' on Wednesday 16th February 1949

[115] LCR Archive: Picture no 12: Map of Harold Hill here shows what it looked like just after most of the building was finished in 1960

[116] LCR Archive: Minutes of the council meeting of the Borough of Romford 27-03-1945

[117] Eileen Interview 5, transcript p. 2

[118] Caitlin (Greater London, 1999; name altered), Interview 2, transcript p. 4

[119] Foster S.M. (1994) *A history of the Diocese of Brentwood 1917-1992*, Brentwood, p. 15

[120] Abercrombie P. *Greater London Plan*, p. 119

[121] Abercrombie P. *Greater London Plan*, p. 119

[122] Ward, G. (1980) *Victorian and Edwardian Brentwood*, Brentwood

[123] Ward, G. (1980) *Victorian and Edwardian Brentwood*, Brentwood

[124] LCR Archive: *The Romford Recorder* Newspaper 9 December 1949

[125] LCR Archive: Council Attendance Sub-Committee, Romford Council meeting minutes, page 9 point 56, 1st June 1954. LCR archive

[126] LCR Archive: Minutes of the Council Attendance Sub-Committee, subdivision of Romford Council 1954 p. 9 point 56

[127] LCR Archive: Minutes meeting of the Council Attendance Sub-Committee, 1954

[128] Eileen Interview 5, transcript p. 4

[129] Eileen Interview 5, transcript p. 4

[130] Young M. and Willmott P. (1957) *Family And Kinship in East London*, London

[131] LCR Archive: *Romford Recorder*, 25th March 1955

[132] LCR Archive: *Romford Recorder*, 15th April 1955

[133] LCR Archive: *Romford Recorder*, 29th June 1955

[134] LCR Archive: *Romford Recorder*, 4th February 1955

[135] LCR Archive: *Romford Recorder*, 11th March 1955

[136] LCR Archive: *Romford Recorder*, 11th March 1955

[137] Minutes meeting of Romford Council Housing Committee, (point 1142: Dealing with a circular from the Ministry of Town and Country planning), 20th December 1949

CHAPTER 5: IRISH WOMEN IN THEIR HOMES

This chapter examines the private worlds of women and their families. It explores the traditions that continued behind closed doors and explores the impact that the Virgin Mary had both upon the expectations of women by their families and on women's own expectations, in order to bring to the forefront the cultural specificity of Irish women's religious beliefs. In the interviews women were reluctant to talk about Mary because she was seen as a mystery, something laywomen would not easily discuss. But they would incorporate the images that the Church taught them of the Virgin into their daily lives. This chapter explores how these mothers were transposing Mary into their own role of mothers. Furthermore it examines how women talk about their role as mothers in which they are acting out and copying the Virgin mother as their perfect example.

This chapter also discusses how the Catholic doctrine on family life and the role of mother influenced the Irish women in their lives on the estate. It explores the difference between siblings of different sexes and how gender roles were enforced. The study looked at the taboo that surrounded sexual conduct and the impact the Catholic Church had with its stance on married women. Furthermore, it investigates the sense of duty and the habits of the old routines and traditions and the rural aspect in their faith. It will examine the strength of the faith and how the Catholic Irish traditions were passed on in families, and also the influence of these concepts on the lives of the Irish women. In doing so it will reflect on the tenacity of and adherence to customs and traditions after migration and it also allows women to talk about their paid and unpaid work in England as this influenced their family life.

Family life

Much emphasis in Catholicism is placed on the importance of the Holy Family and this image of perfect family life is used as an example for Catholics in churches and schools as well as in Catholic literature, especially in the Irish Catholic traditions. One of the mothers on the estate, Nola, of fourth generation Irish descent, had allowed me to study her mother's diary. Nola herself did not wish to partake in this study. Nola's mother Ciara O'Donnell, who was the granddaughter of Irish immigrants, kept a diary as a young girl: her *'Book of Talks'* as has been discussed in the methodology Chapter 3. Nola remembers her mother talking about the family background and that her mother Ciara was brought up in a pious Catholic family which held on to their Catholic roots, which was something that Ciara also passed on to her daughter. Ciara started her diary on January 25th 1938 and kept recording all that she felt was important during the war and afterwards during the fifties when she was an adult. As a young girl, she collected in her *'Book of Talks'* subjects from newspapers and poems. Later on she copied poems into the diary. Initially she recorded her meetings as a Brownie.[1] This diary provides a good example of how girls were prepared on the future role of mothers and the importance of living by example in which the Holy Family was used.

It was not common practice of Catholic girls to join a Protestant club like the Brownies. But Ciara's diary shows that she clearly did attend Brownies and her Catholic poems suggest that she was part of a Catholic pack of Brownies. But alongside it she also joined the Children of Mary: her first entry disclosing this fact is on 05-10-1941.[2] She copied many poems into her diary that all expressed the Catholic ideal of family life and the example of the Holy Family.[3] It was clearly influential and important to the girls who belonged to the Brownies. A good example is *The Famous Carpenter*, which gave the highest approval to Joseph's home building skills:

> *(Not dated but entry is immediately after the previous entry of September 3 1939)*
> "*Saint Joseph built, we like to believe,*
> *His home, and fenced his garden plot,*
> *Repaired neighbour's broken bench,*
> *Constructed a rude chariot*
> *To please his eager little one.*
>
> *We know he built not wondrous bridge,*
> *Or aqueduct, or temple halls;*
> *Yet Solomon nor Hadrian*
> *Is famed as he whose humble walls*
> *Housed Blessed Mary and her Son.*" (poet unknown)[4]

Catholics in England were expected to model themselves on the example of the Holy Family. This subject was a repeated feature in the homilies of the Sunday Mass throughout the Catholic churches. A good example was the sermon course of 1959 given in the diocese of Northampton. A copy of this Sermon course (second year in the religious calendar) was used and kept by the Bishop of Brentwood which stated for the sermon of 11th January 1959 the relationship of the Catholic family and the Holy Family:

> *"The Catholic father presents the first notion of God to his children: their idea of God as father rests on their idea of what father is."*

And that:

> *"The relation of the Catholic husband to his wife is to be modelled of that of Christ to his Church. He is faithful to her, loves her, if need be delivers himself for her. The perfect family of Nazareth we see Joseph as the example for fathers and husbands."*[5]

In his sermon the Bishop directs his laymen, the fathers and the husbands of his Diocese, to be like Christ in their relationship to their wives and said that much of their behaviour was seen as the way in which the Son of God would behave. In their relationship to their children they were to be as perfect and reliable as St Joseph, which left very little space for human error and was far from realistic. The expectations were based on a very strong, well-balanced and able man. These high expectations would have been difficult to achieve for the Irish immigrant men, with their disrupted lives, long working hours and necessity of dealing with an unwelcoming English society.[6] As discussed in chapter 2, McCullough warns that real family life was often very complex and therefore a far cry from the ideal.[7] As for the women, the Catholic Church had always stressed that Mary had only one child, which made her situation very different from the Catholic mothers who were meant to imitate her and use her as an example. As the ordinary women were to receive their offspring willingly and any form of birth control was seen as a sin, they were often left to deal with very large families and great hardship trying to raise their children. The Church itself never studied Catholic mothers and their large families. It continued to stress the ideal without taking into account the reality.[8] The use of the Holy Family as a model, in exhortations to instruct and to live by its example also demonstrates a clear message to the working class laymen. Instruction to copy is a simplistic way of teaching and clearly favoured by the Bishop as role models can be grasped more easily than theoretical discussions on relationships. It also clearly defines the various roles placed on the parents divided in male and female forms of behaviour.

In the interviews, women were often comparing and highlighting the difference between the ideal, which at times they were highly critical of, and their own experience as mothers. Eileen, one of the interviewees, like all of the other interviewees, herself had a larger family than the Virgin Mary (according to Catholic doctrine) and that in Eileen's view made Mary to be less of a mother. When asked if Mary was important to her she hesitated and argued:

> "Well I think so because she was a mother. So I think that if you are a mother yourself, you can see her in the role of a mother, although she only had her son, one son, but she [had] the same role that we had really."[9]

Eileen deliberately played down the importance of Mary as a mother since Mary had, as a mother, less of a struggle than Eileen herself. Eileen had grown up in East London of London and was married with four children. She moved to the Harold Hill estate not long after she was married and worked within school hours at the local hospital as soon as all the children were of a school age. Eileen never had enough money to spend on the household and had to juggle her role as mother and part time worker. Eileen's mother, who had moved to London after her marriage to an English soldier, had struggled to cope with eight children. Eileen, grew up in Greenwich. Eileen's father was invalided out of the army during the First World War after he developed epilepsy as a result of a fall from a horse, Eileen remembered:

> "She used to get a small pension, but it wasn't a lot of money, really – because she had a lot of children – she was quite strong, you know, although she was quite small, she was very strong. Because of the epilepsy he [my father] was often sent away (maybe it was to give my mother relief with the children) in these hospitals that dealt

with men that had been injured during the war. So often he used to go away for up to three to four months."[10]

In Eileen's memory, the poverty and hard work meant that her mother never had enough time for the children or herself. The kindness and patience of Our Lady as a mother was a far cry from the real mother figure, as Eileen recalled:

> *"-she never showed any feelings, really... The baby, whoever was the baby in the family, got the affection until perhaps that was replaced with another one. That one grew up, and there be another baby, and that one would sort of fend for themselves. The baby got a little bit of affection, but she wasn't what you call... She wasn't an emotional mother, and she never demonstrated her love, or she never got hold of you, gave you a cuddle or anything like that."*[11]

The endless chores made it impossible for her mother to spend some time with her daughter. She, like many other families, lacked space, time or money to allow much attention for the individual children. In the interview, Eileen's way of telling this story showed how she was in some way still grieving for this lack of love. Eileen's interview demonstrates the complexity that lay behind an idealised mother-figure whereby girls like Eileen were brought up with the harsh reality alongside this ideal.[12]

The lack of space and the hardship of raising large families was a recurring topic in the interviews. This is where the ideal was most strikingly different from the reality. Women were therefore comparing and highlighting the problems they encountered as mothers. Most also reflected on the place in which they grew up and the way the lack of space had been a constant problem back in Ireland. Some women remembered the simple things such as getting the whole family round the table to eat was a problem in itself. Family meals and the prayers before and after were an important part of family life.

Aoife, another mother on the Harold Hill Estate, grew up in Limerick. She was the daughter of a pork butcher and one of ten siblings. Her parents were very poor and poverty meant a constant struggle about where the meals would come from to the places to sit at the dinner table. She explained:

> *"There were ten of us. We never had enough chairs to sit on. You know my father used to say 'stand up there you fool you go down there further.' We used to stand and have our dinner"*[13] (meaning there is more room if you all stand up)

Aoife herself had four children and although financially better off than her own mother she felt that the first years with her family were particularly hard because they lived in a caravan on a site near Romford in Essex. This meant little room for the growing family. She had to juggle her husband's night shifts and her children's routine. Aoife said:

> *"I had three children in a caravan and he was on nights, he used to do night work."*

Her husband Patrick remembered the times clearly, particularly the lack of space. He added:

> *"And if it was raining like, the kids couldn't get out."*[14]

This meant little or no sleep for Patrick and children who had to be quiet. It was not a happy time for her daughters and one rarely settled:

> *"she never settled in did she and she was a bit... Whinger! She whinged all day long and as her breakfast would go in this side she would be spewing it up the other way."*[15]

The difficulties with the lack of space that Aoife remembered from her childhood were not that very different from her own time as a mother raising a young family. The small caravan in Essex had given her similar problems in England as those of her mother back in Ireland.

Young women and girls were given a very sterile picture of mother figures, which was based on the ever-caring, ever-loving Mother Mary. The ideal of the perfect mother, as has been explained in chapter 4 as a male fantasy, left very little room for the reality young women faced when becoming mothers. As Willmott and Young describe, the closeness in the community in the 1950s between mothers and their daughters often living in close proximity to one another in the East End of London was very much at the heart of the East End community which they did not describe as Irish but as Catholic. They had touched upon the closeness of what were originally predominantly Irish families and the special bond between mother and daughter. What they also noticed was that these women did not find it easy to connect with neighbours who were seen as outside the family circle but in turn the English neighbours did not connect easily and the new estate lacked community spirit at the beginning that in turn created a sense of isolation. The teachings on the Holy Family as a role model, no matter how well meant, left them ill prepared for their actual roles as mothers without their own mothers in close proximity on the new estate. Those whose mothers remained in Ireland, could never really call on their mother for advice and help. They had to find replacements in the form of neighbours and fellow parishioners for family support. Aoife did make contact with one other mother when she lived with her three children in the caravan. Later on she made many friends through the Catholic clubs she and her husband joined.

Cathleen, who already lived on the land just outside Romford where later on Harold Hill was built, could only remember neighbours she got on with but they were definitely outside of the family circle and the Catholic community and she herself was seen by her English neighbours as an outsider. She had to walk up to St Edwards in the town centre of Romford, to go to church, and she was therefore at first not connected with any local parish and lack of contact with other Irish Catholics on the estate.

Edna, as she described in chapter 4, still asked her mother's advice for everything (in her letters) and although on her own on the estate, the bond of her siblings proved strong. When asked if she had felt lonely without her family she said:

> *"No because some of them were here. And we were always, [close] you know. Someone was always coming to take you out for the day [as] I couldn't go out on my own, because I wasn't exactly home anywhere. My older sister would come and get me [to] take me to her place, so then my dad would take me another time when he was here. I didn't really belong with someone… and everything new, you know. As fascinating that was, you know everything was happening"*

Although several members of her family including her father had emigrated to England, Edna only ever saw them one day a week on these outings and she felt it was still hard to be on her own.[16] The huge exodus of young people from Irish rural counties could be viewed as some form of commitment to the family farm, a commitment to one inheriting brother and to the importance of the land itself and therefore other siblings, especially girls were forced to emigrate.[17]

Most women in the interviews referred to correspondence by means of letters with the parents back home. It was also important to include money in the letters to help the family back home, which was more often than not expected of them. As Aoife remembers:

> *"When your dad was dead and your mother used to send him [Patrick] an electricity bill and a letter like, you know she used to say 'I got my electricity bill, God is good!' For the payment, Patrick used to send her the money for the bill."*

But the letters also enabled young women like Edna to receive advice about their role as mothers. On the other hand women also kept in touch with siblings living in England, particularly sisters who were often supportive. Edna kept in touch and also raising her own children she still asked her mother for advice:

> *"You could discuss things with her and she always listen, and she always gave good sound advice, and once she understood anything, you know, then you couldn't do really wrong, because she was very hmm you know...She was dominant I think I suppose, type of woman. I don't see her as that, but he girls reckon she was very, you know, dominant type of person."*[18]

The Catholic Church recognised the need to provide more definitive guidance to mothers and booklets appeared in the fifties to assist the mothers with statements such as; *"The destiny of a woman is marriage and motherhood"*[19] The Catholic Printing Company of Farnworth, Lancaster, originally published it for the Notre Dame High School Mount Pleasant in Liverpool. It clearly states that it was for private circulation only. What is interesting here is that this booklet then appears in the BDA archive and it seems that there was a discussion between the Bishops in England about these booklets and that this one was most likely used to assist laywomen in the diocese. In these booklets the girls are also instructed to ask Mary for help in their development and to use her as an example to them. Some booklets were meant as a discussion to inform girls about what happens during the development of the baby before and after birth. But its emphasis was on the children's need for mothers.[20] The Bishop (Leo) of Northampton wrote on 31st Dec 1958 in a letter to the Bishop Beck of Brentwood:

> *"Prenuptial inquiries should be made carefully. Under question nine of the usual form the attention of prospective parents might well be called to the obligation of telling children at the right age the Fact of Life. There is a good pamphlet for parents on this important subject: 'Sex Instructions in the Home.' it is not to be exposed for public sale."*[21]

The booklet was considered very instructive and because of its subject matter it was to be kept in the hands of the church.

In another booklet *"My Dear Daughter"* the writer (who is not named) refers constantly back to the baby Jesus, his needs and the relationship with his mother.[22] It also discusses the changes girls go through, like menstruation. There were instructions on how to pray to Mary (in honour of her purity) preferably three times a day, and to ask for purity of thought, desire, word or act. It also advises the girls to pray to Joseph and St Maria Goretti:

> *"to be pure does not mean to be ignorant of the Facts of Life - not only to avoid danger and grow in grace but also understand and appreciate the meaning of Christian Marriage, motherhood and fatherhood."*[23]

It then went on to explain in detail sexual intercourse.[24] The booklets appear today to be quite naïve in the way the subject matter was handled. It was, however, a very brave commitment of the Catholic Church and the Diocese of Brentwood to allow the circulation of these booklets in the first place because sexual issues were generally not discussed. It seems to have been an attempt to come to terms with the ever-increasing modernisation of the world around the Catholic Church and it clearly tries to find a position in that world. It needs to be remembered that this was during the 1950s, before the Second Vatican Council took place (1962-1965).

Ciara also copied in her diary work from the Catholic poet Edgar A. Guest, though her entries were not always dated. Again it is not very clear whether she was given this poem and told to copy it, or exercised some choice. But in either case it illustrates the short message she was absorbing about her duties of a mother:

> *"A mother's dreams are always fair,*
> *a mother's hopes are always high,*
> *Nor all life's bitterness and care*
> *can cause her love to change and die.*
> *Still will she speak*
> *Though we are weak*
> *Of tenderness which she has known.*
> *Though far we will fall*
> *she venture all*
> *to claim us proudly as her own.*
>
> *And when a child is ill she stays*
> *Beside the bed all night and day,*
> *So when to shame her black sheep strays,*
> *'he needs me so!' You hear her say.*
> *They little know*
> *Who chide him so*
> *The reasons for his wilful deeds.*
> *Now troubled sore*
> *'Tis more and more*
> *of mother love and care he needs."*[25]

Images of perfection and boundless energy became apparent in the poem, but in much of the copied material there is also a clear message of not making an impact on the world outside the home and to be only able to influence society through the deeds of the husband and children by means of supporting them:

"A woman's world":

I know I cannot speak of great deeds,
Or live as heroes do,
But I can serve my children's needs,
And keep my house for you.

My world is just a humble one,
But I can make it fair;
My windows catch the mighty sun,
A star finds haven there.

My hands can be restoring hands,
And bring, where chaos was,
The order that my soul demands.
My fingers can mend flaws.

And by my will I may create
A place of harmony,
Where happy moments compensate
The friends who visit me.

I know my world, so very small
And narrow in its scope,
Is great enough to bless us all
With happiness and hope! (written by an unknown poet Anne Campbell[26])

These poems ignore the great impact many Catholic Irish women had during their premarital time as nurses, care-officers, nannies or teachers. It also excluded the part they played in creating Catholic parishes and the support of these parishes. By placing the role of women solely in the home as the supportive figure in the background behind the husband and children their importance in their community was either not recognised, was ignored or was taken for granted.

During her time as a Brownie, Ciara wrote, presumably under direction of the important set of rules laid down by the Mgr Giovanni Varishi who was an honorary chamberlain of Pope Pius XI. A life of happiness was based on the Ten Commandments that he had laid down for women, against the seven laid down for their husbands:

1. *Thou shalt not speak internally. The husband must also be listened to.*
2. *Thou shalt lovingly prepare good food and keep thy house in order.*
3. *Thou shalt not embarrass thy husband in business.*
4. *Thou shalt not amuse thyself spreading unfounded gossip about thy neighbour.*
5. *Thou shalt not boast of thy husband before other men, but respect him silently.*
6. *When it is necessary to reprove him thou shalt do it immediately and then forget it.*
7. *Thou shalt be patient over thy husband's defects, and occasionally exalt his good qualities.*
8. *Thou shalt not make of thy husband a housemaid.*
9. *Thou shalt not give all thy thoughts to clothes, since thy first duty is to thy house.*
10. *Thou shalt remember that sometimes it is good for thy husband to be alone. On those occasions thou shalt not disturb him.*[27]

This has an Erasmian ring to it. Erasmus, who advised disappointed wives along similar lines in a mock scenario where Eulalia in a dialogue with Xanthippe, advises her to:

> *"Be agreeable to my husband in every respect, so as to not to cause him any annoyance. I noted his mood and feeling; I noted the circumstances too, and what soothed and irritated him, as do those who tame elephants and lions or such like creatures that can't be forced."*[28]

What makes the material such sad reading was Ciara's entry on the first page of her diary *'Book of Talks'* remembering her Brownie meeting on February 7th 1938; on the subject of ambition the question; *"What is your ambition in life?"* She wrote:

> *"Of course every answer here was different. One girl wished to be a missionary, another wished to be a famous musician. I'm afraid my own ambition is to be an Architect, Inventor or Designer. Seems rather a lot doesn't it? Still maybe they are their only dreams."*[29]

She was allowed her dreams and nobody felt it necessary to enlighten Brownies on the restricted choices set for the girls. She knew she was asking 'too much' because as a girl such career aspirations were untenable. Her words; *'I'm afraid'* and *'Seems rather a lot'* show how she was aware that these dreams were unlikely to be realised. As children expressed their ambitions to participate in a wide range of activities, which were strikingly at odds with the restricted paths being laid out for them by the Church and social class, Ciara's ambition remained only a dream. She married when in her twenties and stayed at home raising her children and looking after the family home.

The ideal of family life recurs in many of the poems copied by Ciara, as the home was portrayed as the place where there was bliss and harmony. Ciara included a poem on the definitions of home that home is the place where:

> *"Definitions of home*
> *The place where we grumble most and are treated the best.*
> *Father's kingdom, a mother's world and a child's paradise.*
> *A world of strife shut out and a world of love shut in.*
> *The place where the small are great and the great are small.*
> *Where one's true disposition is sure to be revealed.*
> *No man is poor who possesses a home and a family."*[30]

The concept of the family unit as a safe environment contradicts findings of researchers such as Hondagneu-Sotelo who when researching migrant and gender roles stated:

> *"Opening the household as a 'black box' exposes a highly charged political arena where husbands and wives and parents and children may simultaneously express and pursue divergent interests and competing agendas."*[31]

The poem refers to the home as a kingdom for a man; a place ruled by him and the entire world for the women; no place outside it exists for her.

The divide between the genders in the case of the Irish Catholic society lies at the heart of the Irish immigration to England. With the marriage bar in place and the dominantly rural communities, where the majority of farms were small family holdings, women were unable to sustain themselves and forced to emigrate. The Irish Republic adopted the Catholic ideal of the family unit where women were placed in a role supportive of men. The large emigration of women is not a clash of that ideal but a consequence of that ideal.[32] Beale discusses how within Catholic culture men preserved three identities for women: that of the virgin, the whore and the mother. She points out that:

> *"The three images are by no means exclusive to Ireland. There is, however, heightened by the dominant sexual ethic in Irish society and by the high degree of separation of the sexes in childhood. Without everyday knowledge of girls as friends boys have little experience with which to counteract the stereotype."*[33]

In Post-Independence Ireland the government had succeeded in creating a society where the man stood above his wife in a way that suggested a relationship between an adult and a child. The search for a distinctive national Irish identity had led them to view the rural family farm as an image of a united Ireland with peasant origins and a classless society. But much of this unity was as a wrapped blanket, which covered with care the great inequalities between siblings and child labour. As Gray argues:

> *"Gender inequality within the 'Catholic Irish family' was naturalised by making the family an 'authentic' source of Irishness while the class implications of the break-up of the peasant families by emigration was largely obscured."*[34]

A major report on emigration and other population problems in 1956 based on the census of that year expressed concern about the large number of women who were leaving the rural areas. It became clear that a shortage of young women would spell problems for the future with a lower birth rate due to an unequal ratio between men and women. But the patriarchal basis of Irish society tied it closely to the ideal of the Catholic Church and the role patterns didn't change, resulting in a continuation of female emigration.

Siblings and gender roles

The Catholic ideal of the family unit proved to be of great importance to the Irish nation.[35] After the turmoil at the establishment of an independent Ireland, the people were in need of stability. With the casualties caused by the painful civil war the Catholic notion of the perfect family unit was a concept that had much appeal.[36] As Ciara quotes in her diary:

"The home was a place where the world of strife was shut out."[37]

It also represented the single unit that the whole of society was based on. With a rural Ireland looking for its own Irish identity distinct from anything British, the rural farming family was the perfect frame to build on.[38] Ireland did not have to create new images, it emphasised what was already there. But as the authorities were promoting the family ties in order to stabilise Irish society, they ignored the reality of family ties.[39] McCullough discussed how the idealisation ignored the reality of this rural society with disputes over land between neighbours and the conflicts between siblings over inheritance. He critiques the classic work of the anthropologists Arensberg and Kimball and argues that it was unable to detect tensions within the family unit in the rural system because of its functionalist approach.[40] Nor did they discuss the huge differences that had emerged as part of this system between the different siblings, in particular between the boys and girls.

One consequence of placing the family unit on a pedestal was the large emigration of young women who were never to inherit, and in general an increase in family tensions between boys and girls with the girls in the weaker position. There was little work for them in rural society and even on the farm many of their own chores such as poultry or pig rearing and cheese making had been transferred to men.[41] Some remained however as wives housekeepers, nurses, teachers or nuns. This inferior role forced many women to migrate. The eventual settlement of Irish women in Harold Hill was a direct result of the lack of space for girls within Irish society. The gender bias back home was however also re-enacted when these women came to raise their own families. According to Nash, the highly differentiated gender roles are much older than the Irish Republic, and were very much part of Irish traditions that date back to well before Irish independence. Out of the suppressed Gaelic society emerged a very masculine image of the Irish man, a reaction to the status that the British oppressor had initially placed him in.[42] It also has to be remembered that in very rural societies strength and healthy physique was very important and men with masculine abilities or bodily strength were valuable to their farming communities. In Ireland the traditional tools of agriculture were still in use in the early 20th century with their emphasis on manual labour.[43]

For Deirdre, one of the interviewees, her gender and the consequent treatment she received continued to impact on her adult life. She described how, when her mother died, her father had decided to send his four daughters to a children's home because he was unable to look after them but he kept his sons at home. Her father, who was an alcoholic with very little money to support him, had two sisters living nearby. Only when her father died was she able to talk with her aunts. Deirdre remembered:

> *"He [father] had two sisters, like my aunties. Very old ladies, in their eighties. And all I wanted, I was saying 'why didn't one of you take care of us... why didn't you take care of us?' And they said 'oh no they couldn't.' Hmm because my dad was adamant that he would put us in the orphanage. But when my [oldest] sister came over [from the United States] and I said 'All this Irish hospitality and people are kind, why couldn't they look after us?' And she said 'because they were horrible... they didn't like my mum because she came from a different part of Ireland.'"[44]*

Her story tells of the divide in families but also between people from different parts of Ireland. Her mother was from Mayo and had met her father when he was stationed as a soldier there. He brought her back home with him to County Kildare where to her in-laws she was always regarded as an outsider. This had added to the lack of value of the girls in the family.

Not all the interviewees had the experience of being treated les favourably because they were girls and for some the realisation that the daughters were to emigrate had persuaded the parents to give preference to girls, giving them more years of education.[45] Edna's mother was able to push her daughters to get a good education but was less successful with her sons.

When she was asked if there was a difference in valorisation between girls and boys, she said:

> *"Hmm, I don't think so really. We weren't anyway. If anything the girls were treated education wise better that the boys. But I think that might have been because the boys didn't want to. But definitely we were, I went to college and everything in Ireland. And hmm, the boys said that often funny enough as a joke when they had a good bit to drink. They said that all the girls are well educated and the boys aren't. But I think the boys were not as keen in school merely as the girls."*[46]

As Mary Kenny points out:

> *"From the late 19th century onwards, there was an emphasis on convent education for girls, and in some cases in rural Ireland, daughters might get preference in education- a farmer might want his son to stay at home and take over the farm, while he would calculate that a daughter could make a better marriage if she had 'the bit of polish' that convent education was said to impart."*[47]

The importance for boys to do well on the farm, to cope with the physical chores, would have had an impact on their behaviour and interest in school. Edna was the only girl in the village who did not go to the local convent school but her mother was put under pressure by other women to send her there because this was seen as a more appropriate type of school for a farmer's daughter than co-educational college, despite evidence that girls were pushed academically in the college.

In immigrant families, Irish gender roles continued to be passed on, stressing a difference in upbringing and positions within the family order of brothers and sisters. Eileen felt that her task of looking after her younger brother was made more difficult because he was able to misbehave knowing that she would get blamed. Eileen told me:

> *"the youngest one of all, he was about... I was seven when he was born, so by the time he was sort of... coming up to school age, I was about ten or eleven, and I had to take him to school, and ooh. I used*

> *to get told off if I was late at school, and it used to worry me. And he was one of these children that needed to go so slowly walking, and the more you wanted him to move along, the less he would do, and I nearly used to tear my hair out! And I used to say "I'm gonna get into trouble." I used to plead with him "Please hurry up, I'll be late, I'll be late". But... No matter. I used to say to her [mum] "He made me late again, for school". But she didn't do anything about it. She just said "Oh... you just have to get Larry as soon as you can". She didn't worry about it, you know."*[48]

Her mother was much milder in her approach to her sons. It could be argued that her suffering husband and the many casualties during the First World War had made her fear their future and the loss of a son during another war. But the fact still remained that as Eileen explained it:

> *"They were boys, so they were sort of a class apart."*[49]

Most interviewees talked about the difference in treatment of their brothers by their mothers. Perhaps this is more keenly felt because mothers spent more time with their children than the fathers. Shiobhan, another woman on the Harold Hill Estate, remembered the difference between her and her brother. Her mother had grown up in Galway Ireland and had met her father there; he had come first to Galway to find work they then both decided to move to London to find work there. They had three children but the oldest, a boy, died after birth. Shiobhan believed that her mother favoured her brother because of the loss of the other boy, Shiobhan recalled:

> *"My brother was younger than me, and he was treated like a God, an absolute God. I think 'cos my mum lost a boy, then had me, and then had a boy whom she named the same name. She lost a John, and then had a John, and he was treated absolutely like a God. Yes, he was an absolute God; different rules to me, completely different."*[50]

The female role of caring and serving was part and parcel of daughters' upbringing and made equal status impossible. As Siobhan explained:

> *"It wasn't until we started to get bigger, and we'd say 'Now look, we do it, they should do it. Why should we run after them, we're not their servants?'"*[51]

For the girls the sometimes-turbulent relationships with their brothers was often part of the preparation of their future roles as wives. All hostilities were to be suppressed so that later in life the girl could take on her subordinate status of wife and mother. It was a way of forcing humility on young girls in order to make them accept their proper place in life. The differences between boys and girls were not simply linked up with the inheritance of the land or the importance to do hard physical labour around the farm. They were also culturally and religiously determined. Girls were to take on the subordinate role in which the Virgin Mary excelled and were therefore preparing for their place in the home sphere and girls like Siobhan were prepared for their lives as mothers and wives. Shiobhan grew up in Islington and moved to the Harold Hill Estate after her marriage. Her mother came from County Kerry and had met her father on her way over to London where she came to work as a nanny and maid in St John's Wood. Shiobhan had a very different upbringing from her brother she remembers:

> *"Yes, my mum did too. You have to be ladylike, very ladylike. The boys... We were told the cooking and cleaning and stuff like that. The boys... didn't do anything, really, it was not expected of them to do that."*[52]

Sex and Catholicism

Preparing girls for life also meant that they needed protection from the outside world particularly when it involved boys other than their own brothers. In Catholic society sex was very much a closed topic. In Ireland after the Irish Free State was established in 1922 and the constitution adopted by the Irish people in 1937 which declared Ireland to be "a sovereign, independent, democratic state," and the Irish Free State was renamed Eire, there was a genuine desire to create a great new pure and above all un-British society. In this new world the Catholic Church became its censor and safeguard against all things regarded as impure and improper. But in the rest of Europe, the First World War had brought about fear of an increase in venereal disease and loosening sexual morals.[53] This created a chain reaction amongst Church leaders but also feminist groups demanding tighter controls on moral conduct. The latter saw venereal diseases as a direct threat to women everywhere. The British National League against Venereal Disease founded in 1924 discovered that one in five soldiers carried at least one of the various venereal diseases. Therefore the concern was based on real dangers to health.[54] But sexuality remained a big issue for the Catholics even after the Second World War and the topics remained the same. At some point sexuality was always connected with the family as Christina remembers. She went to university in the 1950s and read a book that became popular amongst students:

"There was a book by a David Lodge, 'How Far Can You Go' and it is a story of Catholics brought up in the fifties, about sexual moralities and things like that. But it describes perfectly. I mean I smile, he was probably my contemporary at university, probably from a proper Catholic family, going off to university. And these hilarious things about how far can you go sexually shows the whole atmosphere of the London University in the 1950s, for a Catholic and the great questions were nearly as then as is now. It had nearly always to do with abortion. Contraception wasn't an issue because it hadn't come up really. But it was always about mother and baby controversies and ethics was nearly always (the topics)"

On the whole the interest stirred in the general public surrounding matters of birth control made an impact on Ireland. But although birth control was condemned in many quarters it was also an education in others. Mary Kenny writes that:

"Novels and stories began to imply that there were ways and means of preventing the consequences of sex...but the overall view was still having babies was the natural consequence of marriage."[55]

The way in which the Church viewed sex and contraception had an impact on the lives of Irish Catholic women and their families. It was also very important how the local priest dealt with the whole concept of sexual relationships and birth, which automatically affected the women of the parish in Harold Hill.

Aoife felt very confused and affronted by apparent contradiction that the Church forced her to have a family in one sense whilst at the same time forcing her to repent for it in the other. Aoife argued:

> *"You supposed to have committed - what was the sin?... Original sin. It was to be, and yet you were told to get married increase and multiply but you couldn't go into anybody's house when you weren't first in the church to be churched."*[56]

When asked if her husband had to perform a ritual after the birth of their children she said:

> *"No, we were the sinner".*[57]

Eileen remembered it well:

> *"And I think I went to mass about ten days after the baby was born, and the priest said "Oh, if you come to church", he said "I say a prayer over you" and I could never seemed to find out, because, to me I used to think, if you, had... A confinement, and you had a healthy child, you would really be going to church to offer thanksgiving for a safe delivery."*

It became part of Church rituals that were probably connected with the negative aspect of the birth itself. The placenta, for instance, was called *sordes* in Latin, which means filth. In Catholic tradition the whole process of childbirth belonged to the realm of the Devil, it had something dark and sordid about it. Luther brought the concept of childbirth into the light and placed it at the heart of Protestant concept of calling; God had created women to give birth and if a woman should die during childbirth she was still considered clean and was buried in consecrated ground. This was because Luther argued that she had died doing her duty in God's eyes. The sexual act from which the creation of new life sprung was not considered sinful in Lutheran ideology.[58] If a woman had an impotent husband she was even allowed to share her bed with another man who would be able to satisfy her sexual desire and give her children according to Luther:

177

> *Suppose I should counsel the wife of an impotent man, with his consent, to giver herself to another, say her husband's brother, but to keep this marriage secret and to ascribe the children to the so-called putative father. The question is: Is such a women in a saved state? I answer, certainly.*[59]

But under other circumstances the sexual act was an important part of the marriage alone.[60] This is where Catholicism widely differs from Protestantism. To Catholics, intercourse was a necessary evil. The Catholic counter-reformation however maintained the status quo in relation to childbirth and its perception as sinful and unclean remained.[61]

The local priest in St Dominic's tried to turn 'churching' into a family occasion which made it a much more attractive ritual, as Aoife recalled:

> *"I remember when I was being churched after Father put a stole on you in the yard in the front of the church and he would lead you in and would lead all the way up to the altar and [to] Pat and Marian [The kids] he'd say 'come on bring your supporters' he said 'bring them up - in the church [You] with the two girls, that [was] lovely."*[62]

The way in which the parish priest was trying to include the other children is rather interesting, they were after all innocent little children and there was no need for 'churching' them. He appeared to have understood how sensitive this issue was felt by the young mothers and was perhaps not in total agreement with the custom of churching but had to proceed in order to follow rules and traditions. For Edna there were far from positive memories of Irish priests back home who encountered sexual behaviour before marriage amongst the youngsters. Her memories conjure up images of complete control by the parish priest on the whole community and she contrasted this with the attitude of parish priests in Harold Hill. She recalled how the local parish priest in Ireland was obsessed with catching young local courting couples and how he policed the area. Edna described:

> *"The priests were – very strict at that time, you know, very, very strict. I mean the 'creamer', as you go out to our house, in that direction anyway, and he would [go] round the back every night*

> *with a torch and stuff. You know, to see if there were any girls and boys- and would call their names off the pulpit."[63]*

The whole concept of sex was controlled by the Church with help of enthusiastic priests. The parish priest of her little village went as far as to shame couples who 'got caught', she said:

> *"There was one couple [that] got married and they were pregnant. And he would read [it] off the pulpit, which was really, really bad. Even as young as I was I thought that was a terrible thing. And [he] gave a whole speech about it and the bloke got out and went up and punched the priest."[64]*

Edna herself married in 1963, in England, when she was only eighteen and was soon afterwards expecting her first baby. Although living in Britain, she could not be persuaded to take the pill, she said:

> *"Well you could have it here. In this country but hmm, you know.. but it wasn't agreed. You know."[65]*

But unlike the priests she had known in Ireland, the parish priests she met in England were able to help her make her own choice, as she explained:

> *"-The priest was very good, the priests were different here than they would have been in Ireland. The priests were very good, they sort of said that God doesn't expect you to bring a load of children in to the world, that you cannot look after, but you have to go to your own conscience to see whether this would mean, you know the way you deal with it."[66]*

The Irish Catholics in Harold Hill did respect their parish priests but as Edna argued that the men who were sent there to deal with their flock differed from the priests she knew back in Ireland. It suggests that there was not so much an erosion of powers of the priest as Hornsby-Smith argues but a different approach by the priests sent out to work abroad as they dealt differently with topics such as intercourse.[67]

For Catholics, sex was a very complex issue. On the one hand it was never to be explored or consciously experienced by Catholic couples, but on the other hand it was vital for the Church that Catholic families would grow in size and that couples had productive intercourse. But the whole concept of sex was taboo. It was a topic that was not to be touched on by laymen. The laws were laid down by the educated celibate churchmen, laws that were checked rigorously by the parish priests in Ireland as Edna's story explained. To 'church' women after the birth also demonstrated the dirt connected to the birth as it was a reminder of the intercourse and even the possibility of pleasure. But this taboo subject had to be talked about by the Catholic parents when their own children came of age.

Preparing girls for their marriage and sexual intercourse was in a way expected of the parents, but it remained a difficult concept. It was preferred that children would know as little as possible so that they would stay as pure as possible in their thoughts. As has been discussed on page 10 booklets were used by the Catholic Church to guide parents. Most of the booklets used by the Catholic Church were published by the *Catholic Truth Society*, a charity that was operating from London. The reason for the distribution of the Catholic Church's own booklets could well have been a reaction to the increasingly liberal tone used by the British authorities.[68] Many Catholic children received their education in state schools with a Protestant emphasis. As has been discussed earlier the attitude of Protestants' teaching on sexual conduct was widely different and far more liberal than that of the Catholic Church. From their interest in the booklets and their sense of duty to distribute them it appears that the Bishops were concerned about the influence of these schools and the secular/Protestant society that surrounded the Catholic laity.

What parents were allowed to discuss with their children was precisely outlined in this booklet. It claimed that the sex instruction that was encouraged in secular education by the authorities were far too detailed and the author Reverent Aidan Pickering argued this was not necessary. The priest argued further that it was a mother's task to tell children how babies developed during pregnancy and how they were breast-fed. The father's role in sex education was to discuss the marriage act. The mother's role was to teach the girls all about their role as mother and wife, but for both genders the actual sex act itself was not to be explained. What fathers then had to tell the boys was not a description of what actually took place during intercourse but a reference to the need for 'something to take place.' They were advised to speak to their children at the age of 12. The sex acts were referred to in terms of acts of purity and impure behaviour, pure and impure thoughts. Impurity was everything without marriage and impure thoughts were everything based on lust. Pure meant all the sexual activities that were connected with marriage and with the development of new life. Intercourse as such was not to be mentioned to young people and indeed was not mentioned in the entire book. Significantly the book ended with a prayer to Our Lady.

According to the Catholic Church in Ireland as well as England, becoming a mother was the central role in a woman's life. The preparation for that role and the attempt to tell a young girl the facts of life at all was therefore a necessary evil. But she was to model herself on Mary who had not had intercourse to produce her child Jesus. The lesser mortals, ordinary Catholic girls, should be told but told as little as possible to keep them from harm.

Deirdre remembered how she was taught the facts of life by the nuns in her orphanage in Ireland on the day she was to leave its 'safe' walls for work outside in 1951, she said:

> *"When you were leaving hmm, you were taken in the office, the nun said... this was exactly what she said: 'don't go down any lanes with soldiers or you become pregnant.' And those were the facts of life. The other girls, the older ones knew a bit so they tell you little bits, you know."*[69]

In Deirdre's case, the 'lesson' did what it was meant to do, that is scaring her off anybody in uniform. She recalled:

> *"From the convent they used to send a lot of girls from the orphanage to work in different places. And where they sent me to do laundry work you know, poor thing... there was a big army...You can imagine, I saw a soldier I run a mile."*[70]

Preparing girls for their adult sex life and the moral responsibility that came with it appears to have been considered. Although embarrassing to talk about and limited in what should be discussed it was still the view of the Catholic Church that girls needed to be informed. The whole reason for going to the trouble of talking to her in the first place, clearly something the sister felt uncomfortable with and wanted to leave her with as little information as possible, was connected with the expectations and the reputation young girls would have in the community. Especially an orphan girl like Deirdre had to be kept safe and respectable before marriage and that was more important to the convent than helping her with her first experience during her wedding night.

The importance of having babies to Catholic women and their role as mothers determined their future, as Edna explained:

> *"I think one thought really you were a woman and that was your role in life, you got married."*[71]

After children were born, many Irish immigrant women gave up paid work as they would have been obliged to do in Ireland. Some, like Christina's mother, carried on working alongside their husband. Christina's mother, as was mentioned in chapter 4, came from Cork City, where she had done her science degree and had worked in England in 1929-1931 as a science teacher for a Catholic all-girls school before joining her husband in his surgery. But most women in England were not in the situation where they had to assist their husbands after their marriage. They would often spend time at home attending to their children until they were old enough to go to school and a part time job was then possible. Most of the women that were interviewed had a part time job to supplement their husband's earnings around that time. They spent their time working at home which was not only expected of them by their religious background but it was also expected by their spouse. As has been described by Warner, subordination and servitude in Irish women centred round the kitchen and household chores were especially stressed in Irish teaching on Mary.[72]

Although many talked with fondness of their paid working days, lack of childcare facilities and expectations in their own family and community made an outside working life difficult if not impossible. They were to know their place, which was to support the order of things, as Patrick argued:

> *"That is why you have all the break-ups. Here the women do all the work. I said that to Father [the parish priest at the time of St Dominic's, Harold Hill], I said when they took the apron off the woman and put a fag in her hand and a gin and tonic in the other, I said... that's finished."*[73]

Patrick's words are a good illustration as to how the position of working women was defined. Paid work meant a cigarette and alcohol, or enough independence to take time off for the wife/mother to enjoy herself. As the Church had argued, the woman was there to support her husband and family and stay at home and even in England the lack of childcare made choice unlikely. If they had to work they were often forced to leave their babies back in Ireland, as was the case with Caitlin's oldest son and with Siobhan and her siblings. Their parents had to take their children back to Ireland to stay with relatives, whilst their mothers continued to undertake paid work, as the income from the spouse was insufficient or suitable accommodation could not be found. Caitlin remembered her mother's upset when she had to take him back with her to England:

> *"Tim, he was with my mother, my mother wanted to keep him forever, she loved him, she loved him. He was a lovely boy, he had fair hair, and my grandmother was all mad about him. And all the neighbours were I lived, Oh, oh, they were all crying around when I brought him back. But I had to bring him back, because I had to get him into school and that, you know. It was not easy getting them into school, you only had so many places and so hmm, you had to do all that."*[74]

The reason for leaving children with grandparents in Ireland was often job related or a result of the lack of affordable housing as Siobhan explains:

> *"I think the [land]lady died, and I think that my mother had to move out, which was silly, because what they had to do then was to go back to Ireland, leave the children with my mum's parents, my nan and granddad, and then they came here to look for somewhere to live where they could have the children. So it took them six months to find somewhere."*[75]

After the problems were resolved most children went back to live with their parents.

Religious traditions and the Virgin Mary

According to the interviewees, it was typical for the Irish women in England to pass on many of their traditions whilst at home, and to use the Virgin Mary as a role model for their daughters, who were to be future mothers themselves. Shona, a second-generation immigrant, born in East London remembered how Mary was of great importance to her mother:

> *"She is an icon to my mum. She used to say 'what a beautiful woman she is, would you not like to be like her?' And as a child I would think 'Yes I do want to be like her."*[76]

This icon was subject of many prayers and poems. Ciara copied one in her Brownie diary, in an undated entry just after a dated entry of 3 September 1939:

> *Our lady!*
> *She was fair.*
> *Truth in her eye*
> *And love*
> *The sun made gold her chestnut hair,*
> *Her gown was graceful, tied with blue;*
> *Her manner gracious through and through.*
> *No angel could more lightly tread*
> *Than she when through fields she sped.*
>
> *Our lady!*
> *When she went by Old men bowed them low*
> *And though of snow*
> *When she went by;*
> *Young men vowed that they for her*
> *Would gladly die*
> *And little children ceased their play;*
> *To watch her smile and hear her pray;*
> *There was a sweetness in her voice*

That made their little hearts rejoice. (poet unknown)

The characteristics being highlighted here are a mixture of that of a virgin, the pure state for a woman to be in, and the majestic queen to whom all men bow. Even the most respected men of the community, the older wiser men, bow to her. Then there is a beauty in her voice and her whole being is so pure and therefore only beauty is within her. It is a symbolic poem that uses messages that have been part of the traditions of the Catholic faith. It sounds similar to Spencer's *Faery Queene* where Spencer is successfully transferring the qualities of the Queen Mary to his Queen Elizabeth using metaphors and symbolism that was traditionally Mary's terrain.[77] She was an example not only to the family but also in schools. As Siobhan recalled:

> *"You were brought up at school like that; the nuns were like that as well. It was very much to be like Mary."*[78]

Shona in recounting her idea of Mary explained:

> *"Yes it was: Saintly, homely, and not a real person, really to think of it in today's terms, a person who would have done everything for everyone else, but nothing for what they wanted to do."*[79]

Moulding girls in such an image made caring work very honourable and it is apparent that the teachings greatly influenced young minds. Women were told to act out Mary, to be just like her and this internalisation of Mary made it easy for women talk about their work as mothers but difficult to talk about Mary in a more philosophical way.

The place Mary held in Catholic traditions connects directly with the place mothers held in the lives of their daughters. Mary was in a sense a connection point between mothers and their daughters. She was placed at the heart of this bond that glued women together. Mary was the embodiment of motherhood. Central to the future of the daughter was the role of mother, who gave help or advice. The role left to her in the community was an extension of the role she held at home as a mother and the training she received in her childhood was all to prepare her for the role of mother including caring work as teachers and nurses.

Mary was not just an example; the Virgin was also a place of rescue. Women could discuss all their worries in their prayers to Mary in private. They also used the Rosary when saying their prayers with their families. The devotion to Mary and the prayers could also be said anywhere without being in church, and were often said in the home. For Shona's mother it was hard to visit the church as she worked long hours and was only allowed one afternoon off a week. The prayers to Mary were therefore even more important, Shona discussed how:

> *"She used to pray quietly to herself as well, with the Rosary beads, she used to pray in her room. She used to say it was the only thing that kept her sane at times. She didn't stay there, she went to another job then – she used to keep a statue of the Virgin Mary, and that always been with her, in her case [suitcase] when she went from job to job."*[80]

It was often part of a family tradition: Christina told us:

> *"In the family we did try to keep the Irish customs as saying the rosary in the evenings. So family prayers were important. - our Irish family always stuck to it. But my father used to like try and say the rosary if we possibly could even in the car on our way home after a dance."*[81]

But it was not as if people were very intensely concentrating on the prayers said. According to Christina it was speed that counted:

> *"We had what we call a family rosary said at such speed. [she mimics quick mumbling] and we take it in turns to give up the rosary as they say the rosary. So we say the rosary at night at such speed it would take only ten minutes really."*

This did not mean that it would be forgotten about even when visitors came to the house:

> *"And we, we, people who stayed with us became used to the fact that you disappear into the armchair and we used to kneel there and had our heads half set on the armchair so that we were comfortable. And*

> *it was a ritual you know, I mean, you would meditate but you were so busy getting through this so quickly. It was a sort of ritual a mental ritual almost but yes it was an important one for us."*

This family getting together using rituals like praying with the rosary was seen by Hornsby-Smith as that type of Catholicism he refers to as working class. The more personally felt and lived faith in the latter part of the 20th century is considered middle class by Hornsby-Smith.[82] But the story of Christina suggests something different. It suggest that the middle classes were also using rituals and group prayers and perhaps it was more a sign of the times in which society was on the whole based on families and group structures unlike the more recent period when individuality has become more dominant in the whole of our western society. In Ireland especially large families working together on the family farm would have been very much based on this group structure.

Mary was to most Catholics the saint to pray to during illness and particularly when in childbirth. Aoife said:

> *"When anybody was in labour we always say 'Oh Our Lady help them you were in labour yourself.' You know, or anyone losing a son I say 'Help them, you lost a son' you know, I talk to her like I hmm I am talking to you now."*[83]

In the official teachings of the Church Mary was not believed to have suffered labour pains or had a normal labour. This made her so important to the Church as she was not stained with a normal child labour. But women on the contrary held her in high esteem and prayed to her because she could be identified with. As the Church did its utmost with the childbirth theory to set her apart from ordinary women, to women it was the fact that they could identify themselves with her that made her so special. All women interviewed felt connected with her as she was like them and someone who would understand them. As Eileen explains when asked why she was important to her:

> *"Because she was a mother, you see, so I think that if you are a mother yourself, you can see her in the role of a mother."*[84]

Mary would bring relief and could be prayed to: she as well as her son was important in times of need as Christina explained:

> *"My mother's family was prone to diphtheria, three of her brothers died of diphtheria, not one but three. My mothers' family was quite small, but infant mortality and lack of vaccination well that is terrible really in the family. That were disasters but they had these prayers against the burden of these disasters. We had the Sacred Heart, we had pictures of the Sacred Heart on the wall and several statues of Our Lady."*

Visual images were reminders that families were not alone when suffering grief and that they should always find time for a prayer as the almighty and his mother were able to give them strength and comfort. Aoife Caitlin Christina Deirdre and Caitlin had pictures of the Sacred Heart as well as statues of the Virgin Mary in their living rooms. They were hanging along the family photos as if they belonged and were treasured amongst the other relatives.

Conclusion

This chapter indentifies the importance of the Catholic doctrine on family life and shows the importance of the role of the mother. It clearly underlines the difference in status and upbringing between siblings of the two genders and how gender roles were enforced. The study demonstrates the great impact that the Catholic Church's taboo on sexual conduct had on married women and shows the impact of the Virgin Mary on the expectations that were placed on women both by their families and themselves, demonstrating that their customs and traditions were being upheld. Mary had a very central place in the lives of these women, from their upbringing in Ireland, and much of it continued in their lives in England.

Continuities between Ireland and England and the importance of Catholicism in the family lives of women in England are clearly illustrated in women's' personal accounts. Irish ways of life were incorporated into an English suburb, but these traditions were carried on largely behind closed doors in a predominantly Protestant and secular part of England. Irish women's traditions were supported by their parish priests, who were often of Irish descent or from their communities back home, with which most women kept in contact. Most women kept in touch through letters and visits and some even had their children placed with their relatives back in Ireland whilst they searched for work or accommodation. Within the families there was evidence of internal control of mothers over daughters and sons and fathers over mothers but also in the wider family. Young girls objected to the higher status of their brothers and rebelled within the family as powers of control continued to lay in the hands of men supported by their mothers. Within the community the glue of traditions and morals created a more lateral power, which allowed the Church to be at the heart of the community as it was at the heart of family life. Mothers would also use the image of the Virgin Mary to control their daughters and women become silent as Shortall says:

> *"The powerless group is silent about its non-involvement since it has no forum within which it can be vocal."*[85]

Within the Irish Catholic community, women formed the link between home and community. The role that was placed upon their shoulders mirrored the example of a serving Virgin Mary. The serving and assisting role was fulfilled inside the home as daughters, mothers and wives but the spheres of the home and the community overlap, as the next chapter will explore. Women often felt close to Mary because they internalised her and were acting out Mary but were not always close to Catholic teachings on the Mary figure. The next chapter also explores the important role Irish women played in rebuilding the new community on the Harold Hill Estate, the relationship between their faith and their activities in the community through paid and unpaid work and the effect this had on the community in which they lived.

Footnotes

[1] In the early 20th century, Robert Baden-Powell, a famous army general, developed a scheme for training boys. And set up a camp on Brownsea Island in 1907 and the following year published them in a book, Scouting for Boys. The Boy Scout Movement was born. At the Scouts' first rally, at the Crystal Palace in 1909, a small group of girls turned up. In 1910 he formed the Girl Guides, with his sister Agnes in charge.

[2] Ciara Diary study p. 3 (her first entry disclosing this fact is on 05-10-1941)

[3] The Children of Mary, was an organization for young women/girls which was very successful across Europe throughout the 20th century. It was founded by St. Catherine Laboure in 1835 and was based on The Sodality of Our Lady (also known as the Sodality of the Blessed Virgin Mary a society that was founded by the Belgian Jesuit Jan Leunis in 1563. The girls or children of Mary went through a special type training that would prepare them for life later on in which they would be able to serve others with patience and grace like their patron had done. After the six months training they were officially accepted as Children of Mary and where then allowed to wear the Virgin's colour blue.

[4] Ciara Diary 1938-unknown p. 3

[5] BDA files; file 1950-1960

[6] Cowley U. (2001) *The Men that built Britain, a History of the Irish Navvy*, Dublin

[7] McCullough, C. (1991) 'A Tie That Blinds: Family Ideology In Ireland', in: *Economic and Social Review* vol 22 London, pp. 199-211

[8] Ranke Heineman U. (1990) *Eunuchs for the Kingdom of Heaven. Women, Sexuality, and the Catholic Church*, chapt. 25

[9] Eileen (Greater London, 1995; name altered), Interview 5, transcript p. 3

[10] Eileen interview 5 p. 1

[11] Eileen interview 5 p. 3

[12] Eileen interview 5 p. 3

[13] Patrick and Aoife (Greater London), 1999 (names altered), Interview 1, transcript p. 11

[14] Patrick and Aoife Interview 1 p. 2

[15] Patrick and Aoife Interview 1 p. 2

[16] Edna (Greater London), 1999 (names altered), Interview 3, transcript p. 10

[17] McCullough, C. 'A Tie That Blinds: Family Ideology In Ireland', in: *Economic and Social Review* volume 22, (London 1991) p. 206

[18] Edna Interview 3, p. 7

[19] BDA File 1950-160 *on education* : author unknown *My Dear Daughter* Catholic Printing Company of Farnworth, (Lancaster 11th October 1958)

[20] BDA File 1950-1960

[21] BDA File 1950-1960

[22] BDA File 1950-1960 *on education*: *My Dear Daughter* Catholic Printing Company of Farnworth, (Lancaster 1958)

[23] BDA File 1950-160 author unknown *My Dear Daughter*

[24] BDA File 1950-1960

[25] Ciara dairy pp. 4-5

[26] Ciara diary p. 5

[27] Ciara diary p. 3

[28] Thompson, C.R. (1965) *The Colloquies of Erasmus*, London, pp. 88-98
[29] Ciara diary p. 1
[30] Caira diary p. 3
[31] Hondagneu-Sotelo,P. (1994) *Gendered Transitions: Mexican Experiences of Immigration*, California
[32] Daly, M.E. (1995) *Irish Women's Voices Past And Present*, Chapt.: *Women in the Irish Free State 1922-1939. The Interaction Between Economies and Ideology*, Indianapolis
[33] Beale, J. (1986) *Women in Ireland. Voices of Change*, London, p. 7
[34] Gray, B. *Unmasking Irishness: Irish Women*, p. 211
[35] Brown, T. (1985) *Ireland a Social and Cultural History 1922 to the Present*, London, p. 21
[36] Brown, T. *Ireland a Social and Cultural History 1922 to the Present*, p. 21
[37] Chapter 1 p. 4
[38] Brown, T. *Ireland a Social and Cultural History 1922 to the Present*, p. 68
[39] McCullough, C. (1991) 'A Tie That Blinds: Family Ideology In Ireland', in: *Economic and Social Review vol 22*, London, pp. 199-211
[40] Arensberg, C. and Kimball, S. (1968) 'Family and Community in Ireland', in: *A tie that blinds: Family and Ideology in Ireland* in *Economic and Social Review* vol 22, no3 1991 Cambridge, pp. 199-211
[41] O'Dowd, A. (1994) 'Women in Rural Ireland in the Nineteenth and Early Twentieth Centuries-how the Daughters and the Sisters of small Farmers and Landless Labourers Fared', in: *Rural History vol. 5.2*
[42] 'Embodying the Nation – the West of Ireland Landscape and Irish Identity' Cronin, M. and O'Connor, B. (eds), in: *Tourism and Ireland: a Critical Analysis* (Cork 1993)
[43] O'Dowd, A. (1994) *Women in Rural Ireland in the Nineteenth and Early Twentieth Centuries*, Cambridge, p. 174
[44] Deirdre (Greater London), 1999 (names altered), Interview 6, transcript p. 6
[45] Fitzpatrick (1986) *A share of the Honeycomb*, London
[46] Edna interview 3 p. 2
[47] Kenny, Mary (1997) *Goodbye To Catholic Ireland*, London p. 296
[48] Eileen interview 5 p. 5
[49] Eileen interview 5 p. 5
[50] Shona and Siobhan Greater London, 1995 (names altered), Interview 7, transcript p. 6
[51] Shona & Siobhan interview 7 p. 7
[52] Shona & Siobhan interview 7 p. 6
[53] Kenny, Mary *Goodbye To Catholic Ireland*, chapt. 6
[54] Kenny, Mary *Goodbye To Catholic Ireland*, chapt. 6
[55] Kenny, Mary *Goodbye To Catholic Ireland*, p. 152
[56] Patrick & Aoife interview 1 p. 7
[57] Patrick & Aoife interview 1 p. 7
[58] Roper L. (1994) *Oedipus and the Devil*, London, p. 19
[59] Ley D.J. (2009) *Insatiable wives: women who stray and the men who love them*, London, p. 89
[60] Roper L. *Oedipus and the Devil*, pp. 94-95

[61] Roper, L. *Oedipus and the Devil*, p. 19
[62] Patrick & Aoife interview 1 p. 7
[63] Edna interview 3 p. 5
[64] Edna interview 3 p. 5
[65] Edna interview 3 p. 5
[66] Edna interview 3 p. 5
[67] Hornsby-Smith (1991) *Roman Catholic Beliefs in England. Customary Catholicism and Transformations of Religious Authority*, Cambridge, p. 142
[68] BDA file 1950-1960
[69] Deirdre interview 6 p. 2
[70] Deirdre interview 6 p. 2
[71] Edna interview p. 6
[72] Warner M. (1976) *Alone of All Her Sex, The Cult of the Virgin Mary*, London, p. 190
[73] Aoife interview p. 17
[74] Caitlin Interview 2, transcript p. 8
[75] Shona & Siobhan Interview 7, transcript p. 3
[76] Shona & Siobhan interview 7 p. 3
[77] Spencer, E. (1966) *The Faerie Queene*, Reprinted Oxford
[78] Shona & Siobhan interview 7 p. 3
[79] Shona & Siobhan interview 7 p. 3
[80] Shona & Siobhan interview 7 p. 8
[81] Christina (Greater London), 1999 (name altered), Interview 4, transcript p. 7
[82] Hornsby-Smith M.P. (2004) *The changing identity of Catholic in England in Religion identity and change*, London, p. 4
[83] Aoife & Patrick interview 1 p. 17
[84] Eileen interview 5 p. 5
[85] Shortall S. (1992) 'Power Analysis and Farm Wives: An Emperical Study of the power relationships Affecting Women on Irish farms', in: *Sociologia Ruralis* vol. 32 pp. 431-451

CHAPTER 6: CATHOLIC IRISH WOMEN IN HAROLD HILL

This chapter discusses the Irish Catholic women in the community of Harold Hill and explores an under-researched area by their own oral testimonies and local archival and newspaper material. By researching their stories we are able to examine their contribution to the community and the impact their numbers had on the area. It also discusses the reasons for leaving Ireland and the migration patterns that emerge. As the reasons why people leave are often of great consequence to the migration patterns and the lives they lead after settling in their new surroundings, the influence this had on their lives after they settled in Harold Hill needs to be examined. It explores how the paid and unpaid work of Irish Catholic women helped the Catholic community of Harold Hill. Many women undertook paid or unpaid work outside of the family, and raised their children without the support of extended families; therefore their lives differed from the lives of their mothers in Ireland. They had to prove resourceful and able to rebuild their lives. It also shows that changes in lifestyle were also the result of contact with the English community, through places of work, neighbourhoods and intermarriage.

There is an exploration of how their Catholic upbringing and their cultural connections affected their choices in work and their lives on the estate. It examines how their choice of work, paid or unpaid, was related to the influence Mary held as a role model. How the women recreated an Irish social and Catholic community life on the new estate is discussed. Furthermore, this chapter explores their search for a new life and their involvement in parish life and how this new life embraced changes and where it kept the old traditions. It will examine how the unique rural background of these women was transformed into their new community.
It is important to consider the impact the movement of 2,900 Irish Catholics into the estate had on the Diocese of Brentwood during the late 1940s and the 1950s. It will explore why the Church set such importance on Catholic education and its struggle to find school places for children of the newcomers. It will also look at the instructions given to parents of children outside RC schools, the catechism as an education aid and the use of lay catechists. I will discuss the Church's fear of lapsation of the laity in the modern Post War period and specifically explore the work of the Ursuline

Sisters of Brentwood in setting up a new school and how they, with help of laywomen, they succeeded in educating the children on the estate. As many sisters and some teachers that worked in the school were of Irish background, it is important to consider the impact Irish women had on the very young.[1]

As has been briefly discussed in chapter 4, Romford had a thriving Catholic community since the mid 19th century. Its congregation was growing due to the building of the Eastern Railway, which opened on 18th June 1838 and saw the station opened in 1839. The local population remember tales of the Irish navvies who were involved with the building of the railway and who then settled in Romford.[2] In St Edwards Church registers from 1852 onwards, many Irish names appear that back up the argument that their number was growing, but typical English names also appear.[3] In the case of Irish women married to English men, the Irish marker disappears gradually in the registers. The place of birth of the parents is not mentioned in cases of baptism. Only the place name where the Catholics had lived prior to their marriage is reported in the registers making it impossible to track down from these church registers alone where the Irish names originate from or whether they are first or second generation Irish. The registers of St Edwards do reveal that in most cases people had lived previously in local communities in villages either in Essex or in East London.[4] Between 1940 and 1944 there was a steady increase in Irish names in St Edwards's baptism records, and then again an increase during the 1950s.[5]

Harold Hill residents

From the interviewees we get an insight who the new Irish settlers of the Harold Hill estate were and how they had migrated. From evidence provided by the interviewees, we learn that other groups of Irish Catholics that came to settle on the Harold Hill estate had travelled throughout England and Wales in search of jobs. Edna's father had been working as a miner in Wales and he had found her first job there. Edna had served as a domestic worker with many families and had moved gradually to London and from there out onto the estate.[6] Christina's father had been serving as a General Practitioner also in Wales before moving on to London. According to Christina, there was a thriving Irish community working in Wales with several Irish Doctors tending to them.[7] People like Aoife and Patrick had arrived in Harold Hill in the fifties after spending time much closer, in the Dagenham area.[8] Siobhan had settled just outside the estate, moving gradually out of London after growing up in the Catholic community of Ilford, which held very strong Irish links. Her mother came over to London during the 1930s and served as a live-in maid working for a Jewish family in East London.[9] Therefore the background of the Catholic community in the Harold Hill was gradually becoming more than just the Irish community from East London but what they all had in common was their Irish background and the need to leave Ireland.

Reasons for leaving Ireland

It is important to examine why people left Ireland and settled later on in Harold Hill as the reason for leaving often influenced much of the rest of their lives as migrants rebuilding their lives on the new estate. For Deirdre it had not been a matter of choice. She had been brought up in a home in Dublin after her mother had died and her father, an alcoholic of little means, could no longer cope. He brought his four girls to the orphanage whilst still caring for his two sons. Deirdre explained:

> "Then we moved to Kildare and my mother died when I was three. And we had to go into [the orphanage]... there were six of us and – me and my sisters had to go to an orphanage in Dublin. – And –, I stayed there until I was fifteen."[10]

The orphanage was run by the sisters of Mercy. As Deirdre remembered:

> "It was quite harsh. -and you know we had to do work. You know when we were in there, you know cleaning and that sort of thing... laundry."[11]

Her eldest sister stayed a few months but managed to run away from the home at the age of fourteen and was able to find work in Britain after lying about her age. The other sisters promised to look after each other and to get each other out of the orphanage. The second sister kept her promise and brought Deirdre over when she was only fifteen:

> *"Yes,- she was working and saved up and then went over to Ireland and took me. And then consequently when I was seventeen [I]- took my youngest sister."*[12]

The second sister had set up a job for Deirdre in Russell Square, central London, in a hotel as a live-in maid. Two years later, after much saving Deirdre returned to Ireland to collect her youngest sister who was just thirteen.

But the rules had in the meantime slightly changed, she explained:

> *"That was like a Ward of Court over there. That was the sort of the rule, you know, – was like... they took you there, they sign the paper, and you were in there until you were sixteen. They didn't make any fuss when I left, because I think they thought you know because they liked to get rid of me -."*[13]

It was no longer possible just to take her sister out and she had to therefore be careful, she said:

> *"But when I took my sister, I had said to my sister 'I come back for you.' Don't tell anyone, you know. So when I went to collect she couldn't help it but she told someone and someone told the nun."*[14]

Deirdre had to meet the sister and explain the purpose of her visit and the reason why she wanted to spend the day with her little sister outside the walls of the orphanage, Deirdre remembered:

> *"And the nun says to me 'Oh, I think, you are taking her to England, you know it is not allowed?' And I said I was not! 'I am taking her to Kildare you know where I am from!' And -I said 'Do you want to see my sailing ticket?' and she said 'No, no because one thing about you that I always say [is] that you never told a lie' And the reason I never used to lie, was because I was cheeky and I wouldn't you know, I say 'Yeah! I did it.' I wouldn't give them the satisfaction. So that was what they did so she said 'you never used to lie, you were always honest.'"*[15]

Deirdre had already grown accustomed to the world outside but the whole concept was new to her younger sister. Deirdre recalled:

> *"We went into a restaurant to eat. And I am watching my figure, and she is having just everything, you know. And hmm I fall asleep, because I am doing this journey and I had to be back at work the next morning. So... and I am nearly falling asleep and she is shaking me, and I go 'what?' and she says 'where do we wash up?' Thirteen years of age and she had never had anything where she didn't have to work for. And I said 'you never ever have to wash up!' Yeah, she couldn't believe it; you imagine a thirteen year old saying..."*[16]

What Deirdre identified as harsh in the orphanage was that the children had to work for everything: nothing was ever just given. The whole system was based on hard work for very young children. The reason for leaving Ireland for many women and men was, as Tilki examined, a way in which these children could escape abuse from these institutions.[17]

Deirdre told how she and her sister were able to get on board the boat by lying again about the age of the young passenger. When the escape was discovered back home, the orphanage wrote to the sisters in London and promised to send the police after them if the youngest would not return. The correspondence stopped when the Deirdre's eldest sister threatened to expose the harsh regime. Her little sister went on to stay with an aunt from her mother's side in London and even managed to receive an education there.

The O'Neill sisters were not the only ones who helped each other from the orphanage. Years later Deirdre met one of the girls who used to be in the same school. This former orphan girl was now living in the London area with her family. Deirdre said:

> *"But when she, her sister, took her over here she went to night school. And she went to see the doctor and the doctor said the reason she couldn't read or write was that she always associated it with fear. She was so beaten...she was beaten merciful because she couldn't read or write. But the nuns used to give her embroidery, you*

know, to make for clothes and stuff. And she did this so beautiful embroidery."[18]

After arriving in England, this young girl was sent by her sister to evening class to learn. There was a clear desire in the girls to improve on their education and the ambition to find decent jobs in England. It is an example of how difficult life could become after migration that was triggered by abuse and the lack of a home. As Ryan points out this ill prepared migration often caused greater difficulties in the migrants' future but Deirdre's friend also highlights that the abuse was the trigger for the migration and therefore the problems encountered later on in her life appear as a result of both things.[19] What Deirdre also showed was that in the orphanage children learned very little other than how to perform the basic chores and would have been ill prepared for life outside the convent and in particular life abroad.

Despite the anti-British sentiments in the convent Deirdre was determined to emigrate to England and never did regret her move, she said:

"I didn't know but I thought 'oh it sounds great!' Because if they were against it then it had to be great, because they were so awful... But it was greater than I imagined because people were so lovely and when you are fifteen and you meet kindness for the first time oh."[20]

Statements by the Church or figures of authority in the Church, about the degrading or even pagan lifestyle of the English did not deter young girls like Deirdre as Delaney points out:

"Ironically, rather than creating panic or anxiety such statements may have indirectly increased curiosity about life in 'immoral' England."[21]

Children like Deidre and her sisters fell outside the ideal family unit; her father did not run a self-sufficient family farm and her mother had died; there was little room and even less sympathy. The harsh regime of the home was the direct reason Deirdre wanted to go to England. It would give her freedom and independence in the form of a job and away from the powers of the Church. As the sisters of the orphanage held anti English views it made England in Deirdre's eyes a wonderful sounding place. Jackson and Mac Adam refer to England's importance to women shunned by Irish society. It was seen as a place of freedom and refuge. In Deirdre's account the orphans were not very different to them. It also demonstrates how the more vulnerable left for these shores and might explain the mental difficulties they then encountered. Deirdre married and lived for a while in East London, in the Docklands, before the house became too small and the only bigger accommodation available to her and her family was on the Harold Hill Estate.

Deirdre's was not the only example of a family move. Although her story of the orphanage was different from most, the concept of moving with other siblings was not. Siobhan (a daughter of Irish immigrant parents) explained the story of her mother:

> *"She came over on her own. She met her brother, he was already here. Then she stopped with him first of all, then she decided to stay before she found a job, and lived in. Then her sister came, then her other sister came and eventually there was five of them. That was the rule, wasn't it? Not just with my mum, but with my dad's family as well, his brothers, sisters, cousins, and all their friends."*[22]

This migration pattern of gradually moving more siblings/cousins into an area was common to all interviewees with the exception of four examples of immigrating as couples: Aoife, Caitlin, Christina's parents and Peggy's parents. The main difference was the reason for leaving but interestingly enough the way they moved remained the same: family migrating in fits and starts based on siblings entering England with the support of aunts and uncles of earlier migrations.

Edna, another Irish immigrant who had moved to the Romford area, was also one of many in her family to move out to England and like Siobhan's mother she too came from a loving home in County Kerry. Her father was struggling to make ends meet at their farm and was eventually forced to leave for Stoke on Trent, leaving his wife and ten children to run their farm on their own. He ended up working in a coal mine, a big contrast with the work he was used to, which was mostly outdoors. He was not often able to visit his family but was able to help them by setting up jobs for them in England as soon as they were ready to work. Edna came over when she was seventeen, she explained:

> *"I had gone to College and then, been there for a year and a half. Then I left there, I went to trek for three months and you know obviously I couldn't settle anywhere and drove my mum mad, and then I came over here, [to do] housekeeping with two children, my Dad got that for me."*[23]

After several jobs in various places, which she often got through the intervention of her father, Edna settled eventually on the Harold Hill Estate. Edna's migration to the Harold Hill Estate demonstrates clearly this gradual migration pattern where women moved from job to job further eastward. As was discussed in chapter Two, many Irish migrants survived in England by moving often from place to place seeking work.[24]

In Ireland, the lack of available jobs was made worse by the marriage bar and the apprenticeship system by which the parents of the apprentice needed to pay for the time it took to be trained-up for the job. Aoife, who moved to Britain with her husband Patrick shortly after the Second World War, remembers:

> *"I remember I wanted to be a hairdresser, my mother said I can't afford to pay for you to train! She couldn't I mean there was ten of us in the family. [And] when you got out of apprenticeship you only got peanuts didn't you for ages"*[25]

All sorts of jobs required a training of some sort with time spent as an apprentice. As Patrick and his wife Aoife explained:

> *"And [they are] all great tradesmen, because Ireland you served your time even a barman served his time in Ireland and any can come in and pull on, turning on a tap, but filling a pint of Guinness in Ireland is three or four operations."*[26]

The expense of the fees was not the only problem but a shortage of jobs meant that most families kept jobs in trades preserved for their own children. As Aoife recalled:

> *"My dad was a pork butcher, and you had to have somebody in that business for your son to get in."*[27]

Whatever way you tried, without a father with his own trade, your chances of a job were remote and most skilled work was an expense to get into. Aoife remembered:

> *"But you always had to serve your apprentice and you had to pay."*[28]

For parents with so many children, the first child becoming a wage earner was quite an event as in the case of Aoife's sister. Aoife said:

> *"I remember - one of the first girls who got a job, she got a job in the shoe factory. She went up and it was secret, nobody knew she had gone for an interview. Because you couldn't tell anyone or they'd go as well and they might get the job"*

She laughed:

> *"She went there and got the job, well everybody in the whole street was cheering because she got the job."*[29]

Even in a town the size of Limerick the lack of work was so apparent. She goes on to say:

> *"Because she was the first of ten of us to get a job you know and my mother was like ahhh 'gracious put you on the pigs back' that was what we used to say in Ireland; 'we are on the pigs back' -because the country people used to bring their pigs and sell them when they were fat enough. And they would always say 'you are on the pigs back'. I never forget that."*[30]

Her mother still used rural images. As has been explored in chapter Two, town folk kept their rural identity and the close link with country life could be recognised in their attitudes.[31] They continued to use farm animals in their expressions as O'Dowd describes.[32]

After various jobs in factories, which she got with help from her father, Aoife left for England with her newlywed husband Patrick. That England was the land of plenty becomes clear in the example of her husband. When he first moved over without her he had no real plans, no connections and no place to stay once he got there. As Patrick recalled:

> *"I met a fellow on the boat, I thought who was married, [from] my town Limerick as well and hmm, he said 'where are you going?' I said that I was to meet a couple of boys and they were going to fix [to] meet someone, [they] knew someone that would get us a job, just outside London and they weren't there so. And he said 'you have no place to stay', I said; 'no'. So he put me up in Camden Town. His wife was a kind of a..."*

Aoife interjected:

> *"A housekeeper, she was the vicar's housekeeper."*[33]

Although they had never met before, his countryman was also from Limerick and therefore looked after him. This highlights, as Hickman argues, Irish migrants' success at organising themselves and their own migration but also how they were prepared to give things a chance as there was enough work available and the British economy depended on their labour.[34] Patrick travelled from Camden Town to Dagenham and got a job in the Ford factory and found some digs, which is a room, with an Irish landlady who was also from Limerick. Not long after Patrick was able to go back to Ireland and marry his sweetheart. Shortly after their marriage they left again for England. As Aoife told:

> *"We got married on the Boxing Day and we came back here the two of us. Now we had only a week's wages between us...can you imagine!"*[35]

They were willing and also desperate enough to take these risks and leave much to chance but they knew that there was a need for their labour.

Although most women found their way to London when still single, the lack of work for both men and women in Ireland and the opportunities in England particularly in the fifties meant that some also decided to move after their marriage so that they could afford to start a family. Aoife and her husband found a small room in Romford and were afterwards able to buy a caravan that was eventually based at the top of Harold Hill, the place where in the past gypsies and hawkers had paused on their journeys. Afterwards Aoife and her husband were able to buy their own home on the estate.

The reason to emigrate varied amongst the women of the sample but they were certainly not all domestics with an 'unhealthy interest' in Hollywood films or 'unbalanced minds' as the Irish government would have it. Gray explains:

> *"Those women who emigrated in the 19th and early 20th centuries were constructed by commentators as potential wives or mothers of future generations. By emigrating, they were depriving the nation of its rightful national stock. Women emigrants were also seen as being seduced by Hollywood images of 'lavish and romantic American lifestyles', which 'unbalanced already flighty female Minds'. Women emigrants were pathologised for leaving, for being attracted or lured away from the country where they rightly belonged."*[36]

Many could not find work or had husbands who were unable to find permanent jobs with pension-stamps to collect as in Patrick's situation. Without any adequate work on offer for him and his wife there was little option. The restless nature of Edna and her problems to find something permanent made England a good alternative. Her case was only really possible because her father's emigration before her and was necessary because of the dire poverty her family suffered as farmers. Their struggle to survive puts in question the Irish government's attitudes to farming and De Valera's obsession with a totally rural Ireland and the self-sufficient family farms. As Siobhan's explains:

> *[they came] "All from farms, farmers children, the farms weren't big enough to keep that many children, so obviously some stayed behind to work on the farm, the rest came here to live, or to go to Australia."*[37]

To Siobhan it was a simple fact that the family farm produced displacement.

The harshness and lack of love and laughter in Deirdre's case and that of her sisters at the hands of the sisters of her orphanage-convent shows how difficult life could really be in a country that was completely regulated and ruled by the Catholic Church, a country in which the Church's authority was never questioned. Deirdre explained:

> *"-we run away, you know we used to run away...and hmm always be brought back [by the Garda], you know, we be in the city and go to the hospital and get a job; peeling apples or something and we get some money. And then we be picked up, you know and they used to bring you back and we tell the story...how cruel they were. But who do you believe...the nuns standing there looking very angelic and you're there, and you had run away you know... And they wouldn't... they didn't believe us."*[38]

The reasons for leaving Ireland differed with each interviewee but there was a need to look abroad in all cases, as work was not on offer in Ireland. England meant at least opportunities that Ireland lacked for women as well as their men.

Paid work in England

The work in England on offer to Irish women varied. Some came with qualifications; others came to be trained in England where there was no complex apprenticeship system for which the apprentice had to pay. But the group that was best known and often referred to by the Irish government were the domestic workers.[39] It was often the first job available, as in the case of Edna who was to keep house and look after the children of an Irish family in Wales. Some jobs were organised by agencies back in Ireland like that of the mother of Shona Marie, who came over just after the Second World War. Shona said:

> *"-there was a little place in town where they could go, and where they could get a job already lined up in England, and accommodation, so she decided to do that. I think she was about 17 when she done that... And then she was put in to service here. She got the job in Ireland."*[40]

Women were sent out in a system where two parties benefited from the export of potential nurses and nannies from Ireland. As Lambert mentioned in her interview these women were vital for British society.[41] Shona explained how her mother proved ill prepared for what would await her at the other end of the journey as she was unfamiliar with the city of London:

> *"They had a label as well, they had a label on their coat with the name and address of the person she was to live with."*[42]

In case she would get lost she could show her label to whoever was passing and willing to direct her.

There was a strong demand for Irish girls in English families as well as in the caring professions. They had the reputation of being hard workers and would not complain about long hours or heavy physical labour.[43] The immigrant women who came over after the Second World War were often from family farms. They were used to hard work and long hours and could carry the responsibilities of others. This shows how unsuccessful self-sufficient family farms really were and a committee published a report for the Government referring to the lack of work, the lack of social contacts, lack of recreation and psychological and economic malaise as Brown describes.[44] In England the lack of interest in domestic work by English girls and women was only one part of the reason why Irish girls and women were able to get work as domestics so easily; the reputation of the daughters of Irish farmers had also been an important factor and increased their chances of finding work in England.

Whatever jobs they were able to get, it was usually in a caring role for a family, with patients or children, with the teacher as the exception but also here the job was a form of caring. As Deirdre discussed:

> *"I always had a sort of caring nature. You know, help people and make them comfortable. But I don't think I went into caring work hmm with this idea that I am going to help people. It was just a job to begin with and gradually I, you know, I started to like it."*[45]

Her upbringing had made it a natural and obvious step for her to go seek work in the caring professions.

Because young Irish women were brought up in a strict Catholic society, their role in life was mainly seen in a caring function, a function closely associated with their future role as mothers. The Catholic hierarchy along with the Irish government felt that this role was the only one that came naturally to women who had no place in the workforce. After their marriage Catholic women were supposed to stay at home to take charge of their families, which was often the path they followed. In cases of a family business they would then continue to work as assistants of their husbands.[46]

Christina's parents were both from Ireland. Their experiences were significant for the research as they demonstrate the large scale of unemployment in Ireland from the early years of its independence that forced many well skilled middle class professionals abroad, as well as the daughters and sons of poorer farmers. Christina's parents who we introduced in chapter 4 were university graduates. Her parents were able to set up a practice in East London as there was a shortage of general practitioners there. Their practice would not have been possible if English GPs had been interested in working in the area, but the patients of Christina's father were poor and often in ill health.

Most Irish General Practitioners, like Christina's father, continued to help the sick and dying during the difficult times of the Second World War. Their dedication to the poor was of immense importance to the Cockneys and showed what the Irish immigrant GP was prepared to do for them as Christina pointed out:

"My uncle down the road was called up. When my father wasn't, he was slightly older. He therefore had to do the work for two to three doctors basically. And he stayed with his people all during the war."[47]

Much has been discussed of de-skilling in earlier chapters but not enough has been written about the 'de-classing' of the middle class immigrants. In other words, the need to accept the less well paid jobs in the more difficult areas, as was the case with Christina's parents. Both the British and Irish governments always referred to Irish immigrants as working class. This was despite the fact that so many came, particularly in the 20th century, from independent farms and if they had come from English farms would have been regarded as middle class. The women themselves often referred back to their middle class status and their sense of independence. As in the case of Christina's parents there was also a small Irish middle class community operating in various professions in England. There were also a large number of highly skilled but poorly paid professionals from the Irish community working here in the National Health Service, mainly as nurses. There was a shortage of nurses but also General Practitioners in England. Nursing was a profession open to women in Ireland that also had a status that derived from the role of carer/mother and was therefore a respectable profession. According to Walter:

"In Ireland nursing has been associated with middle-class status. A fee for training was charged, which excluded those from poor families."[48]

Women in particular were coached into caring professions even to emigrate in order to work as carers and nurses in England but the status also connected with their own beliefs and that of their family that they were important in a giving role looking after the other. Most of the interviewees refer to the importance to give something to others in work paid or un-paid.

The acceptance in Irish society of women in the paid caring professions created an increase in Irish nurses in Britain. As was mentioned in chapter 3, the Irish paper *The Irish Democrat* had argued in 1948 that about 40% of London nurses were Irish born.[49] The proportion of Irish nurses had dramatically increased in the post-war period. There were also a large number of Irish Nurses working in Romford in the 1950s, as there were also later on during the 1980s when I spent my time working alongside them. Oldchurch Hospital in Romford had a Catholic Nurses Guild in the 1950s with many Irish members. They were involved in charity work after their long shifts. There was much appreciation locally for the Guilds' charity work and some events were mentioned in the local paper; like their concert on 28th January 1955.[50]

The Catholic teachings meant that not all work was considered suitable for Irish women in the eyes of their own community. The Catholic faith made it difficult for Eileen's mother to accept her daughter's conscription during the war: Eileen explained:

> *"When I went, I had to sign, and I was going to be called-up, my mum said to me 'I don't want you to go into munitions'. She didn't want to feel that I was making something that would kill somebody."*[51]

She went into the Wrens, the Women's Royal Navy Service, instead. She was stationed first in Scotland where they placed her in a workshop making landing craft and in 1943 she went as a messenger to the south of England to a secret location, Eileen recalled:

> *"I was working in a secret establishment, where they were planning the invasion of France."*[52]

Again here Eileen explains how her mother really concerned herself with the outcome that the work of Eileen would have on others. Bullets were to end life, not to nurse or care for it and this work was therefore unacceptable. It was important for her Irish mother that the work itself was not destroying life. Caring was the norm in Irish culture where women were concerned. The obedience in Eileen as a dutiful daughter had made her stand out. The fact that she could do as she was told without asking questions made her a reliable and trustworthy worker and singled her out for this particular site, but with accepting this work she disobeyed her mother.

Another caring and high skilled profession that attracted many Irish women was that of teacher. Not all teachers were laywomen. In England many Catholic schools were run or partially run by orders. Christina herself became a member of the Holy Child Sisters and spent many years teaching as a sister before she eventually became a Doctor in Theology. Christina was herself taught by two different orders she said:

> *"We, the Holy Child sisters, had no nuns down in the East End, so I was brought up by the Ursulines in the first place and the Holy Child in the second place."* [53]

In Catholic teaching it was stressed that women had to be of use to others, improve the life of others or to be at least of use to the community with their work. The jobs they were encouraged to take were very different from their brothers. Much of the support and influence on their choice came from their own mothers. Edna told us:

> *"At the start my mum perhaps encouraged the, the boys, as much I would say, as the girls, but none of them...did further schooling they were all working in buildings whereas, I have got - two sisters which are teachers. I have got one which is a community-nurse and - one is in counselling, so all the girls are doing something positive if you like"* [54]

She demonstrates in her answer that the sisters were working in areas that were regarded a benefit to the community whereas the brothers were not.[55] Caring professionals were not all highly trained well skilled workers. Many girls moved in with families to help the mothers to look after the children and the rest of the household. Their work varied and was badly paid. As Siobhan explains when describing the situation of her mum who came here just after the Second World War:

> *"She went what they called in those days service, but the term of it nowadays would be an au-pair, she lived-in because... this is what you did with the richer families. I think she served with a Jewish family in St John's Wood and stayed generally round that sort of area."*[56]

This type of work offered a secure place for young girls and made it easier for their families to part with them. After time in service, both mothers married and moved into Irish communities in East London.

Irish communities

Irish communities in England maintained their Irish identity and were ostracised by their English counterparts. Segregation of the Irish workers from the other working classes had been well established in the early 19th Century.[57] Later when Black African Caribbean and Asian communities developed during the 1950s a similar situation occurred.[58] Segregation can create a stronger awareness of one's own identity and can be in itself a threat to the dominant classes. The education of the Irish children was set-up in such way that it was to highlight their Catholic working class identity to the cost of their Irish identity, and Catholic schools would not teach in the Irish language or give Irish history lessons.[59] Therefore the Catholics in Romford from an Irish background, like the Catholics of East London, were by themselves no longer regarded as Irish after one generation. Whilst communicating with people of the Catholic community during this research, many of them expressed their surprise when being told that they were the descendants of Irish settlers. For instance, in the Catholic school where I taught, children did not always know the Irish origins of their surnames. With this surprise came also often a slight sense of unease with the new information about the identity of their Catholic community, because on the one hand people had clearly identified themselves as English and on the other hand because of the prejudice to Irish settlers. The St Edward Church records clearly show the names of Irish men and women. Unfortunately, as was mentioned before, many women who settled in Romford after having worked 'up town' in London lost their Irish surnames and with that proof of their ethnic background.[60] Of course the other telling association, their religious denomination, stayed.

The disappearance of the Irish names could also be seen in East London where after a few generations the Catholic community flourished without an Irish identity. They saw themselves as English and viewed newly arrived Irish immigrants as outsiders, as Deirdre remembered when she brought her children to the local Catholic school in an area with many Catholic families, Deirdre explained:

> *"This was the Docks [Docklands]. And there were mainly East Enders, the Dockers, there were not many Irish at all. And they were a bit resentful of anybody who wasn't East Ender."*[61]

To be an East Ender was the new identity. Deirdre also viewed them as having a different identity from her own. Willmott and Young never describe the people of Bethnal Green as Irish or of Irish descent but do refer to their Catholic practices when they describe conflict over 'churching' after the confinement period when a baby has been born. They mention:

> *"Between husband and wife...there is the same conflict over Churching. On this, most of the wives were clearly under maternal influence. Both regular Churchgoers, the small minority, and irregular attenders alike thought they should go to Church as soon as possible after the confinement, for the service whose formal purpose is thanks giving for the birth of the child."*[62]

However the Catholics in general continued to be viewed as 'other' by the rest of society. To be a Catholic was seen as being different. Caitlin told the story of the Catholic children who were seen as more difficult than the other children. She recalled:

> *"I remember being on the bus, coming from the shops, one day. And this conductor, all these children got on, and I knew they were coming from a Catholic school. And hmm she said; 'Here they come.' I said; 'Who?' 'Catholics!' she said. 'Why what is wrong [I asked?]' 'O they annoy you when they jump on the bus.' 'Of course they jump on the bus,' I said 'They want to get home, and they aren't doing anything are they?' (laughs). She didn't say anymore she thought 'I say no more.' (laughs)"*[63]

Caitlin realised that the woman connected Catholic children with trouble and there was resentment towards them; Catholics were seen as different.

The Vatican also imposed segregation on its own community. Catholics were not supposed to marry spouses from a different religion. Mixed marriages did occur, particularly in the case of Irish women in London. And for many the only option in marriage was to look for an English partner. Eileen, who got married after the Second World War, was determined that her non-Catholic husband would have a choice in the matter. John was from the Church of England but cared enough for his fiancée that he was prepared to abandon his own Church for hers but she said:

> *"Well, I would have liked him to become one, but he said to me 'If you want me to become a Catholic, I become one'. So I said 'No, I want you to become one because you want to, and not because I want you to'. But he was quite willing to bring the children up in the faith, and...[he said] I will never interfere with you going to mass or anything you want to go; church activities, so there has never been a problem there."*[64]

After the changes introduced by the Second Vatican Council more mixed marriages occurred and more integration was possible. Before the 1960s only one third of the Catholic marriages were mixed marriages compared with over two-thirds in the 1970s.[65] This increased number of mixed marriages was seen as the main reason for lapsation amongst the Irish Catholics in England as Delaney discusses.[66]

Despite the disappearance of Irish identities in England, newly arrived immigrants continued to put 'new blood' into the Irish community and the Irish community continued to be very involved in national politics in England as it was back home. It was only after the independence of Ireland that communities in England concentrated more on their own immigrant status in England and less on the political situation back home. According to Hickman Irish political awareness had been feared by British Government, during the time that Ireland was still part of Britain and was partly the reason behind the segregation of Irish workers and the rest of working class Britain.[67] Politics continued to play an important part in Irish households as Christina remembered:

"We were a very political family, very political, both in England and in Ireland. And [my] family in Ireland was split because my father's family being country were very for the English, they were seen [to be] Fina Gael. And my mother's family were very Fianna Fail. And they were nearly not getting married because they were divided politically."[68]

Because of the many new Irish immigrants, Irish identities were passed on in the Irish communities in and around London, but for the earlier generations of Irish men and women it was more their Catholic identities that remained. Catholic identities were important to all Catholic Irish immigrants as Shona pointed out:

"-and I always think she [her mother] kept her religion. She always kept going to church, or kept some part of it. Or she used to keep a statue of the Virgin Mary, and that she always been with her, in her case [suitcase] when she went from job to job."[69]

Holding on to her little statue gave her support and was part of her Catholic identity.

Women held on to their Irish identity in some ways but were also successful in integrating into a Catholic community often comprised of both earlier Irish descendants and British Catholics, which indicates that they succeeded in making history for themselves. Some women chose very consciously not to marry an Irish man. Siobhan and her sister felt the difference between boys and girls in Irish families made Irish men a bad choice as a husband and an unwilling help in the household. They also feared that so many Irish immigrant men had problems with alcohol, as Siobhan described:

"The pubs become their home, because there's nothing to go back to, is there?"[70]

and how she:

"I always said to myself: I would never marry an Irishman. And I never ever said it to my mum, and I never ever said it to anybody that was Irish, because I didn't want to hurt them, didn't want to

> upset them, but that was how I felt. And I also, till about two years ago, I said it to my sister, and it is funny, she never married an Irishman. She thought exactly the same way."[71]

The fear of alcohol abuse and stories about alcohol related social problems occurred in most of the interviews highlighting its presence in Irish communities in Ireland and in England. As Siobhan and Shona pointed out, that it had been very much part of their Irish communities in London. Tilki refers in her study to the large scale of the problem amongst Irish migrant men in London.[72]

Urban Irish clustering

Most of the Irish immigrants clustered together in the same areas. This was important because, as was the case with most of the women interviewed, the immigrants who arrived first were able to help the later arriving siblings to find jobs and a place to stay. The family unit was also able to help out when the children arrived. The areas where they moved to were obviously areas in need of their labour and the connections that they already had in the area were the reason for the cluster. These communities also made it possible for the Catholic Church to flourish in these urban areas. The Catholic Church became an urban church from the 19th Century.[73] There were enough churchgoers to sustain the church and enough Catholic children to put pressure on the local authorities to allow them a Catholic school as will be further discussed later on in this chapter.

The habit of living within close range of other Irish immigrants, often their own relatives, was seen as supportive, as Siobhan explained:

> ""They tend to stick together, the community of Irish people, in the same sort of areas of London."[74]

And it sometimes created a different identity of the area like Aoife remembered:

> "-[there were] so many Irish people in Dagenham, that they called it little Cork."[75]

Nothing of this was mentioned by Wilmott in his study *'The Evolution of a Community. A study of Dagenham after forty years'*, nor that the Ford company had so many Irish workers, but this is backed up by the building programme in Dagenham of Catholic Churches and schools.[76]

The descriptions of the East End and the community in which 'auntie' and 'nanny' lived a few houses down the road is as much Irish in cultural background as it is Cockney. Within these close-knit communities it was easier to cope away from home and set up your own family and it was also easier to continue to be an Irish Catholic. Although many women married into what had become by then English Catholic families. Eileen's mother had met her English father, a 'stout' Catholic, in Ireland, she said:

> *"She met my father when he was stationed in Ireland in the British Army, because he was English and my mother was Irish and they married and came over to England two years after they were married in 1919 after the war. She already had one child and she had seven children after that and we all lived in London."*[77]

Eileen's mother died in East London. Eileen herself was able to move to the Harold Hill Estate just after it was built and continued to be an active part of the Catholic community there. She like the other interviewees valued their contribution to the parish social life.

Catholic Education in the Diocese of Brentwood and Harold Hill

The settlement of Catholic newcomers in Harold Hill meant a growing Catholic population that was the responsibility of the Brentwood Diocese. The Roman Catholic Diocese of Brentwood was established in 1917, having formerly formed the eastern area of the Diocese of Westminster. It now comprises the Administrative County of Essex, the unitary authorities of Southend-on-Sea and Thurrock, and the London Boroughs of Barking & Dagenham, Havering, Newham, Redbridge and Waltham Forest.

Picture no 13: The coat of arms of the Diocese of Brentwood [78]

The Diocese of Brentwood's existence is a direct result of the growth of London beyond the LCC boundaries into the county of Essex. Places like Walthamstow, East Ham and West Ham became 'East London'. When Brentwood became the centre of the diocese Bishop Ward was appointed the new Administrator of the new Diocese of Essex and became Bishop of Brentwood on 7th Nov 1917.

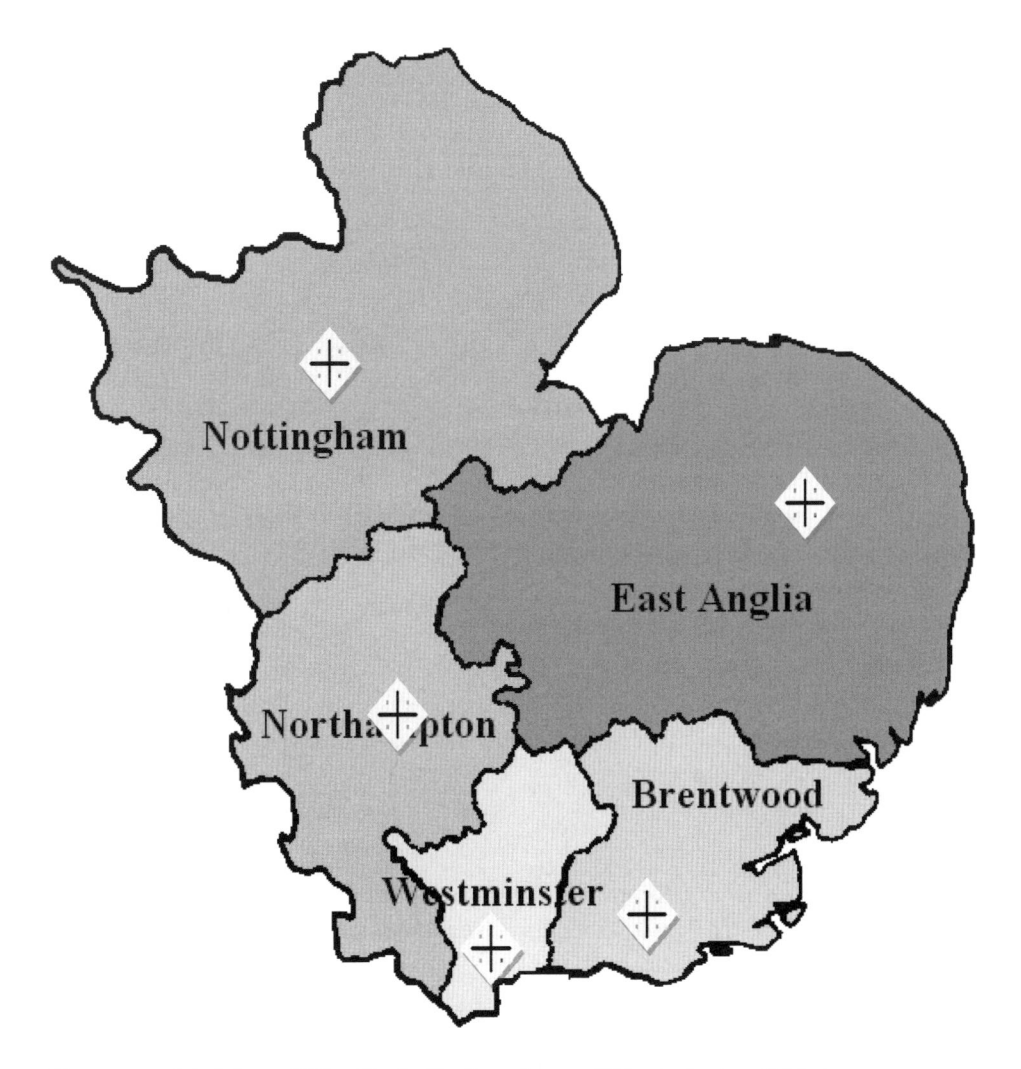

*Picture no 14: Map of **The Catholic Province of Westminster**. This is a current map of the ecclesiastical province in the Catholic Church. The crosses mark where the current Cathedrals of each diocese are located. The specific dioceses are shaded differently* [79]

The diocese was immediately short of funding but also of priests. By 1920 there were an estimated 35,000 Catholics in the diocese, many Irish or of Irish decent, it counted 55 Secular priests, 27 Franciscans, and 3 of other orders. There were also 30 convents of nuns including Sisters of Mercy;

Franciscans; Augustinians, and Ursuline Sisters. When Bernard Wall became bishop in 1956, the diocese still faced a shortage of priests and funds but by then the Catholic population was around 107,000 and increasing with the new and growing Harold Hill Estate within its borders.[80]

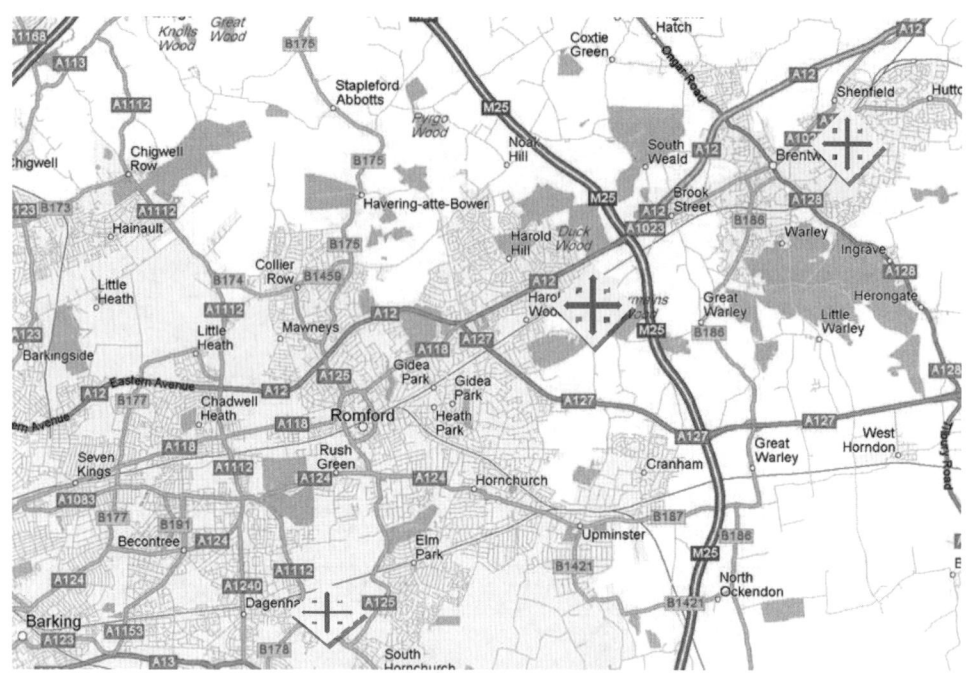

*Picture no 15: Map where **Romford, Brentwood and Dagenham** are shown and the parishes of Harold Hill and Dagenham are indicated by means of a cross.* [81]

Because each Catholic community has at its heart the parish church and right next to it the school it became important to build both on the new estate (see map above picture no 15). The new estate in Romford was not going to function without a school. The inflow of the large number of Irish migrants from East London meant that the Diocese of Brentwood needed solutions in order to educate these Catholic children. Because of lack of financial resources it was a difficult task, which the Ursuline Sisters took upon themselves.

The Catholic Diocese struggled to come to terms with the large inflow of Irish Catholics from East London and the need to provide the children of the newcomers with Catholic education. From the beginning the Catholics received help from the sisters from the Brentwood Ursuline Convent who were to play an active part in the orders' new project; the school on the estate. The following section will examine how the newcomers were viewed from the hierarchy's perspective and the problems that they posed in a period of secularisation and will also look at the diocese's views on the responsibilities it shared with the parents in raising children. The archive work therefore contributes to the thesis as it highlights the voice of the Church as opposed to the interviews where women tell their own stories. It demonstrates the importance of Catholic education as it allowed Irish communities to keep their own Catholic identity but also separated them from the rest of English society by establishing separate schools for their children.

Harold Hill mass centres and serving priests

Two churches and one school were eventually erected for the Catholics of Harold Hill. The mass centre at Petersfield Avenue started on 12th November 1950 (the priest came from Romford to hold mass). It had as first resident priest, Father Foley, on 3rd March 1952. It was considered a unique situation to have a priest moving into a little row of council houses on the newly built estate.[82] The Catholic Herald wrote about him:

> *"To give a picture of Fr Brian Foley's house at 7 Tring Gardens, Harold Hill. Because I have at least never before seen a chapel and priest's house in a row of council houses — a house in this case distinguished by a statue of Our Lady in the lower window, and a crucifix in the window above. One felt that while priests abroad have to experiment with new kinds of priestly apostolate, circumstances in this country drive them into similar work."*[83]

His house stood out by its crucifix and statue of the Virgin Mary. Fr. Foley was considered a kind and humble man who rode his bicycle visiting what were estimated by then the 1000 Catholics of his parish.[84] The Holy Redeemer was eventually opened on 27th September 1953 (see map picture no15 above). The church as it stands today was opened 7th September 1957. As soon as Father Foley moved into the Holy Redeemer, the building of the

St. Dominic's Church was planned. Straight Road had a mass centre in September 1954 with a resident priest. The parish was erected on 7th June 1956 and the church door opened on 15th August 1956. Father Michael Mc Kenna became the first parish priest and dedicated himself to the area from 1954 to 1960. Mc Kenna, a son of Irish immigrants, grew up in Silvertown, an industrialised district on the north bank of the Thames, now in the London Borough of Newham. His humble Irish background and his experience as a parish priest in Dagenham made him an obvious choice. Succeeding McKenna was Father Edmund Tyler, who was parish priest from 1960 to 1972, who in turn was followed by Father Maurice Roche in 1972. It was unusual for an estate of this size to have two churches and a school built in such a short period and shows the interest within the diocese of Brentwood for the Catholics who were moving to the area but also shows that they anticipated an inflow of Irish Catholics from East London. The primary school right next to St Dominic's Church on Straight Road was opened on April 25th 1955 as an infant school for the time being (see map picture no 16 below). In September 1957 the junior school was also opened. But initially this all looked very different as Foster describes:

> *"For example there were no plans initially to provide Catholic churches or schools for the LCC estate at Harold Hill which was first developed in 1948."*[85]

This meant that people were unable to form new parishes. As Foster the historian of the Brentwood Diocese explains:

> *"Many Catholic families moved from the East End to Harold Hill, and because there were no churches on the new estate people returned to their former parishes for Sunday Mass. [therefore] Temporary arrangements were made for the provision of mass, and likewise for the education of the children."*[86]

There was also another reason why the parish seemed so important to the Bishop of Brentwood. In his diary Foley wrote on 14th March 1952 that Bishop Beck felt that:

> *"It was obvious that a serious social problem was arising on the new housing estates."*[87]

Other than the lack of interest of some boys in their education and fights between some school boys, there was very little that stood out in the paper as an obvious social problem emerging at the housing estate of Harold Hill. What Bishop Beck and Fr Foley described as social problems might be a reference to the poverty but also the isolation of the community on this new estate. As local papers recorded there were no facilities on the estate, they all had to be built. Fear of social problems in former slum dwellers, however, was present in Romford as has been discussed earlier. There are no other records that suggest other social problems in any of the archives.

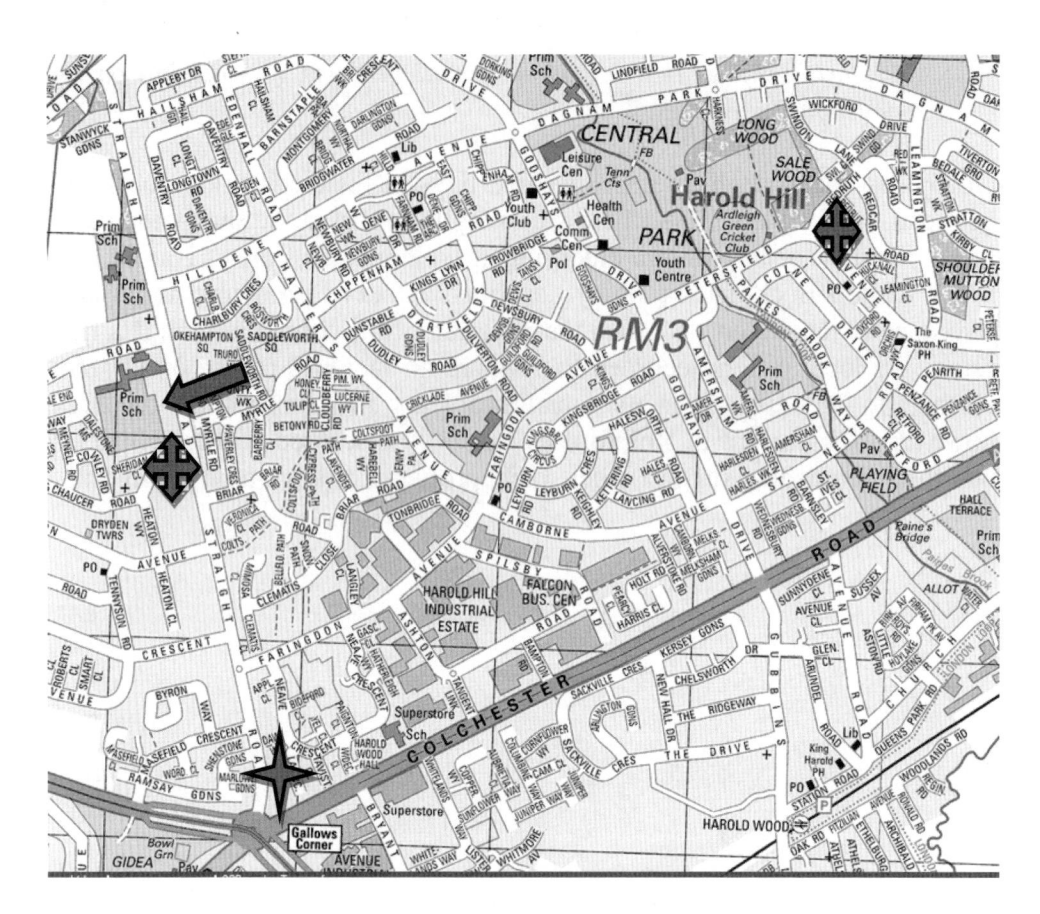

*Picture no 16: Contemporary **Map of Harold Hill** showing Straight Road where St Ursulas School was built with the St Dominic's Church next to it (see arrow pointing towards the school and a red cross situated on the site of the church. Also Petersfield Avenue where firstly the church hall was built and the Holy Redeemer church next to it (see cross on the right side of the map). Visible also is Gallows Corner where the pub the Plough first stood which served as mass centre (see bottom of the map left hand corner). No roads were added after the building program completed in the early 1960s* [88]

Helping the parish and parish social life

During their time at home as mothers, women were often able to assist the parish priest and local school with various unpaid jobs from fundraising to helping in classrooms. Their time off from work proved vital to their own community. All the women interviewees did some work for the parish and had been doing so since their children were born. Most of them would help out with fundraising others would pay visits to the sick and needy. Caitlin was responsible for the opening up of the little room on the side of the Plough pub for the Sunday mass. Caitlin explains:

> *"I'll tell you this, I was, I was with all this young [kids] and on my own you see, and I thought; 'O well, (as we have no church) we got the Plough so that's alright. I go down there, ask the manager'. This very, very, nice man, very good. And every Sunday I go down there."*[89]

Thanks to Caitlin's help the Irish community of Harold Hill were able to go to mass on a Sunday in the estate itself. It meant that they did not have to walk towards the centre of the town each Sunday. Caitlin assisted the priests and set the room up ready for mass:

> *"I help with the congregation lay the tables out and the chairs you know. For the priests, different priests, we had a different priest, I never met so many priests. There must have been, I suppose the war being on, they came from France, Germany, behind the Iron Curtain, Spain, oh what have you. I met so many different priests, there was...You would not have the same one every Sunday."*[90]

This memory of Caitlin stands out as there was nothing found on visiting priests in any of the archives. It became the work of Father Foley to look after the service. Father Brian Charles Foley was ordained priest on 25th July 1937 and consecrated bishop on 13th June 1962 in Lancaster Cathedral. He became resident in Harold Hill in March 1952 but started his involvement when he was still a curate in Romford. He had begun to say mass at Harold Wood hospital in the little chapel for people from the Harold Hill Estate. Harold Wood lies right next to the Harold Hill Estate and also here many houses were built just after the Second World War but in this case by local builders for the council of Romford. Mass would start at 10:00 a.m. and would take no longer than half an hour. Then it was all put back to serve as a bar for the pub to open up at noon. Mass at Harold Wood hospital as well as Oldchurch hospital would be said at 8:00 a.m. so that the many

Irish Catholic nurses could attend. Eventually Fr Foley was able to say mass in the builder's yard of the building company French and use the workmen's canteen not far from Petersfield Road in Harold Hill. The huge hut was a more suitable place to hold mass than a pub. With much fundraising by people like Caitlin, Aoife and Eileen a church hall was finally opened in September 1953 by Bishop Beck who complimented those whose fundraising efforts meant that a hall could now be used for church hall and school purposes and that a workers' hut or pub were no longer needed as venues for Sunday mass. The Bishop of Brentwood Mgr. Beck told the Catholics present at the opening:

> *"You are pioneers laying the foundation of a new community. You can do an immense amount for the estate."*[91]

Caitlin also worked hard to raise the funding needed for the building of the new church of St Dominic. It all started by chance on one of her walks to Noak Hill, when she met someone who was able to help her, Caitlin recalled:

> *"I pushed the pram you know as well, and normal people you know they didn't want to go for walks I suppose. And I go up there and – there was a monastery up there, it was a Benedictine monastery. – The woman that was in there, she was a French lady,-woman that lived – near, – she said ; '- I tell you what,- you can have the garden, the big garden for a feis [Irish party]' I thought 'Good heavens' Fantastic she lent me the money, [and] I was making the teas, and from there we were sort of collecting, helping to get a church."*[92]

Caitlin probably remembered the lady and this monastery incorrectly. Whilst there was a large house on Noak Hill which belonged to a wealthy family and some people even believed that the area had once belonged to a monastery, my research has not been able to indentify it. Caitlin did receive a medal from the Pope and several certificates as a thank you for her fundraising for the new parish. Most people remember the input of the priest Father Foley who became a bishop of Lancaster after he served his time in the Harold Hill community. But not many people outside Harold Hill knew how Caitlin had been the driving force behind the fetes and other money collecting events. On his visitation return of 3rd March 1963 the Bishop asked to congratulate:

> *"Laymen and laywomen helpers, e.g. altar staff. Choir and church cleaners especially"*

And on the visitation return of 16th February 1967 [93]

> *"What points do you suggest for the bishop's address? Perhaps a word of congratulation to the voluntary workers, especially women, who clean the church, agents for the Pool, jumble Sale Helpers, altar staff and choir."*[94]

There were events which were at times also mentioned in the papers as they received well known guests such as 'two ton' Tessie O Shea (the granddaughter of Irish migrants from the maternal side, Tessie was a star and singer known from the music halls) and Ann Shelton a well known singer who worked alongside the Glenn Miller Band, who was also from a Catholic upbringing (in South London).

The big parties that were organised to raise the money needed for a church and a school were important because people did not have much money and it was often difficult to get people to contribute. Parties and fetes were good fundraising events that would get money together. Much of the organising and collecting was performed by women. It was difficult to find ways of raising the cash needed and the collectors were not always successful, as Aoife recalled:

> *"They started the tour club [a fund raising event]"*

Patrick remembered the way it was set up he added:

> *"A shilling for a tour-number."* [95]

Aoife continued:

> *"That money was for the church wasn't it, it was very hard to get money from all that lot here I am not kidding you."*[96]

It was not only raising the necessary money that mattered, there was also the important aspect to the social life of the parish. Their social events were able to give people a good time and the events helped with the various funding. The Irish community always had their own entertainment. Irish pubs and dance halls were good meeting places and many of them were scattered all over London. Siobhan's mother who came over in 1947 met her future husband in one of those places Siobhan explained:

> *"Because they all stuck in this community, they never ventured out of it, they went to [an] Irish dance hall, the Irish pubs, and she used to see him around the Irish dance halls and things."*[97]

The new parishes of Harold Hill were able to run their own social club during the 1950s where they could get together and organise dancing and other events. Aoife and Patrick recalled:

> *"Oh it was lovely down there.-it was the social club for all the Catholics: The association for all the Catholics of Harold Hill."*[98]

It was also an opportunity to see the local priest in a completely different light: Aoife described:

> *"And we used to see the priest up dancing and I thought 'Oh if my mother could see them up there now' you know, a priest up the floor dancing."*

Patrick added:

> *"[and] Drinking brandy."*[99]

The clubs in the Essex area were friendly to one another and club visits occurred, particularly in parishes where people had moved on. These people often kept in touch through the parish's clubs. And regular visits were a way of keeping in touch with the former parish. In the Diocese the halls remained connected to the parish Church and most halls were also called parish halls.

Aoife and Patrick often went back to Dagenham where they would meet up with their old community and work colleagues; they would meet up in the parish hall. Patrick recalled:

> *"Fords was all Irish back then, there were very few English men then."*[100]

For Aoife it was also an important part of her social life, she told us:

> *"We used to go down and loved it. We go down Thursday night Saturday night and Sunday night, always."*[101]

From time to time the club would hire a coach to take them on an outing, often visiting other Catholic clubs. The night would end at someone's place, Aoife remembered:

> *"We would always wound up at someone's house, two or three in the morning, whether here or at any of the others and they were all Irish. I mean we had so much in common."*[102]

There remained contact at least in the area of Romford, Brentwood and Dagenham, between the Hall and the parish church and most dance halls were also functioning as Parish Halls. These places were as Aoife and Patrick explained of great importance to their social life. Delaney describes that:

> *"...the other element that emerges clearly is the extent to which the process of adjustment relied heavily on what were in essence Irish dominated spaces. From the parish church to the dancehall, to the GAA grounds."*[103]

The GAA grounds were the Gaelic Athletic Association stadiums and played an important part in Irish social life.

The Irish clubs or Irish involvement in clubs, are evidence of the ability of the Irish community to organise themselves and to partake in social events. Clubs and social events show that they were a community that functioned well. As Hickman argues, the Irish community did not need a Church to become an organised community during the immigration from rural Ireland to the cities of Britain in the 19th century.[104] They used the public houses as meeting places. This case study shows that the Catholic Church was in need of their clubs and social events as they could raise the cash to build their churches in the new urban estates. The interest of the Irish community in fundraising made the building possible but the clubs did more. They were a way in which the newly born parish could function and grow in strength by means of socialising. The Irish Catholic community in England of the early to mid 20th century ran successful organisations that supported the newly appointed parish priest in his work and helped him pay the bills. The fundraising events were places where the Catholic women could participate without venturing out of their own community; their organisational skills were used by the parish. As McDannell argued, when discussing events in New York:

> "The indoor, semi-domestic environment of fairs made them feminine spaces, and their fund-raising aims chimed with the economic importance of women's work in paid employment sphere."[105]

As Hickman stressed in earlier research it was often assumed that parishes were successful under the watchful eye of the parish priests and that it was the priest that would dictate the direction the parish would go and uphold the structure of the Catholic community, strengthening it and moulding it.[106] Part of this assumption was based on the concept of the Irish immigrants as unable and simple rural people lost in a complex and alien urban world. As has been discussed earlier, Irish populations were able to create their own communities with a strong communal spirit, with or without a Catholic church attached to them. That the parish priest was important to the communities is not denied here but their influence on the social success of the Irish Catholic community was limited. Evidence of this comes from the highly critical way in which the different parish priests were viewed. The interviewees highlighted their disapproval of some priests and their approval of others, which suggests conflicts between parish priests and parishioners. Parishioners also differed in their preferences. One parishioner had mentioned that she had a priest, Father Edmund Tyler (incumbent 1960-1972) who was prepared to walk long distances to make family visits and was seen as a Holy Man. When Patrick and Aoife were asked about another priest Father Maurice Roche (incumbent 1972-181) Patrick's opinion was very different, he described him as *"an oddball"*. But on the whole the extra attention of a home visit of the parish priest was more a hindrance than a blessing for Aoife who had very little time to sit down and talk to Father Tyler despite him being a Holy Man, as she described:

> *"He used to visit, visit all his parishioners, I have to say that. He used to come in.-and some nights, I be having to put a colour in my hair, because I was working then, and he be coming in and I had it back up in a towel and I used to think 'oh will he ever go away my hair will fall out he would be here so long!' And the kids used to disappear of course and I was left with him."*[107]

Father Foley however described the visits in his diary as a necessary part of his mission on the estate. He wrote on 1st April 1952:

> *"Knocked on nearly every door in Dorking Rd, Dorking Walk (completed) and Dorking close, about 100 all told. Found 11 Catholic families."*[108]

And again on 2nd April he found another 15 Catholic families and 3rd April he found another seven Catholic families. His search for Catholics was critically viewed by the parishioners who needed to make time for him. But this in itself differed from the position priests had held in Ireland.

Aoife, like Edna, was more critical of the parish priests in England than she was allowed to be back home. Aoife recalled:

> *"Because I remember I went to confession one time to Father I was only about eight and my mother used to always say to us 'Well what did you get for your penance' you know and all this jazz you know and I said oh and I said 'There is a terrible smell of drink over there'*

The rage, she give me a walloping 'don't you ever say that about the anointed to God'. See and I mean then it was different, you know but today its, the religion is so much different."[109]

Both Edna and Aoife stressed the differences between both societies. The social status was still an important one as Christina's story highlights that even when on visits to the General Practitioner the priest expected to be seen at the doctor's own family home and over a glass of whiskey. Ireland backed its clergy from government to local authorities, with the clergy deciding on everything from teacher appointments to the celebrations of St Patrick's Day.[110] But here in Britain, it was the parish priest who was in need of support and continuous backing from the community. The Irish parishioners were far more critical of their priests and were able to voice their opinions at least to one another. The reason might lie in the fact that the parish priest did not tend to stay on for long. The priests of the parishes of Harold Hill and also the Dagenham Becontree housing estate stayed for approximately five years and then moved on, unlike the General Practitioner and Community nurse who tended their patients often through most of their working lives. These Irish migrants on the other hand continued to behave as a community holding it together socialising with each other and continued to build these communties. The Catholic morals, the rural Irish traditions and the Catholic faith functioned as glue keeping this community together reshaping and moulding its identity. Important aspects of these traditions included the communal displays of Catholic worship such as the community processions in honour of the Virgin Mary.

Involvement in processions on the estate and fundraising

To show the Virgin's importance to the Catholic community processions in her honour continued to be held also on the new housing estate. In these processions the worshipping that mainly happened behind closed doors and in the parish church now poured out onto the street. This was one of the rare occasions that allowed an insight into Irish Catholics' worship to the non-Catholic English neighbours on the estate. Eileen recalled:

"When we first came out here, every May there used to be a procession in honour of Our Lady. A May Procession, and... they

have a statue of our lady, and they have a circle of flowers, they crowned [her with], and one of the favourite hymns was... 'We Crown Thee Queen of the May', I think the words are - and in the actual procession one of the children used to come up and the men would lower the statue, and the children would put the ring of flowers round Our Lady's head, round the statue, and that was held every May. There was always a May procession."[111]

A very important occasion for a procession was the first communion, as Aoife recalled:

"You used to have for the kids' communion and the confirmation, they used to march from our church all down Hilldene, all down to Petersfield and back up again and ah gosh you imagine that now!"[112]

The members of the new parishes also continued to go on pilgrimages as they had done in Ireland, this time to Walsingham which honoured the Virgin Mary. Caitlin remembered:

"[We went] on the fourth of September. - We got a coach and off we went. And we get down there about... I think about oh eight o'clock- it takes about four hours. And - you get there for the mass of one o'clock. -There was quite a lot of us."[113]

It was seen as a welcome break from the daily routine and much of the journey was spent laughing and singing. The trips were enjoyed but also very important as they created solidarity within the community. But this was also a time to join the other Catholics in worship from elsewhere in England. The importance of the use of rosaries, the processions in the streets during the month of May and the pilgrimages show that these women did not move away from their church or faith and continued to pass on their traditions on the Harold Hill Estate. Most traditions were felt as habits as Aoife explained:

"You can't break your habit, you know. Like I mean when I come back from Holy Communion I won't touch a thing, I must have I

must have a drink of water first. My mother used to say 'Always drink water wash down the Blessed Sacrament before you eat anything'; And I go down the shops on morning after mass and I wait until I can drink a drink of water. You know you, your old habits die hard don't they?"[114]

These processions like the fetes drew much attention to the presence of the new Catholic inhabitants. They were markers of the faith of a large and thriving community of the new housing estate. It made them stand out as worshippers. The white clothes of the boys and beautiful long white dresses for the girls with flowers in their hair were meant to make an impact. It was also a celebration of their faith and signified their pride in their religious beliefs. These processions were very much tradition in each Catholic community during this period but it would have shown the world that the Catholics had arrived at Harold Hill. The success of the Catholic community was shown for instance in September 1958 when the Ursuline sisters wrote in their journal the *Fair View Chronicles* in September 1958:

> *"Over a hundred children made their first Holy Communion in Harold Hill. 8 o'clock mass was said at St Dominic's followed by the first Holy Communion on the 8th of June which was followed by the same Corpus Christi procession through the estate as before."*[115]

The local papers often refer to the celebrations of the Catholic community but mostly they mentioned the fetes. For instance *The Romford Times* wrote on Wednesday 8th September 1953 that a large garden fete was opened in the grounds of the church hall of Petersfield Avenue by Count de la Bedoyere, editor of *The Catholic Herald*. What the paper mentions is that the new parish was particularly important to the Catholics on the estate and that in the new estate one in eight was a Catholic. *The Romford Times* wrote quoting the count:

> *"One person in eight at Harold Hill is a Roman Catholic- a much higher proportion than for the country as a whole. (therefore) The new parish was particularly important, for there were 2,900 Catholics on the estate, – an enormous figure in relation to the population of the country."*[116]

The community was much more visible because of the fetes and displays of religious beliefs that spilled out into the streets like the processions of Mary and they were now appearing in local papers with references to their practices and traditions, in a respectable light.

The outings to places like Walsingham would have also enabled Catholics to come out of their community and mix with others from outside their estate. But above all these outings as well as the processions would have helped cement the Catholic community. The imagery of the little girls and boys walking behind the statue was of course a sign of the importance of innocence and purity, again a marker of Catholic beliefs. Other churches on the estate also came out to celebrate their existence as a new community, like the Methodists for instance who appeared in the papers in 1950 when they laid the foundation stone for their new Harold Hill Church in Dagnam Park Drive. The whole community totalling about 350 were present at the laying of the foundation stone that was brought from the Methodist Church in Stratford and which had been previously laid there in 1873. The rebuilding of England after the war years and the new estate seems to connect with the rebuilding of communities and rebuilding was done around the new churches. But what makes the Catholic community in Harold Hill stand out more than any other community was their sheer size. But also the Catholic community was now for the first time given the same positive space in local papers as other churches and little or no references were made to their Irish background or references to public dislike of Irish immigrates or papist views. That would have meant to the new comers of the estate some respectability that connected with their new lives and newly built homes.

There were social gatherings to raise money for a church or as in the case of Harold Hill two churches. The estate proved so large and many of the new occupants were Irish Catholics from East London or Ireland itself, which very quickly provided the need for two churches. But money was also raised for another important aspect of the Catholic community's education: Harold Hill needed a school. There was a Catholic school in Romford and one in Brentwood.[117] For strict Catholics it went without saying that children should and would go to a Catholic school, it only needed to be built. Brentwood had already found a priest willing to dedicate his time to the new estate in Father Foley but also the help from women like Caitlin, and Aoife being available as fund raisers and fete organisers were important participants in the plans of the Diocese to build the schools and churches.

The Need for Catholic schools

The Catholic Church needed schools to enforce Catholic doctrine and to control the community in all its facets. It was part of policing of a community by instilling all the morals that came with Catholicism. If there was no Catholic school available however, Catholic parents were encouraged to see it as their duty to set up a Catholic school and to try and find the funding themselves.[118] It became such an important part of church work that the Cardinal John Heenan had declared public school building its main occupation. Delaney points out that although many new schools were opened in the 1950s, by the mid 1960s only 60% of Catholic children were able to attend Catholic schools.[119] However the reality in England was that the Catholic population were on the whole unable to fund big projects. There were an estimated 1 million Catholic children living in England during the 1950s and only 670,000 were able to go to Catholic schools. Between 300,000 and 400,000 went to council schools.[120]

The Diocese of Brentwood in the post war era was confronted for the first time in its history by such a dramatic increase in the Catholic population and therefore its subsequent challenge was to create both schools and places of worship. It was difficult for the parents to try and find a school as Caitlin remembers:

> "There might not be enough room. I mean, there be too many [children wanting a place at school]. But here that was the same, down in Romford, up at the school they went, a small school [and then] there you had to wait, for a place"[121]

The existing Catholic schools and churches received a circular in the post war years from the Bishop highlighting the problem. The graph below is based on the statistics that were contained within the circular:

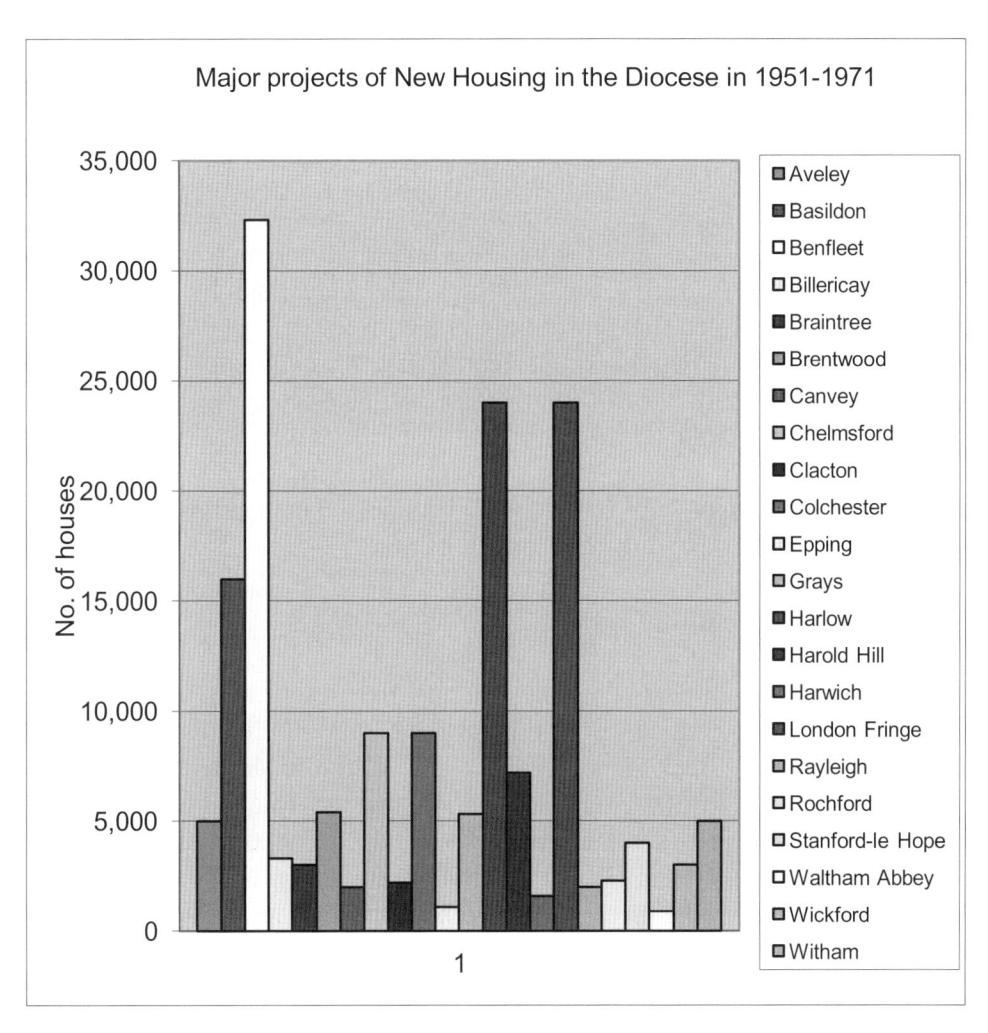

Picture no 17: New Housing Projects Brentwood Diocese, 1951 - 1971[122]

The estimated growth in the Catholic population according to the Bishop of Brentwood during this period was 35,000, excluding new conversions. The new Catholic schools were planned at a cost of £2m, and alterations of existing schools at a cost of £1m in total.[123] In the mean time instructing children in the faith was a problem that parents were left to deal with.

Responsibilities of Parents

The biggest fear of the Church was lapsation, as Delaney pointed out lapsation amongst Irish Catholics was great and London in particular was seen as a city of vice by the Catholic Church in Ireland and held many dangers.[124] The Church's concern was parents would not instil in their children Catholic values and Church teachings. This fear was reflected by the various speakers during the meetings that were held by the Diocese. Most speakers believed that lapsation was a consequence of weak parenting. But Brentwood had two major problems that were unique in a sense: it worried about the influence of the modern secular society but it also lacked provisions for Catholic instruction and Catholic schooling for a rapidly expanding Catholic congregation. It was therefore in a very different situation than parishes in Ireland for instance. The Catholic Education Council therefore assisted the Diocese in its task.

The Catholic Education Council

Bishop Beck encouraged Catholic parents to present the problems and interests of Catholic education to the parliamentary candidates for the 1951 General Election. Beck who chaired the Catholic Education Council adopted a system for levying each parish for the financing of Catholic education so that new schools could be built.[125] The Catholic Education Council which held many of its conferences at St Mary's College in Strawberry Hill, Twickenham proved to be important as many members of the Diocese of Brentwood came together to discuss the various topics that mattered to the Brentwood area. An example of the views expressed in these meetings can be found in the conference held on 2nd to 4th of May in 1962. This conference gives a very good insight into the issues Brentwood Diocese had been dealing with since slum clearance in London. One of the speakers, the Bishop himself, quoted Canon Drinkwater who had written in a booklet *The Religious School Inspector* on role models:

> *"A child is just part of his mother at first, and even after birth is still part of her, mentally and emotionally for some years."*[126]

The Bishop stressed in his talk that father too was in the picture, and of importance to the child, but basically in his summing up he argued that if the roots were not given at home children would lapse in their faith. Many of the new settlers in the Harold Hill estate were also previously members of tight-knit Catholic communities either in the centre of London or rural Ireland, where control by the Church had been important. Particularly in Ireland schools emphasised religion very strongly. Deirdre felt that there was a difference with Catholic schools in England:

> *"Yes, because here [in schools] religion doesn't show so much whereas in Ireland it did."*[127]

However Deirdre did not find it easy to send her children to a Catholic school though. When they still lived in East London they had to find a suitable school but as Deirdre explained this was not an easy decision for her:

> *"In one part that we lived in the East End, we had a choice between two schools, one was a Catholic school and one was Church of England. The Catholic school was definitely better but I was very reluctant to send my children there, although it was the better school. I said they mustn't be beaten and smacked at all because I always knew mums, you know who said that [in the past in the East End, they too] were beaten and I wouldn't have that with my children."*[128]

It was for at least some mothers a difficult choice and the reputation of Catholic schools with their discipline might also be a reason why lapsation occurred in Catholic families. Bishop Beck feared that without schooling, children would not learn Catholic doctrine because parents were not motivated enough to teach them. The Bishop stressed in the conference as he had done on several other occasions the responsibilities to teach children at home and the consequences if this was ignored. He argued:

> *"We must be aware of the number of spiritually handicapped and deprived children who start their Catholic education with the enormous disadvantage just because of parental apathy or*

ignorance. The emphasis on handicapped children is something that is very strong at the present time and it is important that we should think of it not only in terms of physical and mental handicap, but as that much deeper and persistent handicap that falls on children who have been deprived of the early associations with prayer and religion that can be given only in the home and can never be replaced adequately in the school."[129]

Another religious leader who spoke at the conference was the Canon J.J. Crowley of the Southwark Diocese. He felt that the family had become a victim of a particularly troubled period in time:

"First the family seems to have failed in so many cases. The old ideal of a family life has suffered rude attacks in this age. With something approaching an annual average of 25,000 divorces in this country, can we hope that the ideal of family life has remained unassailed among us Catholics living in this polluted moral atmosphere? The industry and Commerce are demanding more and more human bodies, and we see this is reflected in the absence of the mother from the home."[130]

The fear of lapsation and the need for help with instructing children were set high on the agenda of the Catholic Church in general and that of the Diocese of Brentwood in particular.

The Need for Catechists

The discussions at this time at the conferences, immediately after the war and until the 60s, were therefore lack of good parenting and lack of good schools. Another speaker at this conference, Father Larn, connected the two problems; that of the lack of religious instructions at home and the lack of Catholic school places:

"From the material here presented, and from the lively discussions that followed its original delivery, there emerge distinctly two quite dominant notes: that the paramount duty of religious education of children lies with parents, and that there is a desperate need for

> *more provision for the instruction of children who attend non-Catholic schools."*[131]

In the conference the Catholic Education Council was asked to convey to the Hierarchy the very strong feeling that, in view of the enormous numbers of Catholic children in non-Catholic schools, Diocesan catechetical organisations or centres should be established to prepare, in conjunction with the National Catechetical Centre, detailed plans for the recruitment and training of catechists to help parents in the spiritual formation of these children.

The situation in Brentwood however, had left a vacuum that could not be filled with the Lay Catechists alone. The Ursuline Sisters had taken it upon themselves to teach children in the new estates the catechism, but there were not enough sisters to cover the whole area. The Ursuline convent in Forest Gate wrote in the early sixties to the priests of East and West Ham and the Diocesan Inspectors that they had tried to provide religious education to the children in non-Catholic schools. There were simply too many children to cater for in an organisation like the parish schools.[132] Some children did receive Catholic instructions in county schools from catechists who would be allowed to teach them if the Head of the school was willing. One woman wrote to the Bishop that she was unable to attend the conference but that she taught the 5 to 11 year olds in the county school and her pupils were pleased with the lessons. The most popular book was that of the life of Maria Goretti and had been passed on to the non-Catholic girls as well. Also very popular were the Catholic Truth Society's pamphlets especially those with English martyrs.[133]

The conference also disclosed the outcome of the Newman Demographic Survey. The Newman Survey had been commissioned in a number of Dioceses to prepare the report on the requirements in the future of Catholic schooling for children. In 1950, 59% of the five to fourteen-year-old Catholic children were accommodated in RC schools. In January 1961 it was 60.9%.[134] The (Catholic) Newman Demographic Survey was set up as a result of a meeting in 1953 at the London Centre of 'Catholic University Graduates'. They called themselves 'The Newman Association'. The survey was to fill in some of the large gaps in the available authoritative knowledge about Catholics in England and Wales. Voluntary workers of the survey, with the author Spencer, who was mentioned in the archives of Brentwood as the conductor of the Newman survey and the pilot scheme, collected vast amounts of demographic material, and conducted some pilot surveys in parishes and towns. Spencer was a sociologist whose work on English Catholics was well known and well respected. Their first objective was the construction of an independent estimate of the total strength of the Catholic community in England and Wales. Similar research was also carried out by Father Conor from Liverpool who served as an example.[135]

The Demographic Survey was carried out in a large number of dioceses and pointed to the change in the areas where Catholic people were living. The former Catholic areas were in the North's big industrial cities such as Liverpool, Manchester and Newcastle. This picture had changed in the fifties. In 1961 London and Birmingham had the same concentration of Catholics as the more northern cities. The report had checked the number of babies that had been baptised throughout the country. In 1961 Catholic children comprised an average of 25% of all births in London. This was also the underlying cause of the problem of the lack of schools. The report also pointed towards a shift in positive instruction and advised people to avoid negative instruction that was based on fear, as had been the case in the past.[136] Their report shows very clearly a modern approach to religious instruction and a change in Church policies. Spencer's conclusion did not go down well with Irish prelates as Delaney argues:

> *"In the course of his discussion, Spencer suggested that the conditions at home in Ireland explained the problems that arose when it came to integrating Irish Catholics into wider British society."*[137]

They appeared to have only a brief and superficial knowledge of the main teachings of the Church and their children were therefore ill prepared for modern life with its many dangers.

New initiatives and revival of old ones were the major approach throughout the 1950s and 1960s to combat the problem. Again the hierarchy looked to the Catholic working associations for help. They were to contribute with the

Religious Instruction outside the schools. The work of organisations named in various letters and meetings were: The Knights; The Guild of the Blessed Sacrament; The Catholic Women's League and the Union of Catholic Mothers. The Catholic Women's League had as early as 1923 responded to a similar plea when it had set up an organisation called 'Our Lady Catechists' which had been placed under the patronage of 'Our Lady Seat of Wisdom', when Cardinal Bourne asked their help to tackle the problem of leakage in the Church.[138] The emphasis on the role of mother and the charitable work that most women undertook whilst raising their offspring was very much at the heart of the success of flourishing parishes. Another organisation that became active was the Confraternity of Christian Doctrine: C.C.D. The C.C.D. was originally an American movement that held meetings and gave lessons in how to become a Fisher of Men, using the Gospel of St Luke 5:1-7 as their inspiration.[139]

The Inspectors of the Catholic Schools were not only looking at the much-needed increase in catechists but also at the relationship between the parish priests and the schools. In the Demographic Report it was argued that priests should visit schools more regularly. The Diocesan Inspectors backed up these findings and added that there was a need to teach students at the seminaries more clearly on how to teach the catechism. The Hierarchy of the Catholic Church had urged the confraternities and Catholic lay organisations in general to do a lot more to safeguard the Catholic community. But their own input was less than satisfactory and shows a lack of commitment.[140] Another tactic the Hierarchy embarked upon was that of protest; the parents were called up to take children out of R.E. lessons in the non-Catholic schools, as that would increase the pressure on the Ministry of Education to help the Catholics to their teaching training places in the Catholic College. The college referred to in the BDA was St Mary's College, at Strawberry Hill, Twickenham, South West London. Founded in 1850, it is generally acknowledged to be the oldest Roman Catholic college in the UK. For some time there had been a lack of places to train Catholic teachers; this problem was discussed at various meetings of the Education Council.

There was a need for good Catholic teachers but the Minister of Education was not persuaded to make more places available to the teaching training colleges for Catholic students. Teachers were now in short supply. It became too expensive for the Catholic communities to build expensive grammar schools when there were no teachers to fill the posts.[141]

There was a reference to the Education Act of 1944, which clearly states that if parents did not wish their children to receive religious instruction they had the right to withdraw the children from these lessons. The Bishop believed that this would create a strong position for Catholics to get more money or at least more places in the teaching training colleges, they would then be able to teach at the Catholic schools that the Church hoped to build. He referred to the Jews and Quakers who were very consistent in withdrawing their children from Anglican religious instruction lessons. Caitlin had no reason to worry about the reaction of the parish priest when the local Church of England school accepted her child. When asked if that had been a problem for her or her son she argued:

> *"No, no not at all, I mean it didn't hold him back, no he became, [well] he served at the altar, in Romford."[142]*

The history of the Ursuline Sisters and education

Catholic education had been high on the agenda in the Diocese of Brentwood from early on in the mid- to late 19th century. The Sisters of Mercy had established a school in Brentwood, as well as in Romford and the Irish Christian Brothers were active in the Diocese. The order that was to have the biggest impact on the community of Harold Hill and the Becontree Estate in Dagenham were late comers; the Ursuline Sisters.[143] In 1854 the Ursuline Sisters from Thildonck, Belgium, opened a Free School for the Irish immigrants in London. Father Kyne, with the approval of Cardinal Wiseman, had invited the Sisters to London. They were the first nuns to walk the streets of London in traditional habit since the Reformation. But the struggle to find funding and hatred of any Catholic establishment forced them to abandon their project in 1861. They returned however in 1862 and opened a boarding school this time in the small village of Upton, which was very close to Stratford. The Ursuline Sisters became known as an order that was dedicated to the education of mainly poor children.Christine's parents had placed her with the Ursuline Sisters in Forest Gate in East London:

> *"I was brought up by the Ursulines in the first place and the Holy Child in the second place."*[144]

Her experience with the sisters of both orders made such an impact that Christine herself became a teacher of the Holy Child Order in East London dedicating her life to educating children of poor families.

The Ursulines of Brentwood

In the late 19th century there was growing concern that some Catholics were leaving the Brentwood area because it lacked schools for daughters of wealthy Catholic families. Father Norris of Brentwood suggested an all-denominations entry to the new school. At the time it was still uncommon for non-Catholics to enter a Catholic school. Mother Clare accepted the invitation and two other sisters, Sister Philomena and Mother Borromeo came with her.

Originally, they rented a small house, known as Matlock, and opened two schools in April 1900: one for girls of upper social classes and one for Traders' daughters. The two schools containing upper social classes and traders' daughters merged in 1918 with the 1918 Education Act. The school soon became well known for its high academic standards and the wide range of subjects that were taught to girls, which was quite unusual at the time. The community became independent from Upton in 1904. Many of the sisters were either Irish or of Irish descent but they were a very international community with also Dutch/Belgian, German, French, and British sisters.[145] Of the 149 sisters on the register from 1859 to 1954, 36 were of Irish origin and most of them had come directly from Ireland.[146] Many of the Irish sisters spoke with fondness of the role they had to play in the education of the area. One sister, from Tipperary, was responsible for teaching German and was also responsible for teaching the catechism to the children in the new-built estate of Harold Hill during the fifties.

One girl of the *Old Girls Association* I met when visiting the sisters spoke about the chance the sisters had given her. She was from a poor Catholic family and Sister Clare gave her a scholarship and later helped her to gain a place in university, again with a scholarship. Because a large number of girls in the school were from prestigious backgrounds, it was seen as a 'posh' school but the substantial number of poor Catholic girls who attended there free of charge is less well known. Sister Clare did not keep any records of who paid and who didn't.

Most names that appeared at this time have English origins. In 1905 two girls, sisters, with Irish surnames appear on the entry list. The number of Irish names then gradually increased to make a dramatic increase in the entries of 1916 and onwards. By this time they had a substantial day school with an entry of 12 girls with Irish surnames.[147] It is possible that the local girls of Irish descent were unable to enter the boarding school because of their poorer background. The day school opened up new possibilities for these children or grandchildren of Irish immigrants. The two tier system meant that most of the Irish sisters, who came without much of a dowry to speak of, were placed in the lower positions in the order than their English sisters who were often converts and of middle class background. In the 20th century the emphasis was placed more and more on the importance of education which made the Irish sisters without dowry but with good educational background valuable members of their communities.

The input of the Irish women through convents like the Ursuline Sisters and the Sisters of Mercy was of great importance to the Brentwood area and made them invaluable as teachers of the next generation, giving not only the rich but also the poor a chance to improve their financial future. An Irish middle class community would not have emerged therefore in this Diocese without these educational opportunities.

A Catholic school for the Harold Hill Estate

The reason why Harold Hill had a Catholic primary school as early as June 1954 was Sister Clare's interest in the plight of the East Enders who were in many cases bombed out of the slums in which they had lived. She had initiated, and her community had paid for, the St Joseph School in Dagenham that was founded in 1935.

The residents of Dagenham were financially in a better situation than the residents of the new Harold Hill Estate. The only people who were able to settle in Dagenham at the time it was built, were people who could prove never to have been in arrears with their rent whilst still living in East London. This was only possible if they were in permanent occupation. In the Docklands most people were reliant on the arrival of the boats for their wages and therefore were often behind with the rent as there was only money if they had been able to unload or load the ships and the wages also went down in times when labour was abundant. To become a resident on the Becontree estate in Dagenham, you had to be in a very good position. This was in stark contrast to the new dwellers of the Harold Hill Estate, who moved with or without a good pay package.

When the sisters realised that the Diocese was having great difficulties to provide schooling in the newly built Harold Hill Estate they offered to build the school for them and run it.[148] For four years the Reverend Mother Clare arranged with the Diocese Authorities that the Ursuline Community would be responsible for the building of a One Form Entry Infant and Junior School for two hundred and eighty children. Delays were caused however by the *Economy Circular*, a report that looked into the financial challenge of the building and running of the school, and then the plans were changed into a Two Form Infant School for 240 children, and a Two Form Junior School for 240 children. The convent's bid to help was offered before they realised that the schools would attract 50% of displaced pupils, pupils who had been forced to move after the blitz. Displaced Pupils were to receive a special Grant under the Education Act of 1953. The Act read; "-*Displaced-pupils*" must be pupils who have:

> *"ceased to reside in the area are served by some other aided school or special agreement school".[149]*

Children who were born in the area of Harold Hill were not eligible for the grant. Even in cases where their parents and older siblings were forced to move to the estate from the slums. Many of the names that appeared on the first pupils' list were of Irish origin but there were also many English names present which demonstrates the ability of the Irish women to infiltrate into the native communities of East London. Many of the former addresses that appear on the list of pupils roll are from East London places like Bethnal Green, Stepney, Poplar and Hackney. The pupils' roll of 23rd May 1958 gives a more scattered picture but most of the children came from the badly affected areas further into London. Seven children came from children's homes; four were from the Hornchurch Children's Homes.[150] Again this is suggestive of the relatively poor socio-economic background of the new community. When the school was newly built, there were incidences of theft from the school. The theft varied from petty theft to the theft of building materials that could be used privately or sold on. This highlights the problems the area had with theft just as the local papers had been pointing out since the large inflow of newcomers to the area. This is again suggestive of poor socio economic conditions of the residents.[151]

The Ursuline Sisters received a letter on the 20th November 1954 from the Minister of Education stating that a Grant would be given under section 104 of the (original) Education Act of 1944 as amended by section 1 of the Education Act (Miscellaneous Provisions) 1953 at the rate of 50 percent of 85 percent of the expenses incurred by the promoters in the erection of the Infants Department of the school. The new school was to cater for 320 children between seven and eleven and 240 between the age of five to seven. The school was to be mixed boys and girls and also the classes were to be of both genders.[152]

The Ursulines had set up a successful system to pay for schools such as the one in Dagenham and were going to use the same method to pay for the new school in Harold Hill. They used the fees of the wealthy non-Catholic pupils in their private school in Brentwood to fund the costs of the building and running of both primary schools. On the ninth of November in 1950 a Mrs. and Miss Barnes were prepared to sell to the Ursuline Sisters the land on which the school was to be built for £340 pounds. The sisters were able to claim £247 pounds by the Town And Country Act. The cost of building the Infants school alone was an estimated £43,120 and the sisters were adamant that the cost should not go above the set price. The final cost of the Junior school was a total of £60,318.[153]

Although Reverend Mother Clare had initiated the building of the schools she never lived long enough to see the success of her project. She died on

22nd November 1954 at the age of 92 shortly after she had retired. Sister Angela took on the task of leading the convent and was much involved with the new school. She meticulously documented the costs of the building of the school, appeared well informed of the various stages of development of the school and kept a close eye on the running of the school later on.[154]

The Beginnings of St Ursula's School

Because there were so many Catholic children it was decided that the school would start in the hall in Petersfield Avenue, Harold Hill which became later on the Holy Redeemer Church with added Church Hall. At the opening of the Hall Bishop Beck announced the plans for the building of two infant and junior schools on Straight Road on the estate. He wanted the community originally to build two primarily schools with one on Straight Road accommodating 560 children and a second on the estate for 280 children. (The latter was never built.) The priest Fr. Foley, who was referred to in the paper as the priest in charge of Harold Hill told *The Romford Times* on 28th September 1953:

> *"More than 400 children leave the estate each day to go to Catholic schools in the neighbouring districts, and there are at least another 100 children under school age to be accommodated in the future."*[155]

In this article the number of Catholics on the Harold Hill Estate was referred to as one in seven and again their numbers were shown as an important aspect of the new estate.

The first school day for the new and improvised Catholic school started on the 14th June 1954. The builders were by that time digging the foundations of what was to become the Infant School on Straight Road in Harold Hill, on the other side of the estate. Two classes of Infants were held in the hall and the authorities would not allow more than 92 children. One of the sisters who helped run the classes in the hall, Mary Bernadine Irish and was closely connected with the setting up of the new school. The hall was not really suitable as a school and was difficult to run. The sisters had to clear up all the materials they had used because in the evening it was used for the clubs and at the weekends for mass. At this time there was no real Catholic church on the estate and the Hall drew large numbers. During the break the sisters could use some grassland next to the building, as there was no playground. This piece of land was also used for their P.E. lessons.

Women from the parish volunteered to cook the dinners and the food had to be paid for by the parents of the children who came mostly from very poor backgrounds. At least 50 per cent came from East London and fell in the category of displaced pupils. The women who were doing the cooking were not paid wages and neither were they given the bus-fare.[156] The task to cook something wholesome for the small amount of money that the children's parents were able to afford was far from easy. It was the ladies' voluntary work that made it possible for the children to receive a meal during school time. As previously discussed free milk was not available to the children in the Hall. Despite the objection of the Education committee and the Romford Council, the Minister of Education ignored the needs of the displaced pupils, the poorest of the population and his dealing with the case showed his clear irritation that the Catholic community had fought for a school of their own. Only when the buildings in Straight Road were ready, did the children get free meals with the help of government money. But again there were many complaints when the two schools wanted one canteen with one area for cooking shared by both schools. This was more efficient and cheaper to build and cheaper to run with fewer kitchen staff.

After the Easter holiday on 25th April 1955 the infant school was completed, but not all children could be moved, as there was not enough space. The buildings were used for both infants and juniors; the class sizes were sometimes as big as 54 children. The noise of the building carrying on next door to the school was sometimes so loud and distracting that teachers used to play loud music on gramophone records to drown out the noise and keep the children occupied. The game store and the hall were also used as classrooms and when the hall was being used for dinner the class in that hall had to move off to the cloakroom where the class would continue.[157]

The Building of St Dominic's

Until July 1956 St Dominic's congregation would go to the school hall to have their mass. They would make their confession near the entrance of the school. It was the community's responsibility to raise the money for the costs of their own church. The Diocese was unable to help, especially now that it was aware of the increase in newcomers.[158] The funding for the schools was a priority. The fundraising of parishioners like Aoife and Caitlin made the start of the building possible. For Caitlin it was simple: her son Tim needed to go to a Catholic school but it was difficult to get him a place and it was a long walk into Romford town:

> *"It was not easy getting them into school, you only had so many places and so, you had to do all that [fundraising]."*[159]

Although she never felt that the first school he attended, an Anglican school, held him back, it was still important to find a place in a Catholic school.

It is very unlikely that the Catholic community would have been able to fund both churches plus the two schools. Therefore the input by the Ursuline Sisters was instrumental in the building of the schools. Bishop Beck laid the Foundation Stone of the church on 31st July 1955 and finally, on 15th August 1956, St Dominic's was blessed and opened by the new Bishop of Brentwood, Bernard Patrick Wall. 15th August is the Feast of the Assumption of Our Lady and it was considered an appropriate opening day. It was a miserable and wet day but a large crowd assembled in front of the little church. There were not enough places for the congregation but the atmosphere was one of rejoicing. The church was referred to in the *Fair View Chronicles* as '*the most precious jewel*'. The Church was named after St Dominic because the Bishop of Brentwood, Bishop Beck, who later on was to become the Bishop of Salford, had received £2,000 pounds from a donor provided they would call the church St Dominic's. It demonstrates how names of church buildings have often come about due to the pressure of one wealthy individual and is rarely a reflection of the background of the parishioners. Neither does it reflect the large input of the parishioners.[160]

The newly built church in Straight Road was seen as a modern building reflecting the hope and future for the community. It also meant more space in the school next door. The sisters in the St Ursula's school were supportive and enthusiastic about their new neighbour. Their interests were often voiced in the school meetings when all that was happening with the church building was carefully recorded in the minutes of the meetings. When St Dominic's Church was opened the whole school was able to use it at the end of the week for a Benediction of the Blessed Sacrament on Friday afternoon, which involves the blessing of the children and the teachers, and for confession in lunch hour. The church therefore aimed to both support and extend the religious education and practices of the school.[161]

The Junior School is opened

In September 1957 the Junior School opened with eight classes and the infants had their school to themselves. Now that the Junior School was in operation the classes in the hall in Petersfield Ave were closed. Sister Mary Bernadine was made Headmistress of the Infants and the sister who had run the 'Hall School', Sister Mary Paul, became Headmistress of the Junior school. It was important for the community that their children were able to attend a Catholic school because they were always seen as a very different denomination. There was also much more involvement of the community with their parish church.

The school was placed under the protection of St Joseph the Carpenter. And the *Fair View Chronicles,* published by the Ursuline Sisters in Brentwood in January, May and September, wrote jubilantly in the May edition of 1957:

> *"Our school building has been under the special protection of St Joseph since it was started, and so we tried to give him special honour during his own month. His feast day, March 19th, coincided with the Silver Jubilee of Father McKenna's priesthood. A special concert was arranged in Father's honour."*[162]

Again use was made here of St Joseph as the worker and shows a clear reference to the Holy Family in the daily life of the Catholic community of Harold Hill, particularly his help during the construction time would safeguard the building works. He was also an example for hard work and dedication as the article shows:

> *"Providence must have had something to do in arranging that the last term of school should begin on May 1st, the Feast of St Joseph*

the Worker, because we all knew that it was going to be undoubtedly the busiest time of the whole year and St Ursula's would have no room for drones."[163]

The Saints therefore were a constant reminder to the children and their parents of the strength of individuals who lived in the faith of the Lord.

As Eileen had discussed in her interview, the Virgin Mary's celebrations were also important and processions through the area were part of the festivities. The processions continued to make the link between the two parishes on the estate; the Holy Redeemer, which had been only a hall until 1965, and the church in Straight Road, St Dominic's. As the *Fair View Chronicles* reports:

> *"On the last Sunday in May a procession in honour of Our Lady took place at the Church hall of the Most Holy Redeemer in Petersfield Avenue. Our Lady's statue was carried in procession by the children of Mary, while the choir and congregation sung hymns in her honour. On arriving back in the Church Hall the statue was placed in the sanctuary and was crowned by the May Queen, attended by her 6 small helpers."*[164]

The strength of the community and the number of children that were church attendants becomes clear when the writer in *Fair View Chronicles* describes the large number of children that made their first Holy Communion and the involvement of the parishioners:

> *"Almost a hundred children belonging to the Parishes of St Dominic and the Most Holy Redeemer made their first Holy Communion on Sunday, June 23rd. They were served breakfast in the school hall and then went home to rest in preparation for the procession of the Blessed Sacrament which took place that same afternoon. The weather was ideal for the occasion, and a great crowd turned out to do honour to Our Blessed Lord. The procession began at the Church hall of the Most Holy Redeemer and then followed as direct a route as was possible to St Dominic's Church, where Benediction brought the day's proceedings to an end."*[165]

These celebrations were fondly remembered by most of the interviewees. The large number of children at the Holy Communion was based on the fact that the Bishop would perform the service and children would wait until he was in the area again rather than scheduling the first Communion around the child's age. Some children had a double celebration as a result; As Aoife explained:

> *"the Bishop only used to come every three years to do the confirmation then. And our girl then was only seven when she did her Holy Communion. She was already at school like"* [166]

Aoife recalled:

> *"she was seven when she did her Holy Communion, the Bishop just happened to come a couple of months after so she had the same clothes for Communion and Confirmation, she was only seven when she made both."* [167]

The whole layout of the two schools was considered very modern and the materials used were new in school buildings. The Catholic schools therefore attracted many visitors. The County Inspector of Schools was able to see the schools for herself in October 1957. The sisters reported how impressed she was. The Borough Education Officer also viewed the schools the next day. He had been able to help the church hall in Petersfield Avenue with school materials such as tables and chairs that he had been able to salvage from schools that were either closed or refurbished. He had also been very critical of the way in which the school went about appointing their two headmistresses. The Ursuline Sisters had appointed their own members as heads as was their custom. It kept the schools in close contact with the Reverend Mother of the community, but the Borough Education Officer demanded that the posts were advertised and that official interviews were held. This created much protest from the Bishop who refused to pretend that there were going to be open interviews and who therefore did not agree with the posts being advertised. The Mother Superior Sister Angela was very clever in her correspondence and refused to move an inch. With the backing of the Bishop she got what she wanted and her own sisters took the posts. It had made the Borough Educational Officer more critical of their project but he admired the two schools on 22nd October 1957 and was pleased with the way the schools were run.[168]

Other important visitors were the Mayor and Mayoress who had their daughter working at the school as a member of staff and Bishop Petit of Menevia, who had paid the sisters a visit and who was interested in their project. They had to open the schools especially for him, as it was the half term holiday. The interest of the hierarchy of the Church shows the importance of the new school buildings. The Sisters had arranged a visitor's day after both schools were opened and many of the visitors complimented Sister Paul on the wisdom to have a huge crucifix placed on the large wall of the Junior School. The crucifix could be viewed from the road at the time and was a clear image of the faith taught behind the school wall. The other important piece of artefact was the statue of Our Lady of Lourdes between both the schools. It was surrounded by flowers and was also clearly visible from both the schools as well as the road. One anonymous visitor wrote in the *Fair View Chronicles* after congratulating the sisters on their new project;

> *"Thanks be to Him and to those who have given so generously and have prayed and toiled so hard to give them [the children] these two beautiful schools."*[169]

One of the regular visitors was the parish priest of St Dominic's. He was much involved with the schools and paid regular visits. He was also the chairman of the schools and was closely involved in all the decisions of the running of the schools.

The school itself paid various visits to other schools in the area, mostly to schools of other denominations and participated in inter-school sports-days and concerts. The interest in the other non-Catholic schools shows that integration was encouraged and although there was a keen interest in the setting up and running of a Catholic school the pupils were no longer kept separate from children of different faiths.

As for the Ursuline Sisters, they were and still continue to be of great influence in the education of Catholic children. Although most sisters are now retired and their numbers are dwindling they are still present on the school Boards of Governors and show an interest in the teaching of the children in the area. Ursuline Sisters are still active in the Diocesan Council of Education and they continue to contribute to the Religious Education of the children in the area. They started the battle for a Catholic secondary school on the estate as early as the mid fifties, and predicted at the time that there would be a lack of school places for Catholic teenagers in the area. They proved to be right as the total of secondary school places in Romford still proves to be insufficient with a shortage for school places in the secondary Catholic schools. The correspondence between the Reverend Mother Angela, the Minister of Education and the Education Department of the Borough was frequent and she tried her best to convince them of the need for a Secondary Catholic School in Harold Hill. They were not successful in achieving their goal however but their record is a remarkable one. By the end of the 1950s the number of Roman Catholic children educated by the Ursuline community was around 1700 at no cost to the Diocese itself.[170]

Conclusion

The research indicates that there has been an Irish Catholic presence in the South East area since the 19th century. After some generations many Irish immigrants had lost their Irish identity as many of the women married local men, but they often remained Catholic. New Irish people arriving into the community in the nineteen fifties revived the Irish Catholic identity. Some settlers moved directly to the estate from Ireland but most moved in stages from areas like Wales into London and from there further out into Romford, Essex. Women often left Ireland because of poverty and the lack of apprenticeship opportunities or money for professional training for girls. The migration of Irish women from the countryside was a direct result of the place women held in Catholic Ireland. Some young women like Deirdre simply escaped from church-controlled society. For others social exclusion and condemnation of their behaviour, as in Christina's father's case, made leaving the only option. But they also left because it had become the norm to leave and many mothers expended much energy in training their daughters to enable them to leave.[171] Most migrant women came from a rural background in which communal life was the norm, and which was something they transposed into the new community. Their upbringing had turned them into dutiful, caring, disciplined and hard working workers who were family and community orientated. The emphasis in Irish Catholicism on the role model of the Handmaid Mary had greatly influenced the choices and opportunities of these women, also in their new lives. The local Catholic Church benefited greatly from these Irish women as they helped build their parishes and helped finance them. But also the wider community benefited from these women as they often looked for socially engaging jobs.

From the interviews the migration pattern that emerged was a more gradual migration moving in stages from area to area; most migrant women moved into already formed Irish clusters. Most of them had sisters or brothers also migrating and families were aiding new comers to find work or accommodation. The interviews only showed three migrant couples: Aoife and Patrick: Caitlin and her husband and Christine's parents. All three couples had moved to England shortly after marriage or just before with the plan of getting married. The second generation was often from mixed Irish/English background and came from East London in search for accommodation in the Romford area. Irish communities held on to their Irish identity as a result of the inflow of 'new blood'. Many did not venture outside their Irish community and when moving on to other parts of the South East did so within newly formed Irish communities. Their spare time was often spent in local Irish clubs or dance halls with the exception of mostly young mothers who were more active in social events organised by the local church or school.

Ireland backed its clergy from government to local authorities with the clergy deciding on everything from teacher appointments to the celebrations of St Patrick's Day. But in England it was the parish priest who was in need of support and continuous backing from the community. The Irish parishioners were far more critical of their priests and were able to voice their opinions at least to one another. These Irish migrants continued to behave as a community holding it together not venturing out of Irish areas. The Catholic morals, the rural Irish traditions and the Catholic faith functioned as glue keeping this community together, reshaping and moulding its identity. To the Catholic Church, doctrine was always taught in parish churches by the priests and in schools by men religious and women religious. They were the 'right arm' of the Church. In England Catholic sisters often came from abroad as the Catholic community had dramatically decreased during the penal laws. Many of the women religious dedicated to teaching came from Ireland. Like the Irish priests they were to supervise the flock of migrant Irish workers. Irish women religious in particular dominated the local schools in Romford and were assisted in their task by Irish secular women teachers. Schooling was a way of controlling and policing the community but it also offered a way out of poverty and kept communities close and was therefore not only an important feature of Catholic life but also a feature of hope of a future for the Catholics on the new estate.

In this chapter the importance of the increase in Catholic children in the Diocese as a result of the building of the new estate has been explained. It also showed how the Ursuline Sisters were of great influence on the education in the area. It has demonstrated how in general the large number of Irish women, both women religious and to a lesser extent laywomen, were involved in educating the young. The need for places in schools for the Catholic children and the struggle to succeed in building the school were discussed and the importance of Catholic education for the dioceses of Brentwood demonstrated. As has been explained in the methodology chapter, archive material triangulates with the interviews and this chapter used the archives and to some extent interview data to demonstrate the involvement of the Catholic Church in the settling of Catholic newcomers on the Harold Hill estate. This evidence also provides a background to the personal stories.

Catholic education was used to instruct girls on their place at home and in society, which emphasised women's position as inferior to man and saw women in a caring capacity as the interviewed women explained in chapters 5 and 6. The Feast days of Mary were celebrated but Joseph was also introduced as the saint for the schoolboys as an example. Both saints were direct role models for Irish Catholic children, but Mary was more dominant in the instruction of girls. Marian ideology continued to have a strong impact on Irish migrant women in England through education and highlighted their cultural differences from English women.

Footnotes

In Romford a permanent school for 58 children was built in 1856 in St. Edward's Square. It was receiving annual government grants from 1880. In 1892 it was rebuilt to in 1911 67 children attended in 1911. In 1951 this school was granted Aided status and was reorganized in 1954 for juniors and infants. In 1968 it was moved to a new building in Dorset Avenue.

[1] The order was founded by Angela Merici at Brescia in 1535 and had spread over the whole of the continent. Various bishops had been keen to introduce the Sisters in their Diocese but often feared the highly educated background from these often very young and wealthy women. The teaching of Christianity was their main apostolate and they became quickly known for their work in schools.

[2] CLR Lingham B.F. (1969) *Harold Hill and Noak Hill*, London
[3] ECA records baptism 1850-1900
[4] ECA records 1900-1940
[5] ECA records baptism 1940-1944
[6] Edna (Greater London) 1999 (name altered), Interview 3, transcript
[7] Christina (Greater London) 1999 (name altered), Interview 4, transcript
[8] Aoife (Greater London) 1999 (name altered), Interview 1, transcript
[9] Siobhan (Greater London) 1995 (name altered), Interview 7, transcript
[10] Deirdre (Greater London) 1999 (name altered), Interview 6, transcript, p. 3
[11] Deirdre (Greater London) 1999 (name altered), Interview 6, transcript, p. 1
[12] Deirdre (Greater London) 1999 (name altered), Interview 6, transcript, p. 1
[13] Deirdre (Greater London) 1999 (name altered), Interview 6, transcript, p. 7
[14] Deirdre (Greater London) 1999 (name altered), Interview 6, transcript, p. 7
[15] Deirdre (Greater London) 1999 (name altered), Interview 6, transcript, p. 7
[16] Deirdre (Greater London) 1999 (name altered), Interview 6, transcript, p. 7
[17] Tilki M., Taylor E., Pratt E., Mulligan E., Halley E. (2011) *Advances in Mental Health*, pp. 221-232
[18] Deirdre (Greater London) 1999 (name altered), Interview 6, transcript, p. 4
[19] Ryan L. (2006) 'Depression in Irish migrants living in London: case–control study', in: *The British Journal of Psychiatry*
[20] Deirdre (Greater London) 1999 (name altered), Interview 6, transcript, p. 6
[21] Delaney E. (2007) *The Irish in Post War Britain*, Oxford, p. 160
[22] Siobhan & Shona (Greater London) 1995 (names altered), Interview 7, transcript, p. 1
[23] Edna (Greater London) 1999 (name altered), Interview 3, transcript, p. 4
[24] See Literature chapt. p. 27
http://www.movinghere.org.uk/galleries/histories/irish/working_lives/working_lives.htm
[25] Aoife (Greater London) 1999 (name altered), Interview 1, transcript, p. 7
[26] Aoife (Greater London) 1999 (name altered), Interview 1, transcript, p. 7
[27] Aoife (Greater London) 1999 (name altered), Interview 1, transcript, p. 18
[28] Aoife (Greater London) 1999 (name altered), Interview 1, transcript, p. 7

[29] Aoife (Greater London) 1999 (name altered), Interview 1, transcript, p. 19
[30] Aoife (Greater London) 1999 (name altered), Interview 1, transcript, p. 19
[31] Humphreys, A.J. (1966) *New Dubliners: Urbanisation and the Irish Family*, London, p. 236
[32] O'Dowd, A. (1994) 'Women in Rural Ireland in the Nineteenth and Early Twentieth Centuries-how the Daughters and the Sisters of small Farmers and Landless Labourers Fared', in: *Rural History* 5.2, p. 175
[33] Aoife (Greater London) 1999 (name altered), Interview 1, transcript, p. 1
[34] Hickman M.J. (1995) *Religion, Class and Identity*, p. 107
[35] Aoife (Greater London) 1999 (name altered), Interview 1, transcript, p. 2
[36] Gray, B. (1997) 'Unmasking Irishness: Irish Women, the Irish Nation, and the Irish Diaspora', in: *Location and Dislocation in Contemporary Irish Society*, Cork, p. 201
[37] Siobhan & Shona (Greater London) 1995 (names altered), Interview 7, transcript, p. 1
[38] Deirdre (Greater London) 1999 (name altered), Interview 6, transcript, p. 4
[39] Rossiter, A. (1992) 'Between the Devil and the Deep Blue Sea' Sahgal G. and Yvval-Davis N. (eds), in: *Refusing Holy Orders*, London
[40] Siobhan & Shona (Greater London) 1995 (names altered), Interview 7, transcript, p. 2
[41] Lambert S. (2011) interview about her research (Online) Available: http://www.virtual-lancaster.net/reviews/interviews/lambert.htm (accessed May 2011)
[42] Siobhan & Shona (Greater London) 1995 (names altered), Interview 7, transcript, p. 2
[43] Walter B. (2001) *Outsiders inside; Whiteness, place and Irish women*, London, p. 144
[44] Brown T. (1985) *Ireland a Social and cultural History, 1922 to the present*, London p. 142
[45] Deirdre (Greater London) 1999 (name altered), Interview 6, transcript, p. 11
[46] Walter B. *Outsiders inside*. p. 20
[47] Christina (Greater London) 1999 (name altered), Interview 4, transcript, p. 4
[48] Walter B. *Outsiders inside*, p. 181
[49] Walter B. *Outsiders inside*, p. 180
[50] CLR Weekly paper The Romford Recorder 1955- January 28
[51] Eileen (Greater London) 1995 (name altered), Interview 5, transcript, p. 9
[52] Eileen (Greater London) 1995 (name altered), Interview 5, transcript, p. 10
[53] Christina (Greater London) 1999 (name altered), Interview 4, transcript, p. 4
[54] Edna (Greater London) 1999 (name altered), Interview 3, transcript, p. 2
[55] Fitzpatrick D. (1986) 'A share of the Honeycomb: education, emigration and Irish women', in: *Continuity and Change*, London
[56] Siobhan & Shona (Greater London) 1995 (names altered), Interview 7, transcript, p. 1
[57] Hickman, M. J. *Religion, Class*, pp. 89-93
[58] Kofman E., Phizacklea A., Raghuram P. and Sales R. (2000) *Gender and international migration in Europe. Employment, welfare and politics*, London, pp. 35-39
[59] Hickman M. *Religion Class*, chapt. 4
[60] ECA
[61] Deirdre (Greater London) 1999 (name altered), Interview 6, transcript, p. 9

[62] Young M. and Willmott P. (1957) *Family And Kinship in East London*, London, pp. 56-57

[63] Caitlin (Greater London) 1999 (name altered), Interview 2, transcript, p. 9

[64] Eileen (Greater London) 1995 (name altered), Interview 5, transcript, p. 2

[65] Walter B. *Outsiders inside*, pp. 177-179

[66] Delaney E. (2007) *The Irish in.* p. 167

[67] Chapter 2 *'Immigration'* of this thesis

[68] Christina (Greater London) 1999 (name altered), Interview 4, transcript, p. 6

[69] Siobhan & Shona (Greater London) 1995 (names altered), Interview 7, transcript, p. 5

[70] Siobhan & Shona (Greater London) 1995 (names altered), Interview 7, transcript, p. 3

[71] Siobhan & Shona (Greater London) 1995 (names altered), Interview 7, transcript, p. 8

[72] Tilki M. (2006) 'The social contexts of drinking among Irish men in London: Evidence from a qualitative study', in: *Drugs: Education, Prevention and Policy*. 13(3), pp. 247-261

[73] Chapter 5 of this thesis

[74] Siobhan & Shona (Greater London) 1995 (names altered), Interview 7, transcript, p. 1

[75] Aoife (Greater London) 1999 (name altered), Interview 1, transcript, p. 7

[76] Willmott P. (1963) *The Evolution of a Community : A study of Dagenham after forty years*, London

[77] Eileen (Greater London) 1995 (name altered), Interview 5, transcript, p. 1

[78] Picture no13: The coat of arms of the Diocese of Brentwood Archive Catholic Herald (Online) Available: http://archive.catholicherald.co.uk (accessed August 2011)

[79] Picture no 14: Map of The Catholic Province of Westminster. This is a current map of the ecclesiastical province in the Catholic Church. Catholic Herald (Online) Available: http://archive.catholicherald.co.uk (accessed August 2011)

[80] BDA file 1950-1960

[81] Picture no 15: Map where Romford, Brentwood and Dagenham are shown and the parishes of Harold Hill and Dagenham are indicated by means of a cross. (Online) Available http://maps.google.co.uk/ accessed September 2011

[82] http://archive.catholicherald.co.uk/article/24th-july-1953/4/in-a-few-words

[83] http://archive.catholicherald.co.uk/article/24th-july-1953/4

[84] http://archive.catholicherald.co.uk/article/24th-july-1953/4

[85] Foster S.M. (1994) *A history of the diocese of Brentwood*, Edmundsbury, p. 82

[86] Foster S.M. (1994) *A history of the diocese of Brentwood*, Edmundsbury, p. 82

[87] BDA Foley papers Dairy

[88] Picture no 16: Contemporary Map of Harold Hill (Online) Available http://maps.google.co.uk/ accessed September 2011

[89] Caitlin (Greater London) 1999 (name altered), Interview 2, transcript, p. 5

[90] Caitlin (Greater London) 1999 (name altered), Interview 2, transcript, p. 5

[91] CLR Romford Times Wednesday Sept 27 1953

[92] Caitlin (Greater London) 1999 (name altered), Interview 2, transcript, p. 3

[93] Code of Canon Law: 'The Bishop is bound to visit his diocese in whole or in part each year, so that at least every five years he will have visited the whole diocese, either personally or, if he is lawfully impeded, through the coadjutor or auxiliary Bishop, the

Vicar General, an Episcopal Vicar or some other priest' *(Canon 396 # 1)*'The Bishop is to endeavour to make his pastoral visitation with due diligence. He is to ensure that he is not a burden to anyone on the ground of undue expense.' *(Canon 398)* cf. *Directory for the Pastoral Ministry of Bishops (2004),* nos. 220-224

[94] BDA Harold Hill Visitation Forms 1960-1967
[95] Aoife (Greater London) 1999 (name altered), Interview 1, transcript, p. 8
[96] Aoife (Greater London) 1999 (name altered), Interview 1, transcript, p. 8
[97] Siobhan & Shona (Greater London) 1995 (names altered), Interview 7, transcript, p. 5
[98] Aoife (Greater London) 1999 (name altered), Interview 1, transcript, p. 3
[99] Aoife (Greater London) 1999 (name altered), Interview 1, transcript, p. 3
[100] Aoife (Greater London) 1999 (name altered), Interview 1, transcript, p. 6
[101] Aoife (Greater London) 1999 (name altered), Interview 1, transcript, p. 6
[102] Aoife (Greater London) 1999 (name altered), Interview 1, transcript, p. 6
[103] Delaney E. (2007) *The Irish in Post War Britain,* Oxford, p. 175
[104] Hickman, M. J. (1995) *Religion, Class,* pp. 106-107
[105] Walter, B. *Outsiders inside.* p. 58.
[106] Hickman, M. J. *Religion, Class,* chapt. 3
[107] Aoife (Greater London) 1999 (name altered), Interview 1, transcript, p. 7
[108] BDA Foley papers Dairy
[109] Aoife (Greater London) 1999 (name altered), Interview 1, transcript, p. 3
[110] Cooney J. (1999) *McQuaid: The ruler of Catholic Ireland,* Dublin
[111] Eileen (Greater London) 1995 (name altered), Interview 5, transcript, p. 3
[112] Aoife (Greater London) 1999 (name altered), Interview 1, transcript, p. 7
[113] Caitlin (Greater London) 1999 (name altered), Interview 2, transcript, p. 10
[114] Aoife (Greater London) 1999 (name altered), Interview 1, transcript, p. 15
[115] UCA File journals Fair View Chronicles Journal : September 1958 no. 210
[116] CLR Romford Times Wednesday Sept 08 1954
[117] British history on line (2011) (Online) Available: http://www.british-history.ac.uk/report.aspx?compid=63844 (accessed May 2011)
[118] Schuck M.J.(1991) *That They Be One, the Social Teaching of the Papal Encyclicals 1740-1989,* Washington D.C., p. 80
[119] Delaney E. (2007) p. 158
[120] BDA file 1950-1960 Spencer survey
[121] Caitlin (Greater London) 1999 (name altered), Interview 2, transcript, p. 7
[122] Picture no 17 UCA files Education file referred to as Figure x
[123] UCA files Education file.
[124] Delaney E. (2007), pp. 159-170
[125] BDA file 1950-1960 administrative papers relating to Roman Catholic education including the Director of Vocations
[126] BDA file 1950-1960
[127] Deirdre (Greater London) 1999 (name altered), Interview 6, transcript, p. 11
[128] Deirdre (Greater London) 1999 (name altered), Interview 6, transcript, p. 11
[129] BDA file 1950-1960

[130] BDA file 1950-1960
[131] BDA file 1950-1960
[132] BDA file 1950-1960
[133] BDA file 1950-1960
[134] BDA file 1950-1960
[135] Conor, K. (1961) *Priest and People, on the Sociology of Religion,* Liverpool, p. 1
[136] BDA file 1950-1960
[137] Delaney E. (2007), p. 165
[138] BDA file 1950-1960
[139] BDA file 1950-1960
[140] BDA file 1950-1960
[141] BDA file 1950-1960
[142] Christina (Greater London) 1999 (name altered), Interview 4, transcript, p. 7
[143] St. Helen's Roman Catholic junior and infant school stood at Sawyers Hall Lane and Queen's Road. In 1839 there were two small Catholic schools, but they had closed by 1845. But they were replaced by a school started by the Revd. Eugene Reardon before 1848. For this new school project the local patron Catherine Adams gave £300 for a schoolroom to cater for around 15 children. In 1861 the school took over and enlarged the former St. Helen's Chapel. It received annual government grants from 1872 onwards and attendance grew from 54 in 1874 to 150 in 1893. The school was again enlarged in 1913 and was granted Aided status in 1950. By this time buildings at the convent in Queen's Road were adapted and used for the infants. The school was again reorganized for juniors and infants in 1954. From: 'Parishes: Brentwood', A History of the County of Essex: Volume 8 (1983), pp. 90-109. URL: http://www.british-history.ac.uk/report.aspx?compid=63844 Date accessed: 14 July 2011
[144] Christina (Greater London) 1999 (name altered), Interview 4, transcript, p. 4
[145] UCA files on Ursuline Brentwood: school register
[146] UCA files on Ursuline Brentwood on beginnings of the order in Brentwood
[147] UCA files on Ursuline Brentwood on beginnings of the school in Brentwood
[148] UCA files on Ursuline Brentwood correspondence Reverend Mother Clare
[149] UCA files; Ursulas file
[150] UCA files; Ursulas file: school registers
[151] UCA files; Ursulas file: school registers
[152] UCA files; Ursulas file
[153] UCA files; Ursulas file
[154] UCA files; Ursulas file
[155] CLR Romford Times Wednesday Sept.30 1953
[156] BDA file 1950-1960 papers relating to the Ursulas School at Harold Hill Estate
[157] UCA files; Ursulas file
[158] UCA files; Ursulas file
[159] Caitlin (Greater London) 1999 (name altered), Interview 2, transcript, p. 8
[160] UCA files; Ursulas file
[161] UCA files; Ursulas file

[162] UCA Ursulas file *Fair View Chronicles* journal, anonymous, (May 1957), p. 16
[163] UCA Ursulas file *Fair View Chronicles* anonymous, (September 1957), p. 23
[164] UCA Ursulas file *Fair View Chronicles* anonymous, (September 1957), pp. 23-24
[165] UCA Ursulas file *Fair View Chronicles* journal, anonymous, (May 1957)
[166] Aoife (Greater London) 1999 (name altered), Interview 1, transcript, p. 19
[167] Aoife (Greater London) 1999 (name altered), Interview 1, transcript, p. 19
[168] UCA files: Ursulas file
[169] UCA files journals :*Fair View Chronicles* Anonymous, (January 1958), p. 1
[170] UCA files; Ursulas file
[171] Fitzpatrick D. (1986) 'A share of the Honeycomb: education, emigration and Irish women', in: *Continuity and change,* London

CHAPTER 7: CONCLUSION

This study has examined the lives of Irish immigrant women in the newly-built Harold Hill Estate in Essex in the post-war period, with reference to the influence of the cult of the Virgin Mary upon those lives and brought an important new perspective to understandings of the persistence and nature of cultural difference. It highlights the hidden effects of cultural difference within 'English' working-class neighbourhoods, as most cultural difference defines itself in the homes, churches and schools of the Irish Catholic immigrants. The research suggests that localities represented as 'English' working class neighbourhoods and 'English' Catholic communities may contain a crucial Irish dimension which is usually overlooked.

The importance of the ideology of the Virgin Mary to Irish immigrant women has been examined and highlights that the Virgin Mary was used by the Catholic Church to instruct young girls on their subordinate position in their families and their place in society. Women were to act out Mary or encouraged to be Mary, which meant obliging and obedient behaviour. The Church and school were policing mechanisms that sustained cultural ideas outside Ireland in Irish communities like the one in Harold Hill. There was also an aspect of self-policing as families allocated gender related roles for their sons and daughters, husbands and wives. Mothers also used the ideology of Mary in order to keep their daughters in check.

Few interviewees considered the difference in position between themselves and their brothers negligible. The cultural past therefore continued to play an important part in the lives of the Irish immigrant women. However women did make changes in their own lives or those of their daughters. The interviewees were able to work outside their family in paid work unlike their counterparts in Ireland because most had been encouraged during their childhood to have an education to make emigration for work possible. Another contributing factor was the economic situation in England just after the Second World War when their labour was in high demand unlike the Irish economy where possibilities on the labour market were scarce. Their choice of work was often in a caring capacity where social and serving aspects were the most important. The lives of women on the estate were affected by migration and differed from the lives of their mothers in Ireland, as many undertook paid work outside of the family, and raised their children without the support of extended families.

But it also shows that changes in lifestyle were also the result of contact with the English community, through places of work and intermarriage ('mixed marriages') and that the interviewees continued to play an important part in the functioning of their community and had an impact on the wider community as they dedicated their working lives to local hospitals, children's homes and schools.

Looking back at the lives of the women in this study, sifting through the interviews and archive material what strikes me is the effect that moving to England and in particular moving to Harold Hill had on them. Migration meant change for all of them. They had their whole lives changed and despite that, they were able to hold on to values, traditions and identities that were important to them. They were able to work and earn money to supplement their husband's wages. When single they had to earn a living away from the family farm, where they mostly came from. Reflecting on their past, the parish priest back home was more critically viewed whereas the parish priest in England played a less dominant role within their community. The interviewees described the parish priests in England as friendlier and more at the same level as the parishioners, as Aoife described when the parish priest got on the floor and danced with his parishioners in chapter 6. The interviewees also had to work outside the family framework, raising their children without the support of their mothers and when in need of a parish they had, in Harold Hill at least, to set up their own. But through the Catholic Church they were able to tie in their own traditions and values that they had brought with them into this new community.

The women interviewed in this study described how their lives changed after the migration. Some changes have to be connected with the way the Irish community was viewed by their English neighbours. It meant that within the community the roles, formerly gender based, were also changing. As Walter demonstrates Irish immigrants in English society were not only marginalized but also racialised. Irish women were perceived more positively than Irish men as more positive images of Irish women allowed them more room within English society. The study shows that their value of Mary and the usage of her as a role model to Irish women meant that they emerged at the heart of English families and society in the role of the patient and obedient nanny, nurse or domestic. Irish women were sent or came to England to work.

In England, they were allowed to make money, which was unlike their traditional role back home. The study shows that the main reason for most to migrate was to earn a living and to send some of that back home. Their income had made them valuable members of their community both in England and Ireland. This and the more positive image of Irish women allowed them to attain a higher profile within Irish communities in England.

The Irish women in the Romford area were successful in integrating into the English community, mostly by means of marriage and many lost their surname as a marker of their Irish identity. Chapter 4 (Christina) and chapter 6 (Deridre) show that this clearly meant a change to the future of their families as gradually Catholics saw themselves no longer as Irish, despite the fact that they formed a community on its own. The remaining identity marker was mostly their Catholic background and the women were often able to pass this on successfully to their children.

The large families of many of the Irish immigrant women increased the number of Catholics that were part of the Brentwood Diocese and changed the shape of the local Catholic communities as is demonstrated in chapter 6: one person in eight at Harold Hill in the 1950s was a Roman Catholic – which was higher proportion than for the country as a whole. The research has demonstrated that Irish Catholic women made use of their position in their families and communities as the bearers of tradition and were often the source of the Irish Catholic identity. They passed on their Catholic faith to their children and included them in the various events of the parish. They sent their children to Catholic schools as soon as they became available to them, even when this was no more than a small church hall without any real school facilities. This was despite the fact that they could have accepted places for their children in the newly built local state school. Their involvement in their Catholic community also demonstrates how many different tasks women were able to perform.

Women stand at the intersection of many different facets of their lives. Consequently women develop knowledge about a wide range of subjects, their lives being connected with a wide range of disciplines. This was and is often at the heart of the various roles that they have to perform in their homes and outside in their community. This way of using knowledge is often viewed as less important but on the contrary it weaves different academic disciplines together. Therefore to analyse women's lives is to use the many different disciplines and create a coherent picture. The research allowed the Irish immigrant women to become more visible by studying their contribution to one geographical area. The study contributes to the debate on Irish immigrant women by bringing more information on their role in their local community. This will help make data on Irish immigrant women more complete in order to get a better understanding of the lives these women lead. The research demonstrated that it is important to study specific areas and how this can add to the understanding of Irish immigrant communities in general.

This research dealt with a small location but the Irish Catholic women in the Harold Hill estate demonstrated the significant influence that they held in the local Catholic Church and it would be desirable if more research could be done in other areas in order to see how great their influence has been in the Catholic Church in England. This could give us more information about the cultural stamp they placed on the Catholic Church and whether this changed the course of history for the Church and in what way. There is also a need for more research in the roles women performed within Catholic traditions and the symbolic meaning behind role models such as Mary, so that we get a better understanding of the lives of these women. As Kristeva writes:

> *"Christianity is doubtless the most refined symbolic construct in which femininity, to the extent that it transpires through it – and it does so incessantly – is focused on Maternality."*[1]

This symbolic construct connects specifically with Catholicism as Catholic understanding of the essence of femininity is infused with the women's roles as mothers and based on the ultimate mother, the Virgin. I believe oral history can add a great deal of information especially to women's role in history. It gives us information about the roles that women play and can give an understanding of the position of women in Catholic societies. From the perspective of Marian ideology, women's position in society is far more closely linked to an ideal concept than that of men. Therefore to analyse the lives of women is to get a glimpse of the real identity of women behind these layers of meaning that surround their position in the wider society. That a large part of the women's lives took place in the home keeping much of it hidden from view further complicates the research leaving a lot of history to be uncovered. With this study I have attempted to uncover information that could be found in individual and communal histories and this information is still very much part of what women are today but more research should be done to get a clearer picture of the lives women led in the past.

The thesis has shown how the Irish community through its Irish Catholic identity retained its distinctiveness as the people of the community continued to live out their lives as Catholics with communal celebrations and worship. Because many of their religious traditions continued out of sight and because the Irish were less visible as a white English speaking migrant community their unique difference was often unrecognised. This is very different from the Muslim community, for example, which is far more visible because of the language and cultural differences. But there are parallels here as faith was a dominant part of Irish migrant culture as it often is in Muslim culture, which also has a distinct role set aside for their women. As new East European communities are emerging into English society I believe that there is a need for further research into migrant communities and lives of migrant women in England.

This research explored how Irish immigrant women contributed to the moulding of the Catholic Church and helped shape its future. Evidence from the research found that Irish immigrant women contributed by means of fundraising in order to establish the new parishes, which had to be paid for by the communities themselves. They were also involved in social events and aided social events for the Church. They took part in pilgrimages and the local processions held by the Church. They contributed to local Catholic clubs in the area, some of which had mainly Irish members and they were therefore clearly visible as a foreign community. Irish women were also influential in the founding and running of the local Catholic school and in teaching the catechism in general to the children. Women took their role from the example of the Virgin Mary whom they were brought up to worship and idealise. This meant that they were structured to be mothers and to suppress their own needs in order to serve for the needs of others. Women were therefore highly active within the community to aid the community. They were also forced to see themselves in comparison with the Virgin Mary. This was at times at cost of their own personal development as Shona and Siobhan explained in chapter 5 and education was very much restricted and based on parental instructions as was highlighted in chapter 6.

The Virgin Mary was internalised by the women and became part of the identity of the women themselves. The study has examined how the cult of the Virgin Mary was used to prepare these women for motherhood and it is almost as if the inability to translate or explain the abstract doctrine left women with their own way of dealing with Mary as a mother and as an example and icon and that was how they were brought up; to act out Mary. The evidence in the research suggests that the influence of their Catholic Irish background, with a strong emphasis on the Virgin Mary as the ultimate role model, was clearly visible in their choices of role fulfilment. They were important to the community at large as a consequence of their choice to work in the more caring professions such as nurses, teachers or care officers and because of their interest in charitable work. The Irish immigrant women contributed to their community in their supportive and caring roles and their paid and unpaid work was based on the Catholic Church's teachings on the Virgin Mary as was expected of them. On the other hand Mary was used to teach young girls their lower status within the community as well as within the family. To be like Mary was to suppress the needs of the individual for the greater good of the community.

But as has been discussed in chapter 2, Mary in the Gospels differs from Mary in the devotion of the Catholic Church. The Virgin's union with the Almighty was so important that it became the focus point of her existence within Catholic traditions and the basis for later doctrine and devotion. This ideology had its origin in the apocryphal writings, which, although rejected by the Church, were still very influential in the way in which the Virgin Mary was interpreted. The Mary in the Gospels of particularly John and Luke is far more closely linked to the mothers on the Harold Hill estate. She too was actively involved in the life of her son and part of his community. Mary was present at the marriage feast of Cana where, according to John, II, 3-5, Jesus performed his first miracle, changing the water into wine, at his mother's request. She is also found at the bottom of the Cross at his crucifixion, John, XIX, 25-27.[2] Beyond the figure of Mary other women played an important part in the Gospels, the other three Marys – Mary Magdalen, Mary the mother of James and Joseph and Mary the mother of Zebedee – were the first to learn of the Resurrection and communicate the news to the Disciples as described in Matthew, XXVIII, 55-61; Mark, XVI, 1-9, Luke and XVIII, 27-28. In Acts of the Apostles, I, 12-14, women were also present at gatherings of the disciples and Luke VIII, 1-3 refers specifically to the many women who served Jesus and his followers with whatever they possessed.[3] So the public, as opposed to the strictly maternal and therefore private, role of the Virgin Mary and other women, which was not emphasised by the Church, is clearly in evidence in the Gospels. This means that there is potentially a divergence between Tradition, i.e. the teaching of the Church, and the Bible on which Tradition is supposed to be based.

Without knowing it the women in the interviews who had to act out Mary and try to be Mary came in my opinion much closer to the woman Mary, the mother Mary, than their Church would recognise. They were like Mary right at the heart of community life and took on a far richer and more varied version of Mary's role than the rigid stereotypical one prescribed by the Church. The Irish women in the research were sometimes critical of the image of the silent Mary but never critical of her as a mother. They tried to act like mother Mary and would seek in her refuge but also use her as an example. As Shona demonstrates:

> *"I say I fed her (her daughter), and changed her, and she still cried, I'll get really upset, and I think 'What would do?' Yes, I did, what would Mary do? Mary would not get annoyed, like you, would she? I would be talking to myself. Now, would she? Yes, so Mary was there talking to me (laughs), and telling me to calm down, then I would stop crying when I thought what would Mary do."*[4]

Using Mary and identifying themselves with her in a way the Church had never instructed them to do, allowed Irish women to be much closer to the ideal woman that the church had placed so high above ordinary women; the daughters of Eve.

Footnotes

[1] Moi T. (1986) ed. *The Kristeva Reader*, London, p. 161
[2] *The Holy Bible, Douai Version*, London, CTS, 1955
[3] *The Holy Bible, Douai Version*, London, CTS, 1955
[4] Interview Shona p. 11

Bibliography

Primary sources

Archives:
Brentwood Diocese Archive (BDA)
    BDA file 1940-1950
    BDA file 1950-1960
    BDA file; 1950-1960 administrative papers relating to Roman Catholic education including the Director of Vocations
    BDA file; 1950-1960 Pickering, A.(1951) .a booklet *Sex Instructions in the Home*, by the Catholic Truth Society London. 1st December
    BDA file; Harold Hill Visitation Forms 1960-1967
    BDA file; Father Foley papers and diary
    BDA file; BDA file relating to the Spencer survey 1950-1960

Ursuline Convent Archive (UCA)
    UCA files; journals :*Fair View Chronicles* 1950-1970
    UCA files; Ursulas file
    UCA files; Ursulas file: school registers 1950-1960
    UCA files; Ursulas file: school registers 1960-1970
    UCA files; Ursuline Brentwood correspondence Reverend Mother Clare
    UCA files; Education file Figure x
    UCA files; Education file

St Edwards Church Archive (ECA)
    ECA records baptism 1850-1900
    ECA records baptism 1900-1940
    ECA records baptism 1940-1944

Central Public Library of Romford Archive (CLR);
    CLR; Minutes from the council meetings 1940-1970
    CLR; The Romford Recorder local newspaper 1940-1970
    CLR; The Romford Times local newspaper 1940-1960
    CLR; The Brentwood Gazette 1940-160
    CLR; Abercrombie P. (1944) Greater London Plan London

CLR; Coffin R. (1986) 'Moving Out To Harold Hill' in *Romford Record Journal*, London

Archive Catholic Herald (Online) Available:
http://archive.catholicherald.co.uk

Diary:
Ciara 1938-unknown

Interviews:
Patrick and Aoife (Greater London), 1999; names altered), Interview 1, transcript
Caitlin (Greater London, 1999; name altered), Interview 2, transcript
Edna (Greater London, 1999; name altered), Interview 3, transcript
Christina (Greater London, 1999; name altered), Interview 4, transcript
Eileen (Greater London, 1995; name altered), Interview 5, transcript
Deirdre (Greater London, 1999; names altered), Interview 6, transcript
Shona and Siobhan (Greater London, 1995; names altered), Interview 7, transcript

Archive Catholic Herald (Online) Available:
http://archive.catholicherald.co.uk

Maps, figures and photos

Picture no. 01: Aerial photo of the Becontree Housing Estate Dagenham 1966 p. 55

Picture no. 02: Picture no 02: A map of Inner London including the twelve central boroughs plus the City of London source from Simmie J. (2002) *The changing City* Oxford p. 56

Picture no. 03: Map from just before 1850 showing the small hamlets and towns of Essex and urban developments p. 59

Picture no. 04: Map from just before 1911 showing an increase in urban development and the spreading of London developments p. 60

Picture no. 05: Map of the London boroughs as they are known today p. 62

Picture no. 06: Photo of Dagenham Village from the church tower taken in 1954 p. 65

Picture no. 07: Map of East London in 1950 p. 128

Picture no. 08: The map that was used in the Greater London Plan to show the way the area had been built up before the Second World War p. 146

Picture no. 09: Map of Essex showing where Romford lays in relation to Dagenham (online) available http://maps.google.co.uk/ accessed September 2011 p. 148

Picture no. 10: Map from the Greater London Plan as a way to keep green areas like parks working for the population of London p. 152

Picture no. 11: Map also shown in the greater London Plan, with the classification of the arterial roads exploring accessibility of various sites based on the old road system with additional new roads added p. 153

Picture no. 12: Map of Harold Hill showing what it looked like just after most of the building was finished in 1960 in LCR Archive p. 160

Picture no. 13: The coat of arms of the Diocese of Brentwood, from the archives of the Catholic Herald (Online) Available: http://archive.catholicherald.co.uk (accessed August 2011) p. 242

Picture no. 14: Map of The Catholic Province of Westminster. This is a current map of the ecclesiastical province in the Catholic Church p. 243

Picture no. 15: Map of Essex where Romford, Brentwood and Dagenham are shown and the parishes of Harold Hill and Dagenham are indicated by means of a cross p. 244

Picture no. 16: Contemporary Map of Harold Hill p. 248

Picture no. 17: New Housing Projects Brentwood Diocese, 1951 – 1971 p. 263

Secondary sources

Abercrombie P., (1944), *Greater London plan,* London

Adolph A., (1991), 'The Catholic Marriage Index in Family History' in *Journal of the IHGS* vol. 16, np 129, NS 105. October

Ahrentzen S. (1997) 'The Meaning of Home Workplaces for Women', in: *Thresholds in Feminist Geography; Difference, Methodology, Representation*, Oxford

Alexander S. (1994) *Becoming a Woman*, London

Alexander S. and Davin A. (1979) 'Labouring Women: A reply to Eric Hobsbaw', in: *History Workshop Journal, vol.8,* pp. 174-182

Arensberg C. and Kimball S. (1968) *Family and Community in Ireland*, Cambridge

Arensberg C. and Kimball S. (1968) 'Family and Community in Ireland in A tie that blinds: Family and Ideology in Ireland', in: *Economic and Social Review, vol 22, no3*

Aspinall P.J. (2002*)* 'Suicide amongst Irish Migrants in Britain: A Review of the Identity and Integration Hypothesis', in: *The International Journal of Social Psychiatry vol. 48 December*

Barthes R. (1992) 'Death of an Author' Sim S. (eds.), in: *Art: Context and Value*, London

Beale J. (1986) *Women in Ireland: Voices of Change*, Dublin

Beyer-Sherwood (2006) 'From Farm to Factory: Transition in Work, Gender, and Leisure at Banning Mill, 1910-1930', in: *Oral History Review, vol. 33 Issue 2*

Bible Version (1955) *The Holy Bible*, *Douai Version*, London, CTS

Boal A. (1992) *Games for Actors and Non-Actors*, London

Booth C. (1889–91, 1892–97, 1902) *Life and Labour of People in London, vol. 17*, London

Bornat J. and Diamond H. (2007) 'Women's History and Oral History: Developments and Debates', in: *Women's History Review, vol. 16*

Boss S. (2000) *Empress and Handmaid, on Nature and Gender in the Cult of the Virgin Mary*, London

Bourke J. (1993) *Husbandry to Housewifery: Women, Economic Change and Housework in Ireland, 1890-1914*, Oxford

Brown T. (1985) *Ireland a Social and Cultural History, 1922 to the Present*, USA

Buckley M. (1997) 'Sitting on Your Politics: The Irish Among the British and the Women Among the Irish', in: J. MacLaughlin (eds), *Location and Dislocation,* Cork

Cairns D. and Richards S. (1988) *Writing Ireland, Colonialism, Nationalism and Culture,* Manchester

Clapson M. (2010) *The Blitz and the 'Break-up' of Working Class London, 1939-1960* a paper presented 13 October, London (University of Westminster)

Connolly, G. (1985) 'Irish and Catholic: Myth or Reality? Another Sort of Irish and Renewal of the Clerical Profession among Catholics in England, 1971-1918', Swift, R. and Gilley, S. (eds), in: *The Irish in the Victorian City,* Kent, England

Connor K. (1961) *Priest & People- A study on the sociology of Religion,* Liverpool

Cooney J. (1999) McQuaid *The ruler of Catholic Ireland,* Dublin
Coppa F. J. (1999) *The Modern Papacy Since 1789,* Harlow, England

Cortes J. and Cameron D. (1989) *Women in their Speech Communities: New Perspectives on Language and Sex,* London

Cowley U. (2001) *The Men that built Britain, a History of the Irish Navvy,* Dublin

Daly M.E. (1995) 'Women in the Irish Free State 1922-1939. The Interaction Between Economies and Ideology', in: *Irish Women's Voices Past And Present,* Indianapolis, USA

Delaney E. (2007) *The Irish in Post War Britain,* Oxford

Dion Committee, (Online), Available: *http://ics.leeds.ac.uk/papers/vp01.cfm?outfit=ids&folder=112&paper=113* (accessed April 2011)

Donnelly J.S. (2000) 'The Peak of Marianism in Ireland 1930-1960' Brown S.J. and Miller D.W. (eds), in: *Piety and Power in Ireland 1760-1960, Essays in Honour of Emmet Larkin,,* Notre Dame, Indiana USA

Douchen C. (1994) *Women's Rights and Women's lives in France 1944-1968,* London

Dowd, A. (1994) *Women in Rural Ireland in the Nineteenth and early Twentieth Centuries,* Cambridge

Dye R. (2001) 'Catholic Protectionism or Irish Nationalism? Religion and Politics in Liverpool, 1829-1845', in: *Journal of British Studies vol. 40, No. 3 July*

Figlio K. (1987) 'Oral history and the Unconscious in Psychoanalysis', in: *History Workshop Journal, vol. 26* pp. 120-132

Fitzpatrick D. (1986) 'A share of the Honeycomb: education, emigration and Irish women', in: *Continuity and Change Journal, vol. 1 issue 02,* p. 137

Foster S.M. (1994) *A history of the diocese of Brentwood,* Brentwood

Freud, S. (1990) *Case Histories I,* London

Gearhart S. (1979) 'The Scene of Psychoanalysis: The unanswered Questions of Dora', in: *Diacritics Journal vol.1 March (Spring),* pp. 14-126

Giles J. (2004) *The Parlour and the Suburb. Domestic Identities, Class, Femininity and Modernity,* Oxford

Gray B (2006) 'Migrant Integration Policy: A Nationalist Fantasy of Management and Control?', in: *Translocations Journal vol. 13 issue 1,* pp. 121-141

Gray B. (2006) 'Changing Places: The Irish Migration, Race and Social Transformation Review', in: *Translocation Journal vol. 1 Issue 1 autumn* pp. 5-21

Gray B. (1996) 'Irishness – a global and gendered identity?', in: *Irish Studies Review vol.16, Issue Autumn*

Gray B. (Online) Available: *http://website:ttp://migration.ucc.ie/oralarchive/testing/breaking/about.html* (accessed May 2011)

Guyot J., Padrun R., Dauphinet E., Jospa Y., Fischli E., de Mestral M., Giudici D., Scheidecker C. (1978) *Migrant Women Speak,* London

Hawkes T. (1983) *Structuralism and Semiotics,* London

Heimann M. (1995) *Catholic devotion in Victorian England,* Oxford

Hickman M , (1995) *Religion, Class and Identity: The state, the Catholic Church and the Education of the Irish in Britain* Aldershot, England

Hickman M., Morgan S., Walter B. (1998) *Recent research into the needs of the Irish in Britain* (Online) Available:

http://ics.leeds.ac.uk/papers/vp01.cfm?outfit=ids&folder=112&paper=113
Accessed June 2011

Hobhouse H. (1994) 'Public Housing in Poplar: The 1940s to the early 1990s, in Poplar, Blackwall and Isle of Dogs', in: *A Survey of London:* vol. 43 and vol. 44, London

Hoffer C. (2000) 'De Dynamiek van Cultuur en Religie: volksgeloof Onder Moslims in Nederland' (translation: The dynamics of culture and religion; popular beliefs under Muslims in the Netherlands) in *NAK Magazine. vol. 13, Issue Autumn*

Hondagneu-Sotelo P. (1994) *Gendered Transitions: Mexican Experiences of Immigration,* California

Horney, K. (1950) *Are You Considering Psychoanalysis?,* Amsterdam

Hornsby Smith M.P. (2004) *The Changing Identity of Catholics in England in Religion, Identity and Change: Perspectives on Global Transformations,* London

Hornsby-Smith M.P. (1991) *Roman Catholic Beliefs in England. Customary Catholicism and Transformations of Religious Authority,* Cambridge

Humphreys A.J. (1966) *New Dubliners: Urbanisation and the Irish Families,* London

Humphries S. (1995) *Hooligans or Rebels,* Oxford

Humphries S. and Weightman G. (1984) *The Making of Modern London 1914-1939,* London

Jackson P. (1987) *Women in 19th century Irish emigration* London

Jonkers M. (2003) *Een miskende revolutie. Het moederschap van Marokkaanse vrouwen,* (translation: A misunderstood revolution, motherhood of Moroccan Women) Amsterdam

Kelly K. and Choille T.N. (1990) *Emigration Matters for Women,* Dublin

Kenny M. (1997) *Goodbye to Catholic Ireland,* London

King R. And O'Connor H. (1996) 'Migration and Gender: Irish women in Leicester', in: *Geography Journal* vol 81 (4), pp. 311-325

Kneafsey M., Cox, R. (2002) 'Food, Gender and Irishness – How Irish Women in Coventry Make Home', in: *Irish Geography* vol. 35 (1) pp. 6-15

Kofman E., Phizacklea A., Raghuram P. and Sales R. (2000) *Gender and international migration in Europe. Employment, welfare and politics,* London

Kristeva J. (1977) 'Stabat Mater, the Heretic of Love', in: *Tel Quel vol. 74 Winter,* Paris

Labrianidis L., Lyberaki A., Tinios P. and Hatziprokopiou P. (2004) 'Inflow of Migrants and Outflow of Investment: Aspects of Interdependence between Greece and the Balkans', in: *Journal of Ethic and migration studies (JEMS)* 30(6)

Lambert S. (2011) Interview about her research (Online) Available: http://www.virtual-lancaster.net/reviews/interviews/lambert.htm (accessed May 2011)

Lambert S. (2002) *Irish Women in Lancaster 1922-1960,* England

Lambert, S. (2004) 'Irish women's Emigration, 1922-1960: the lengthening of Family Ties', in: *Irish Women's History,* London,

Laws G. (1997) 'Women's Life Courses, Spatial Mobility, and State Politics and Thresholds', in: *Feminist Geography Journal*

Lee, J.J. (1978) 'Women and the Church since the Famine', pp. 37-45, in: M. MacCurtain and D. O'Corráin (eds) *Women in Irish Society: The Historical Dimension,* Dublin

Ley D.J. (2009) *Insatiable Wives: Women Who Stray and the Men Who Love Them* London

Lentin L. (2007) Synopsis of Dear Daughter (Online) Available: http://www.alliancesupport.org (accessed July 2011)

Lingham B.F. (1969) *Harold Hill and Noak Hill,* London

Luddy M. (1995) *Women in Ireland 1800-1918: a documentary History,* Cork

Lyberaki, A. (2002) 'Social Capital Measurement in Greece', in: *Journal of International Migration. September Issue*

Lyberaki, A. and Tsakalotos E. (2002) 'Changing Society without Society: Social and Institutional Constraints to Economic Reform in post-1974 Greece', in: *New Political Economy Journal, vol. 7 no.1*

MacAmlaigh D. (1964) *An Irish Navvy: The Diary of an Exile,* Dublin

Markus H.R., Kitayama S. (1991) 'Culture and the self: Implications for Cognition, Emotion, and Motivation', in: *Psychological Review*, vol. 98(2), April, 224-253

Mauthner N. and Doucet A. (2003) 'Reflexive Accounts and Accounts of Reflexivity', in: *Qualitative Data in Sociology vol. 37(3),* London

Mac Laughlin, J. (1997) 'The New Vanishing Irish', in: *Location and Dislocation in Contemporary Irish Society'* Cork

McAdam M. (1994) 'Hidden From History: Women's Experience of emigration', in: *Irish Reporter vol. 13*

McCullough, C. (1991) 'A Tie That Blinds: Family Ideology in Ireland', in: *Economic and Social Review volume 22*

McCurtain M. (1995) 'Late in the field: Catholic sisters in Twentieth Century Ireland and the New Religious History' Hoff J. Voulter M (eds), in: 'Irish Women's voices: Past and Present', in: *Journal of Women's History 6.4, 7.1*

McEvoy and Boyle (1998) 'Putting abortion in its social context: Northern Irish women's experiences of abortion in England', in: *Health and Interdisciplinary Journal for Social Study of Health, Illness and Medicine, July 1998 vol. 2 no. 3 283-304*

McKenna Y. (2002) *Negotiating Identities: Irish Women Religious and Migrations,* unpublished PhD thesis for University of Warwick, England

Moser P. (1993) 'Rural economy and female emigration in the West of Ireland 1936-1956', in: *Women's Studies Centre Review vol. II*

Murphy B.P. (2005) *The Catholic Bulletin and Republican Ireland 1898-1926*, Belfast

Murphy J. (1975) 'Ireland in the Twentieth Century', in: *The Gill History of Ireland*, Dublin

Nash C. (1993) 'Remapping and Renaming: New Cartographies of Identity, Gender and Landscape in Ireland. Women of the West: gender, nation and landscape in early 20th century Ireland', in: *Feminist Review vol. 44*

O'Brian C. (2005) 'In Buildings of England, London 5: East', in: *Victoria County History, A History of the County of Essex: vol. 7*

O'Dowd A. (1994) 'Women in Rural Ireland in the Nineteenth and Early Twentieth Centuries-how the Daughters and the Sisters of small Farmers and Landless Labourers Fared', in: *Rural History vol. 5.2*

Oliver P. (2004) *Writing Your Thesis*, London

Owen D (1995) *Irish-Born People in Great Britain: Settlement Patterns and Socio-economic Circumstances*, Coventry

Parr J. (1998) 'Theoretical Voices and Women's Own Voices. The Stories of Mature Women Students.', in: *Feminist Dilemmas in Quality Research*, London

Passerini L. (1979) 'Work ideology and consensus under Italian Fascism', in: *History Workshop Journal, vol. 8 autumn*

Platt E. (2000) *Leadville, A biography of the A40*, London

Pollard J. (1999) *The Unknown Pope Benedict XV (1914-1922)*, London

Portelli A. (1981) 'The Peculiarities of Oral history', in: *History Workshop Journal vol. 12 autumn*

Porter R. (1994) *London, a Social History*, London

Powel W.R. (1994) 'Roman Catholicism', in: *The Borough of Colchester- A History of the County of Essex: vol. 9* (Online) available:
http://www.british-history.ac.uk/report.aspx?compid=42701 (accessed June 2011)

Powel W.R. (1966) 'The Growth of Population and the Built-up Area 1850–1919 of Metropolitan Essex since 1850 (Online) available:
http://www.british-history.ac.uk/report.aspx?compid=42701 (accessed July 2011)

Powell W.R. (1973) (eds.) 'West Ham: Roman Catholicism, Nonconformity and Judaism', in: *A History of the County of Essex:* vol. 6 (online) available:
http://www.british-history.ac.uk/report.aspx?compid=42701 (accessed June 2011)

Ranke Heineman U. (1990) *Eunuchs for the Kingdom of Heaven. Women, Sexuality, and the Catholic Church*, London

Ribbens J. and Edwards R. (1998) 'Living on the Edges. Public Knowledge, Private Lives, Personal Experience', in: *Feminist Dilemas*, London

Ribbens J. Edwards R (1998) 'Introducing Our Voices', in: *Feminist Dilemmas*, London

Riccards M.P. (1998) *Vicars of Christ. Popes. Power, and Politics in the Modern World*, New York

Roberts E. (1995) *Women and Families: An Oral History*, Oxford, England

Roper L. (1994) *Oedipus and the Devil*, London

Rossiter A. (1992) 'Between the Devil and the Deep Blue Sea, Irish women, Catholicism and Colonialism', in: *Refusing Holy Orders, Women and Fundamentalism in Britain*, London

Ryan L. (2007) 'Migrant Women, Social Networks and Motherhood: The Experiences of Irish Nurses', in: *Britain Sociology Journal* vol. April

Ryan L. (2006) 'Depression in Irish Migrants Living in London: a Case-control Study', in: *The British Journal of Psychiatry vol. 188*

Ryan L. (2004) 'Family Matters: (e) Migration, Familial Networks and Irish Women in Britain', in: *Sociological Review vol. 52 (3)*

Ryan L. (2002) 'I'm Going to England. Women's narratives of leaving Ireland in the 1930s', in: *Oral History Workshop Journal*, Spring

Sangster J. (1994) 'Telling Our Stories: Feminists Debates and the Use of Oral history', in: *Women's History Review,* vol. 32

Serra A. M. (1999) 'Magnificat; Remembrance and Praise', in: *Marian Studies Journal, vol. L*

Shepard C. (2010) 'Irish journalists in the intellectual diaspora: Edward Alexander Morphy and Henry David O'Shea and in the Far East', in: *New Hibernia Review*, vol. 14, no. 3 autumn

Shortall S. (1992) 'Power Analysis and Farm Wives: An Empirical Study of the power relationships Affecting Women on Irish farms', in: *Sociologia Ruralis vol.32*

Simmie J. (2002) *The changing City: Population, employment and Land use change since the 1943 county of London plan*, Oxford

Spencer, (1961) *The Demographic Survey,* London

Spinley B.M. (1953) *The Deprived and the Privilege,* London

Spretnak C. (2004) *Missing Mary: The Queen of Heaven and Her Re-Emergence in the Modern Era*, New York

Thompson P. (1988) *Voices of the Past*, London

Thompson P. (1975) *The Edwardians: The Remaking of British Society*, London

Thurer S. (1994) *The Myths of Motherhood, How Culture Reinvents the Good Mother*, London

Tilki M, Taylor E, Pratt E, Mulligan E, Halley E. (2011) 'Older Irish people with dementia in England', in: *Advances in Mental Health, vol. 9(3)*

Tilki, M. (2006) 'The social Contexts of Drinking Among Irish Men in London', in: *Drugs: Education, Prevention & Policy vol. 13 no 3 June*

Todd S. (2005) *Young Women, Work, and Family in England 1918 – 1950*, Oxford

Valiutis M.G. (1995) 'Power, Gender, and Identity in the Irish Free State.' in J. Hoff and M. Coulter (eds) in 'Irish Women's Voices Past And Present', in: *Journal of Woman's History vol.6. No.4*

Villarreal M. A. (2006) 'Finding Our Place: Reconstructing Community Through Oral history', in: *Oral History Review vol. 33 Issue2*

Walter B. (2001) *Outsiders Inside; Whiteness, Place and Irish Women*, London

Walter B. (1989) 'Irish Women in London, the Ealing Dimension', in: *London Borough of Ealing Women's Unit (1989)*

Walter B. and Hickman M. (1995) 'Deconstructing Whiteness; Irish Women in Britain', in: *Feminist Review no. 50*

Ward G.A. (1980) *Victorian & Edwardian Brentwood: A Pictorial History*, Brentwood

Warner M. (1976) *Alone of All Her Sex, The Cult of the Virgin Mary*, London

Werner A. (2011) *Migrant Communities and Health Care in the Home, the Influence of Cultural, Religious and Migration Factors* (Online), Available: http://buurtzorglive.com accessed May 2011

White H. (1978) *Tropics of discourse: Essays in Cultural Criticism*, London

Widowson J. (1986) *A Marsh and Gasworks: One Hundred Years of Life in West Ham*, London

Willmott P. (1963) *The Evolution of a Community: A study of Dagenham after forty years*, London

Worth J. (2010) *Tales from a midwife*, London

Young M. and Willmott P. (1957) *Family and Kinship in East London*, London